ECONOMICS OF AGEING

A Study based on Kerala

ECONOMICS OF AGEING

A Study based on Kerala

D. Radha Devi
A. Asharaf
Nandini Das
S. Santhosh
S. Sureender

SERIALS PUBLICATIONS
NEW DELHI

First Published - 2008

ISBN : 978-81-8387-166-2

Published by

SERIALS PUBLICATIONS
4830/24, Prahlad Street, Ansari Road
Darya Ganj, New Delhi-110002 (India)
Phone : 23245225 Fax : 91-11-23272135
E-mail: serials@satyam.net.in

CONTENTS

PREFACE

Independent India made a persistent effort to bring down the fertility and mortality level of the country to control its rapid population growth. Though the effect was not uniform across the different constituent parts of the country, reduced fertility is becoming a reality. Mortality level has already come to a low level with very few exceptions. The net immediate effect of these changes is also visible in the form of an increase in the working age group population. Moreover, the working age population is slowly graduating to the aged group thereby increasing that proportion. These changes are visible across the country with degrees of differences.

In this context Kerala, a state situated in the southern part of India has already attracted attention of both administrators and scholars alike by achieving a below replacement level fertility, a very low mortality and a fairly high proportion of population in the age group sixty years and above. According to the Census of India 2001 the share of persons aged at least sixty years in this state was 10.5 percent, the highest in the country. This proportion has been increasing fairly consistently over the decades and is projected to reach 16 percent by 2021. Among the elderly, the share of the younger age groups is slowly decreasing and that of older age groups is increasing fast. In 2001 those aged 80 years and above formed 12 percent of the total aged persons.

With below replacement fertility, the number of children available to take care of the elderly has also declined. Added to this is the increasing trend of nucleation of the family where older parents can hardly fit in. As a result of these demographic and social changes, care of elderly is emerging as a social issue in this state. One consequence of this situation is the development of old age homes. But the majority of the elderly need love, care, understanding, compassion, etc. in their old age and would like to be an essential part of their household sharing their happiness and unhappiness rather than in an old age home. Thus, old age homes cannot be a substitute for home from the point of view of the older persons.

However, family is the major supporting system for most of the elderly in Kerala to-day. But in a fast changing society where people are trying to fulfill their ambitions and that of their children, how long this informal support system will continue remains to be seen. With only nominal welfare schemes available to financially support the elderly; one of the major concerns is their financial security. They are becoming an additional economic burden to their care givers, as their needs, though reduced from what it was in their adult life, still involve some expenditure. It is apprehended that the financial status of the elderly will influence their status and various aspects of their life in the household. This is an issue that needs to be addressed as lack of finance can create problems for the elderly.

The economics of ageing has three dimensions: (i) the money required to take care of the elderly, (ii) the money available to take care of the elderly and (iii) how the economic status of the elderly is likely to affect the different aspects of their life in the household. The present work deals with the last of the three dimensions mentioned above. To be specific, this book will look into the relationship between the financial status of the elderly and their perceived health, their involvement in family decision making and their participation in household activities.

Data used for this study is from Ernakulam and Kozhikode districts of Kerala, which was collected in 1996-97 by the International Institute for Population Sciences (IIPS), Mumbai, for a larger study, entitled *The Aged in a Changing Society: A Case Study of Kerala*. This book is a modified version of a report, "Economics of Ageing", based on the above data submitted to the International Institute for Population Sciences.

D. Radha Devi
A. Asharaf
Nandini Das
S. Santhosh
S. Sureender

1 INTRODUCTION

IMPORTANCE OF POPULATION AGEING

"As the proportion of the world's population in the older ages continue to increase, the need for improved information and analysis of demographic ageing increases. Knowledge is essential to assist policy makers, formulate and evaluate goals and programmes, and to raise public awareness and support for needed policy changes" (United Nations, 2002a).

The world is undergoing a tremendous change in its population age structure. In 2005 there were 672.8 million older persons (aged 60 years and above), which is expected to increase to an unbelievable 2.0 billion by 2050. By then the older population will be more than the young population aged 0-14 years of age (United Nations, 2007).

The proportion of older persons in the world has increased from a mere 8.1 percent in 1950 to 10.3 percent in 2005, a two percentage point increase in just fifty five years (Table 1). This proportion is expected to increase to 15 percent by 2025, and 22 percent by 2050, i.e. doubling in the course of the next forty five years from its present situation. In other words, currently one in every 10 persons is aged 60 years or more which in the course of the next four decades will become one in every five persons, as per the projection of the United Nations.

But there is a difference in the age structure of more developed countries (MDC) and less developed countries (LDC). Ageing of the population of LDC is more than fifty years behind in comparison with the situation in MDC. When almost 12 percent of the population of the MDC was old in 1950, even in 2005 the corresponding proportion in LDC was only 8.1 percent. By 2050, the LDC will reach the situation in which the MDC were in 2005 – still 45 years behind.

Also to be noted is the fact that there are more females than males in the old age group, suggesting that ageing is an issue, which affect women more than men as they live longer than their male counterparts.

Though ageing slowly, two-thirds of the world's elderly populations are accommodated in the less developed countries of to-day. Of the total estimated 672.8 million elderly in the world in 2005, 428.2 million (63.6 percent) were inhabitants of the LDC and the remaining 244.6 million (36.4 percent) were in MDC (United Nations, 2007).

Table 1
Indices of ageing: World and major regions

Sl. No.	Indices of ageing	1950	1975	2005	2025	2050
I	*World*					
1	Older population (Percent of 60+ to total)	8.1	8.5	10.3	15.0	21.8
2	Index of ageing*	23.7	23.0	36.5	62.2	109.9
3	Median age (years)	23.9	22.4	28.0	32.7	38.1
4	Life expectancy at birth (years)**	46.4	58.3	66.0	70.9	75.4
5	Sex ratio (males per 100 females)	30. 4	71.8	82.3	84.6	84.9
II	*More Developed Countries*					
1	Older population (Percent of 60+ to total)	11.7	15.5	20.1	27.3	32.6
2	Index of ageing*	42.9	63.8	118.3	175.0	213.9
3	Median age (years)	29.0	31.2	38.6	43.0	45.7
4	Life expectancy at birth (years)**	66.1	71.3	75.6	79.0	82.4
5	Sex ratio (males per 100 females)	73.7	66.7	72.1	76.4	78.3
III	*Less Developed Countries*					
1	Older population (Percent of 60+ to total)	6.4	6.1	8.1	12.7	20.1
2	Index of ageing*	17.0	14.7	26.1	49.4	97.9
3	Median age (years)	21.5	19.4	25.5	30.8	36.9
4	Life expectancy at birth (years)**	40.8	55.0	64.1	69.4	74.3
5	Sex ratio (males per 100 females)	86.7	88.9	89.5	88.1	86.6

Source: World Population Prospects : The 2006 Revision, United Nations, 2007
* Computed
** Relates to 1950-55, 1970-75,2000-05,2020-25 and 2045-50.

The various indices given by United Nations (2007) indicate that sometime between 2005 and 2025, India will have more than 10 percent of its population in the 60 plus age group (Table 2). Note that all the indices are showing a rapid ageing of the Indian population. Even though the overall sex ratio of the country has almost always been favourable to men, the sex ratio after age 60 indicates more women than men beginning twenty first century.

In absolute number, the increase of elderly population in India had been very striking. From a mere 20.1 million persons aged 60 years and above in 1951, this segment of population has increased to 77 million in 2001 – an increase of almost four times in five decades. United Nations' (2007) medium variant projection of aged population in India is 117 million by 2015 forming almost 9 percent of the total population. This increase is expected to speed up during the next three decades and will reach an unbelievable 335 million by 2050 (United Nations, 2007) due mainly to the expected rapid decline in fertility (Radha Devi, 1998). Further, about one percent of the total population will be aged 80+ years which constitutes eight percent of the elderly (60+) population of India.

Table 2
Indices of ageing in India

Sl. No.	*Indices of ageing*	*1950*	*1975*	*2005*	*2025*	*2050*
1	Older population (percent to total)	5.4	5.6	7.5	11.5	20.2
2	Index of ageing*	14.4	14.1	22.6	46.3	111.1
3	Median age (years)	21.3	19.7	23.8	29.9	38.6
4	Life expectancy at birth (years)**	37.4	50.7	62.9	70.0	75.6
5	Sex ratio (males per 100 females)	100.5	105.9	95.8	91.4	89.2

Source: United Nations, 2007
*Computed
**Relates to 1950-55, 1970-75,2000-05,2020-25 and 2045-50

Since the elderly persons in India are living longer than they used to, and since their income is likely to stop or reduce as age increases, meeting their economic need is of primary importance. India, with an officially estimated 26.1 percent of its population below poverty line (Guruswamy and Abraham, 2006)[1], this problem assumes gigantic proportions.

IMPORTANCE OF ECONOMICS OF AGEING

In old age, the money flow will not be the same as in adult working age. But the needs, though reduced, still will involve some expenses. This will necessitate economic dependency for those elderly with no financial means of their own. In poor societies many of them have no financial support or care except from their own poor families. Such a situation can create a great deal of mental strain. Moreover, when the elderly are economically dependant, the caregivers will have to stretch the available resources to cover the needs of the elderly, besides their own needs and that of their children. This, in some circumstances can create problems for both the caregivers and the older persons.

The economics of ageing has three dimensions: (i) the money required to take care of the elderly, (ii) the money available to take care of the elderly and (iii) how the economic status of the elderly is likely to affect the different aspects of their life in the household. The present work deals with the last of the three dimensions mentioned above.

Generally income from work is the most important source of economic support for an individual. The labour force participation rate of the elderly in the different regions of the world is given in Table 3.

Table 3
Labour force participation rate

Sl. No.	*Region*	*Labour force participation rate*				
		1950	*1975*	*2005*	*2025*	*2050*
1	World	31.9	24.6	19.9	18.8	17.9
2	More developed	23.3	15.0	9.1	8.4	7.7
3	Less developed	40.1	33.9	28.4	25.9	23.9

Source: United Nations, 2002a

The world over, there is a decline in the labour force participation rate of the elderly. In more developed countries only one out of 10 is in the labour force (which could be mainly to while away the time rather than to obtain a livelihood) in 2000, whereas almost every third elderly person in the LDC is found to be engaged in some economic activity. The current situation of the labour force participation of the men and women in the old age group is also reported by the United Nations (2002b). In 2002, it is found that only 21 percent of men and 10 percent of women in the MDC were engaged in some economic activities. Compared to this, the labour force participation rate of older men and women were 50 percent and 19 percent respectively in the LDC and 74 percent and 42 percent respectively in the least developed countries. This shows that in very poor countries old people usually will have to work until fragility or ill health force them to stop (Beck, 1996).

This indicates that with development, due to the several changes that take place in the economic sphere, the economic dependency of older persons will decline. Most of the developed economies have built-in welfare systems besides the savings made by the persons in their adult days to take care of them in their old age. However, this is not the situation for the less developed societies. Neither the society nor the family is economically prepared to meet the needs of the increasing number of elderly persons. Thus the last years of life of a person in these societies will be filled with stresses and strains. It is in this context that the studies of economics of ageing assume importance.

According to the various censuses of India, the work participation rate of the elderly in this country has consistently declined from 49.5 percent in 1961 to 43.2 percent in 1971, to 40.4 in 1981, to 39.1 in 1991 and to 40.3 percent in 2001. The economic activity rate for India based on International Labour Organization (1998) projection is 36 percent in 2011and 35 in 2020. The decline in the participation rate shows a slow growth of employment opportunities for the elderly in comparison to their increasing number.

Though the Indian labour force is ageing slowly with an increase in its median age from 33.3 years in 1971 to 34.6 years in 2001, and though the economic activity rate for the elderly in this country declined consistently, the increase of elderly workers in

Fig. 1
Relative change in the economically active elderly population in India (1961=100)

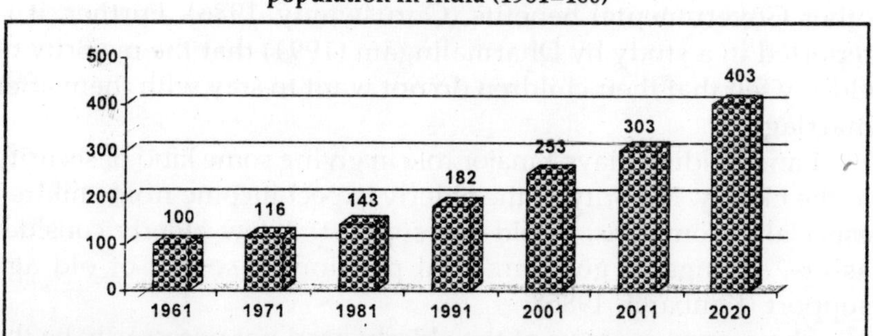

Source: Computed from LABORSTA, Economically active population estimates and projections, version 5: 1980-2020, ILO, 1998

absolute number is very striking. The enumerated and projected numbers of economically active elderly persons shows an increase from 12.2 million in 1961 to 49.2 million in 2020. The relative change in the economically active population is given in Fig.1 calculated from the data published by the International Labour Organization (1998).

However, a large segment of elderly who are out of labour force might have been engaged in agricultural and related activities or in informal sector activities during their adult ages. These are persons who retire without having enough resources for post retirement life. And for those who were working in some pensionable job, the income reduces to only a fraction of the original salary.

Furthermore, many of the aged are living longer than they used to in olden days, which means the present day families will have to take care of them for a period longer than was the case with the previous generation. It is in this context the financial status of the elderly assumes importance. In old age their consumption pattern changes due to reduced material needs, increased health care needs and shrunken budget. But the changed pattern also involves some expenses. In this context, if they have their own financial means, even if it is a small amount, it is expected to make a big difference in the attitude of others towards them and their feeling of belonging to the household.

Expectation of familial support in old age is reducing (Asharaf, 2000). According to Krishnan (1976), elderly in Kerala are neither in a position to maintain themselves nor are receiving support from their kin. Options for aged are retaining some land, seeking some form of employment and living on old age pensions and other Governmental benefits (Guruswamy, 1986). Further, it is reported in a study by Dharmalingam (1994) that the majority of elderly felt that their children do not want to stay with them after marriage.

Land holding plays a major role in giving some kind of security to the elderly. Majority of the elderly expect income from children especially from sons, as old age support. A few elderly consider assets, savings or governmental pension as source of old age support (Kanbargi, 1985).

The economic status of the elderly need not necessarily be the same as that of the household. The difference will be adverse to the elderly as they are past their productive age with none or only some income. In an average household that consists of children, adults and elderly the chances of the elderly getting a fair share of the household income of the family is least likely. On the contrary, if the elderly has his/her own financial means, it could be a different matter altogether.

Of late there has been a spurt of studies on ageing in this country using primary and secondary data[2]. Nonetheless, studies dealing with the economics of ageing directly or indirectly are comparatively negligible. Some of the relevant studies are reviewed below.

REVIEW OF SELECTED LITERATURE ON AGEING: GENERAL

In writings on the political economy of ageing it has been suggested that the twentieth century society had deliberately promoted the marginalization and dependency of the elderly people (Clark and Spengler, 1980). The economic status of the elderly is determined by four factors viz. their employment status, their access to state pensions, their access to private savings and their receipt of financial support. The relative shares of these four categories have changed over time with the decline in employment income roughly matching the rise in state benefits. In terms of their asset ownership, there are fewer dependants on the goodwill of their relatives than was the case in the early years of the twentieth century. Employment opportunities of the older men have declined in the last eighty years. Townsend (1963) writes that the concepts of retirement and pension status have been developed in both the capitalist and the socialist countries in ways, which have created and reinforced the social dependency of the elderly rather than economic dependency.

The choice of living arrangement is an important aspect of the well being of the elderly because of its effect in the provision of care and the physical environment that this choice provides. As reported by the American Annual Housing Survey (Wise, 1989), more than two-thirds of the elderly population lived independently. This proportion increased steadily from 1974 to 1983. There is a large income gap between the elderly living as head of a family and the elderly living as subfamilies. Elderly parents who head a joint household with their adult children exhibit larger average income than those living independently. If elderly are staying in a household headed by the children, the latter is likely to have a higher average income.

Among the determinants of population ageing, a very gradual decline in fertility and mortality became manifest in some Western countries in the nineteenth century (Laslett, 1978). During the last quarter of the nineteenth century, ageing became apparent in North-West Europe, Australia and New Zealand. Later the decline spread to south and East Europe. By the early 1970s, expectancy of life at birth in Sweden and Norway had attained 72.1 and 71.3 years among males and 77.5 and 77.6 years among females. Old age has come to be recognized as a distinct period of life likely to be marked by poverty should the family and complementary institutions prove incapable of supplying adequate support.

Interest shown by International Labour Office in retirement and related problems of individuals contributed largely to the growing of interest in demographic studies on ageing. In France, even as early as the Franco-Prussian War (1870-71) concern was expressed about the decline of young adults (Laslett, 1978). In 1933 Thompson and Whelpton (1933) estimated that by 1980 population greater than 64years of age would comprise of approximately 13 percent of the population. During the second quarter of the twentieth century, Chaddock (1936) had pointed out the increasing need to provide jobs for the older workers and the need for agencies and institutions to take care of the aged. The burden of old age pensions and the costs of dependency, he pointed out, will increase rapidly.

The National Resources Committee in 1938 (Clark and Spengler, 1980) indicated the need to keep older persons in the labour force and to avoid too early retirement. According to the Royal Commission on Population (1950), premature retirement and limitations upon the employment of older persons limited the work force and produced forces that lead to an imbalance between consumption and production. Lord Keynes (1948) has pointed out that there is a danger of increasing ratio of retired dependant people to productive workers leading to a risk of decline in output per head. Sauvy (1948) examined the ways in which population ageing decreased the ratio of persons of working age to those of retirement age. There was a slow down in the increasing output per worker by increasing the cost per worker of providing support for the aged.

In 1950, as well as in 1960-61, in America, proportional expenditures for food, housing, household operations and medical care became increasingly larger with the rising age of family head, especially after age 65 (Sidney, 1968). The data on the contribution of the various age segments of the population to the aggregate expenditure for consumer goods and services points to the relationship between age of consumers and the consumer market. The relative contribution to aggregate expenditure does not vary by age of head of the household, being greatest for those in the age-group 35 to 44 years and very low for the aged. The rise between 1950 and 1960 in the relative number of aged units in America has resulted in some increase in the aged population's proportionate share of aggregate income and expenditures. Changes in number alone may not have altered significantly the aged group's share of aggregate expenditure. A much more important factor possibly affecting the aged's share of the market was changing income level. The big spenders for all categories of consumption were the above average income families in every age group. This was true for the aged also. Between 1950 and 1960 the average income of the non-elderly units grew at a higher rate as compared to the elderly units. This gave rise to a possibility that the aged may continue as a relatively unimportant segment of the consumer market, except for those specific items of goods and services which may be unique to the needs of the older persons.

In economically advanced societies there is a possibility of conflict between the desire of older individual to be gainfully employed and the availability of suitable employment. In advanced industrial countries, unlike the less developed ones, older workers and older jobseekers are relatively numerous (Long, 1958).

In the Central and East European (CEE) countries pensions for older persons were a major responsibility of the Government. Beginning of the demographic transition, dependency ratios were in the range of thirty to forty-five retirees for every hundred workers with country-wise variations (Fultz and Ruck, 2001). This had mixed consequences for the Central and East European Economies. For pension schemes the impact was negative. Contributions fell and benefit payments increased implying a major deficit in financing. From the mid-1990's most of the CEE countries undertook major pension reforms. Some CEE countries sought to improve the collection of contribution through a unified collection system. The second category of reforms brought about a mixed pension system. Here the two sources of pension were public schemes and a commercially managed individual savings account. Privatization of pension proved to be expensive because of reduced economies of scale. In a case study of Hungary (Vukovich, 1994), it was pointed out that both the cultural demand and job requirements affecting continued employment of the elderly beyond retirement age are influenced or even determined by their education levels. Expenditure on pensions grew very rapidly in the decade between mid-1970s and mid-1980s. The number of employees working beyond retirement age had decreased significantly since pensions formed 65 percent to 75 percent of former wage or salary levels, whereby the retirees could maintain previous incomes by undertaking part-time occupations involving reduced number of working hours. As a result of other modified financial regulations, employers found it increasingly profitable to pension older workers, in order to limit employment. Among those elderly who expected to receive support from relatives more than a million did not perform any household work.

In Netherlands, according to Krishnaraj (1999), the social security systems have built in gender biases that adversely effect women's life course. Insurance for sickness, widowhood, unemployment and old age developed only after the Second World War. There is a fierce debate in the Netherlands on the erosion of family values, rise in individualism and loss of social cohesion. This concern is regarding the care of the elderly. Earlier acute housing problem was the reason for pushing old people into old age homes; now cost calculation is pushing them back into their homes.

The widely used cut-off point of 65 years was decided as the age of benefit in the first public social security legislation in Germany in 1873. Broadly, in surveys of those over 65 years in established market economies, nearly half consider themselves to be in good health and less than a quarter report poor health. The concept of healthy ageing as a goal of lifetime health promotion requires that the elderly share in the general facilities available to the population at large.

The principal reason for the relative lack of attention to the elderly in developing countries has been the presumption that they continue to be well cared for by their families and communities (Naik, 2001). Women have specific health and socio-economic problems relating to family responsibilities as well as the types of occupation in which they were engaged in their younger days. The situation of the elderly in the rural areas was worsened by the migration of the young to the urban centres and the deterioration in the rural farming economy.

In an ASEAN (Association of South East Asian Nations) aging survey in 1988 by Jones (1990), it was found that income from own economic activity and from pensions was more important for men whereas children and grandchildren were a major support for elderly women. It is generally considered that the high labour force participation rate among the aged in the agricultural societies represent the relatively strong economic position of the old people. As a consequence of the high cost of hospital use and technology in the care of an ever-increasing elderly population, growing attention has recently been directed towards taking care of the aged patients at home or in the community. The empirical fact that many elderly persons make substantial bequests merits attention because elderly persons might implicitly trade bequests for care from children or other beneficiaries should it be required or in return for assurance that care would be provided.

Martin (1990) points out that with the exception of Nepal half or more of the female elderly in each country have lost their husbands. On the other hand, three quarters or more of the males are still married. The existence of a married son did not guarantee that co-residence would occur. But greater incidence of widowhood and low status among women contribute to the differences in living arrangements. There is some evidence that those with more economic resources in urban areas may choose to live apart from their children.

Kono (1993) states that in an ageing society people are worried about the death of young labour force, loss of economic vitality, increasing financial burdens upon the prime age adults supporting the elderly, difficulty of recruiting the armed forces and so on. But from the children's side it may be pointed out that they will receive bequests from the parents in the form of house, stocks and bonds which might compensate their support for their parents.

In the case of Philippines there exists a predominant pattern of co-residences mainly with spouse and/or their children (Cruz and Natividad, 1997). The overall proportion living alone increases with age. There are more rural residents than urban residents who live alone. Ownership of the house where the elderly respondent currently resides most commonly remains with the elderly couple. Percentage of the elderly living with a single son is higher than that living with a single daughter. With increase in age there is an inclination to live with a married child with a slightly higher percentage co-residing with a married daughter. The proportion of elderly who regularly care for their grandchildren is quite sizeable - more common among widowed females and urban residents. There is more openness to the idea of putting up old age homes. A sizeable percentage indicated willingness to live in such a home when they become too old.

The Government of Singapore had reacted to the graying of the population in a variety of ways. Some of these include raising the retirement age from 55 to 60, implementing laws governing support for the elderly, continuous campaigns to promote familial care of the elderly and so on (Chan, 1997). Male elderly persons are more likely to be living with a spouse compared with females as they tend to remarry and marry younger wives. Divorced or separated seniors are more likely to assist children with housework, provide financial assistance to children and consult on family matters as compared to currently married or widowed elderly. In the context of Singapore, Shantakumar (1990) stated that since aged women have lower educational endowments, they would find employment mostly at the lower occupational categories. They may prefer to continue in household chores. Health considerations and increased desire for leisure may be interrelated factors that contribute to early retirement decisions. Lack of education seems to depress the economic participation among the aged.

In the case of Thailand improved economic situation in recent years has facilitated the construction of separate dwelling units for married adult children next or near to their elderly parents

(Knodel and Chayovan, 1997). Declining co-residence is observed for the elderly in rural areas where obtaining land for a new home is not a major problem. More Thai elderly persons live with an ever-married daughter than an ever-married son. This is largely a rural phenomenon.

In a study in Bangladesh it was seen that the programmes designed for elderly people were available only to the elite - retired military persons, Government employees and industrial workers (United Nations, 1996). But these people form a negligible fraction of the total elderly in that country. To a great extent there is no public safety net for the aged people living in poor families especially in rural areas. In another study in Bangladesh it was pointed out that the principal persons of the elderly's support system were their sons, daughters-in-law, their daughters, sisters, grandchildren, friends etc. in that order. The population that remained in the rural communities was in a chronically depressed condition. There were no formal programmes by the Government for their welfare.

As per the Chinese constitution, the citizens who are aged, ill or losing ability to work enjoy the right of being supported materially by the state and the society (Cangping, 1994). In their marriage laws it is stipulated that children are duty-bound to support parents. The pension amount of the elderly depended on the length of the service and the number of years of participation. Those who made special contributions enjoyed higher pensions. With increased age, pension and wages took a backseat while support from the children increased in proportion. Chinese parents have reinforced filial loyalty through control of property, marriage age and choice of marriage partner for their children. But this has gradually weakened as in many urban areas employment based pensions, community based health care and old age clubs are emerging.

In Japan the child population is provided with social expenditures in areas like education and hygiene whereas the aged population is provided with large expenditures in the form of old age pensions, old age social welfare and so on (Okazaki, 1967). In 1920 the Japanese population was beset with the burden of large families. From 1950 onwards the ratio of dependant population declined. In the context of economic support, the idea of children taking care of the elderly declined after the war. However, according to Ogawa and Retherford (1997), father and son tend to have the same occupation and thus by virtue of the father's longer experience parental authority over children is reinforced in Japan. Under these circumstances co-residence of parents and adult children extending to care of elderly parents by adult children makes both economic and social sense. This holds true in case of an agrarian economy. In recent years the Japanese elderly have tended to transfer home ownership in return for services from co-residing children. They also found that feminism dominates in the provision of physical support.

A project titled 'Value of Children' addressed a common questionnaire to more than twenty thousand married adults in nine countries in the mid 1970s (World Bank, 1994). Questions on expectation of care by children received a low response of eleven per cent in the USA to as high as 91 per cent in Turkey. There was a preference for sons as caregivers.

In old age sibling's support is more common in Africa than in Asia. Non-formal institutions such as kin, community and tribal support networks are more important in Africa. But Africa's poor economic performance has made it difficult for the younger generation to support the old. Two kinds of risks are particularly important in old age – the risk of becoming unproductive through ill health or disability and the risk of living long and needing income for consumption. Greater mobility and less communication between rural based parents and urban-based children reduce parental control and social pressure for parental support.

El-Badry (1986) wrote about the social security system existing in the developing countries. Contribution by the private sector is through its participation in schemes providing post-retirement financial support, provident funds and private pension schemes. But they are confined only to large establishments in urban areas and coverage usually does not stay at the beginning of retired life. In the area of housing, the special arrangement made for accommodating the elderly in developed countries like institutions and planned housing are not needed in the near future in most of the developing countries on any large scale, as neither the size of the elderly population nor the pattern of living arrangements prevalent in developing countries warrant this. While family can shoulder the main responsibility of food, housing and personal care, Governments in developing countries have to take action in other areas. It seems inevitable to provide organized public financial support in the form of social security. Such schemes take a fairly long time to establish and expand and therefore, should be given immediate attention.

REVIEW OF SELECTED LITERATURE ON AGEING IN INDIA

A quick look around the ageing scene in India reveals that an overwhelming majority of the elderly population is working in the unorganized sector where the age of superannuation is not applicable.

Dandekar (1996) gives the rural-urban differences in the economic status of the elderly. It states that there is a lack of medical care facilities for the old irrespective of the place of residence. In terms of poverty, the states of Kerala, Tamil Nadu and Maharashtra had comparatively higher proportion of poor elderly as compared to the states of Assam, Bihar and Himachal Pradesh. The percentages of males living alone are more than the females and the percentage of men living alone in rural areas was more as compared to those in the urban areas. They preferred living alone, as the alternative was Old Age Homes.

Gulati (1993) categorized the needs of the aged into (a) physical needs due to decline in health and mental faculties; (b) financial needs due to incapacity or reduced capacity to earn and with hardly any savings to fall back upon; (c) psycho-social needs due to decreasing role and status even within family, feeling of loneliness and unwantedness; (d) recreational needs due to decreasing participation in socio-religious ceremonies; and (e) housing needs arising from inability to pay rent needed for the accommodation. It appears that most of the needs barring the psychological needs can be met if one has sufficient economic means.

There are the different types of caregivers available. The main care providers for the aged are informal caregivers such as family, friends, neighbours and formal institutions such as state, private sector agencies and non-Governmental organizations (NGO) including trusts, charities, cooperatives and mutual help societies (Gulati, 1993). The forms of care differ from nation to nation depending upon the magnitude of the problem of caring for the elderly and the extent to which informal systems are able to provide satisfactory care, public perception of the role of the state in providing assistance and services, political weight of the elderly in the electorate and their ability to influence the Government policies in regards to more allocation and services, stage of development of the economy and the extent of resources that can be allocated for social security, emergence of a new market for private sector care agencies and growth of NGOs providing care services.

D'Souza (1985) explained the position and role of older people in pre-industrial society of India and the changes since then. Older people in the past enjoyed a higher status in the society. Decline in the status of the older people has coincided with certain fundamental changes in the socio-cultural conditions. Social interaction has changed from group oriented to an individual oriented affair.

Discussing the problems of retired people in Greater Bombay, Desai and Naik (1982) spoke about three major problems, viz. health, financial and psycho-social adjustment. The pre-retirement and post-retirement phase showed a change. The instances of illness increased in the post-retirement phase. There existed problems of financial commitments and repayment of loans. The single most recurring liability was marriage of their children. This was followed by financial commitment on education of children and building a house. Phenomenon of pooled income declined with an increasing level of financial position.

There are several socio-cultural factors in India, which positively influence the living conditions of the aged and have helped in reducing the adverse impact of change on them (Husain, 1997). This study was primarily for the state of Karnataka. A large number of sixty plus persons are economically active. A fall in employment is observed only in the primary sector. Traditionally it was only the destitute amongst the old who were provided with care and maintenance. The Government employees are entitled to house building advance at concessional rates of interest. The National Housing Building Policy 1988 has recognized the aged as a specially disadvantaged group for whom housing schemes will incorporate dwelling units of appropriate designs formulated to meet their specialized requirements. The States Transport

Corporation also provided schemes such as fifty percent travel concession to citizens over sixty years.

In the Indo-UK workshop on the Public Health implications of Ageing in India, the top four common illnesses identified among the rural aged of Madurai were visual handicap, joint pains, insomnia and backache (Shah, 1993). A significant proportion of the elderly had mental health problems. There was a huge demand on health care services. Often health service providers were ill equipped and ill trained to provide adequate diagnostic, therapeutic and rehabilitative support to the elderly.

On the basis of some surveys conducted in Delhi and Lucknow, in 1982 D'Souza (1985) also states that old people who are economically independent try to live on their own. Easwaramoorthy (1999) found that in Tamil Nadu health awareness among women is poorer and he attributes this to their poor educational background. A higher proportion of females have rated their health as poor and this may be due to their physical distress and higher dependency on daily activities. Males are not as mentally depressed as women and this could be due to education, active profession and fewer health problems. Prevalence of health problems and psychological morbidity among women could be a consequence of widowhood and other social problems.

Pant (1997) states that the property owned by parents is generally shared with adult children in inter-generational co-residence. Wealth in the form of land is likely to determine the elderly person's status in family settings.

Vijayakumar and Suryanarayana (1989) point out that the old people are more secure in joint families. He suggests that since widowed women generally outnumber widowed men, widow pension programmes in relation to the aged needs top most priority in the welfare programmes.

Joseph (1991) carried out a study of the Kottayam district of Kerala and pointed out that the elderly in this district were found to be living in the community with their kith and kin. The elderly living with families had lesser number of physical ailments than the institutionalized old. Females had more physical problems than males. The most frequently reported economic hurdles of the home where the old are living were lack of savings, lack of stable income and difficulty in settling children. The most frequently reported mental problem of the home living is a sense of worthlessness. Memory failure and inefficiency are the other common mental problems of the old. The old-old are emotionally better off as compared to the young-old. But economic dependence of the old led to interpersonal problems within the family.

According to Gulati and Rajan (1988) the problems of the aged would differ by (a) family type, (b) control of assets by the elderly, (c) older person's access to independent income, (d) family's access to regular income of its own, (e) marital status and (f) sex of elderly. The number of married sons living with heads of the household is higher in India as compared to Kerala. Vast majority of elderly in Kerala do not have any independent means of support except when they have a pensionable job. Thus, the aged continue to work beyond what is normally regarded as working age. The low income, households generally have a pooled arrangement i.e. all the working members of the family, males and females, contribute towards support of their elderly non-working parents (Rajan *et al.*1999).

There are more than thirty-five social security and assistance schemes that have been implemented in Kerala. Among the thirty-five, sixteen are completely financed by the state exchequer (Rajan *et al.*, 1999). Kerala continues to enforce a retirement age of 55 years for its employees because of its serious unemployment situation reflected in the high rate of unemployment among the youth in the state (United Nations, 1992).

A study on the perceptions of the elderly in Andhra Pradesh (Jamuna, 2001) revealed that given the opportunity many elderly parents with functional capacity and finances would like to live by themselves than with their children's family or in institutions for the elderly. Caring becomes mechanical in any situation if restricted to physical help without the psychological component. The pattern of older care is culture specific. It varies from a predominant state care, to predominant self care to family care depending on the prevalent contemporary practice in the country. The author says that intergenerational contacts and interactions are expected to become more complex in the coming years. To motivate family members and maximize dyadic interaction, provision of family incentive becomes important.

Realizing the importance of ageing of population in India, the Government of India, has brought out a National Policy on Older

Persons (1998), which identified among others, financial security as a major area of concern. The aim of the policy is to strengthen the elderly's legitimate place in society and help them to live the last phase of their life with purpose, dignity and peace.

OBJECTIVES AND ORGANIZATION OF THE STUDY

The primary objective of this study is to understand the relationship between the economic status of the elderly and their health, their involvement in decision-making and involvement in household activities. The latter two will make the elderly feel that they are part of the household, and that sense of belonging will be of immense importance in assessing one's own health. This research used some of the data collected in 1996-97 by the International Institute for Population Sciences (IIPS), Mumbai from Ernakulam and Kozhikode districts of Kerala, for a larger study, entitled *The Aged in a Changing Society: A Case Study of Kerala*. The justification for the selection of Kerala for this study is provided in Chapter II with the help of various indices of ageing calculated from the census and other published data.

Though the data used for the main study came from a previous survey of aged, as has already been mentioned, it was thought appropriate to provide a brief account of the methodology adopted in that survey to acquaint the reader of the same. This, along with the general background characteristics of the study population forms the content of Chapter III. The main analyses form the subject matter for the following three chapters, one each for the health of the elderly, their involvement in household decision making and involvement in household work in that order. Chapter VII, the last chapter, gives the summary and discussion of major findings.

NOTES

1. Guruswamy and Abraham (2006) describes how inadequate the computation of poverty rate done by the Government of India is, as it takes into account only nutrition for computing poverty line. Thus the authors computed a holistic poverty rate taking into account all aspects that are required to live with a "modicum of dignity" like nutrition, health, clothing, energy consumption, sanitation, housing etc. and found that the poverty rate in rural and urban India to be 84.6 percent and 42.4 percent respectively giving a weighted average of 68.5 percent for all-India.
2. For a detailed annotated bibliography see Karkal, 1999.

2 AGEING IN INDIA: A STATE-WISE ANALYSIS OF CENSUS DATA

INTRODUCTION

A state-wise analysis of ageing situation in India in the last four decades is given here to understand the trend of ageing and its variations across different states. Only the states with a population of 10 million or more according to 1991 census are included in this chapter and they are referred to as the major states. Thus defined, 15 states in 1991 could be classified as major. These are Andhra Pradesh, Assam, Bihar, Gujarat, Haryana, Karnataka, Kerala, Madhya Pradesh, Maharashtra, Orissa, Punjab, Rajasthan, Tamil Nadu, Uttar Pradesh and West Bengal. These states together accounted for 95 percent of the total Indian population in 1991 and 90 percent in 2001[1]. Aged persons are defined as those who have completed at least 60 years of age.

According to 2001 census the total Indian population was 1028.610 million of which the contribution of Kerala was only 31.841 million forming 3.1 percent of the Indian population. But the quantum of elderly population in India and Kerala for the same years was 70.686 million and 3.362 million respectively, thus making the share of Kerala in this segment of population to 4.8 percent. Further, it is projected that Kerala will have 5.833 million aged population in 2021, an addition of 2.471 million during a short span of two decades. In the same period the national elderly population will reach an unbelievable 143.244 million, an increase to the tune of 103 percent during the twenty year period. This is due mainly to the rapidly ageing population of almost all the states and Union territories of the country. The details can be seen below.

INDICES OF AGEING

The ageing of population is measured in terms of proportion of population aged 60 years and above among the total population, median age, index of ageing and expectation of life at birth. With population ageing, the share of older people will increase and that of children and youth will decrease resulting in a rise in the median age. The median age is the most important single measure, which summarizes the age structure by dividing the population into two equal parts. Thus higher the median age, older will be the population. Index of ageing is the aged-child ratio, which takes into account the number of persons at both ends of the age distribution simultaneously. It is usually expressed as percent.

Shryock and Siegel (1980) have given round limits to three of the four different indices mentioned above to decide whether a population is "young" or "old". They suggested that a population with less than five per cent of its people in the older age group can be categorized as "young" and those with ten percent or more can be taken as "old". In general, it is said that, if the value of the index of ageing is below 15, the population can be described as "young" and above 30 can be described as "old". Similarly, a population with a median age under 20 years may be described as "young" and those with a median age of 30 years and above as "old". Since those aged 60 years and above are considered as aged in less developed countries perhaps, an expectation of life at birth of less than 50 years may indicate an "young" population and 65 years and above an old population. The stages in between any of the categories given can be taken as transitional stage from young to old population.

Percent old, median age, index of ageing and expectation of life at birth are given in the following sections. The first three indicators are given for five census years from 1961-2001 and for the last one, effort is made to obtain for years closer to the above. Changes in the age structure of all the 14 states (excluding Kerala, as its age structure is provided in the text itself) are given in the appendix to this chapter in the form of age pyramids.

PERCENT SHARE OF ELDERLY IN THE POPULATION

The percent of aged to the total population of India is 5.6, 6.0, 6.5, 6.8 and 7.4 respectively for 1961, 1971, 1981, 1991 and 2001 as can be seen from Table 1. Also see that the proportion of aged women is consistently higher than that of aged men at the all-India level and in eight states (Andhra Pradesh, Karnataka, Kerala, Madhya Pradesh, Maharashtra, Orissa, Rajasthan and West Bengal) during the period 1961-2001, which can be attributed to the high female life expectancy at birth. In 2001, in all but two states (Bihar and Uttar Pradesh), the share of elderly females exceeded that of aged males. The highest proportion of elderly females and males is observed in Kerala (11.3 and 9.6 percent respectively) and the lowest in Assam (5.9 and 5.8 respectively).

There are only four states (Andhra Pradesh, Karnataka and Kerala from the South and Punjab from the North.) with the proportion of aged population consistently equal to or higher than the national average during 1961-2001. During the period 1961-81 Punjab had the highest proportion of aged population (6.6 to 7.8 percent) but in 1991 Kerala out-stepped Punjab by attaining the highest proportion of older population with 8.8 percent. In 2001, Kerala retained this position with 10.5 percent - differencing itself by 1.5 percentage points over that of Punjab (9.0 percent). Also in 2001 there were eight states having a proportion of the aged exceeding that of the national average of 7.4 percent. The states are Andhra Pradesh, Karnataka, Kerala, Tamil Nadu from the South, Punjab and Haryana from the North, Maharashtra from West and Orissa from the East.

The population projected by the Technical Group on Population Projection of the Government of India (Registrar General, 2006) shows that by 2021 the population of Kerala will have 16.0 percent of its population in the age group 60 years and above compared to 10.7 percent at national level. With this kind of increase the age pyramid of Kerala will show a very constricted form, even though the process of constriction started as early as 1981.

The tempo of ageing process of the population in various states can be visualized by comparing the proportional changes of the aged (Santhosh, 1994) which is presented in Table 2 for the period 1961-2001. The tempo of ageing is the highest in Kerala (81 percent) followed by Maharashtra (64.2 %),Tamil Nadu (57.1 percent), Orissa (45.6 %), West Bengal (42.0 %) and Gujarat (40.8 %).The other states which exceed the national average of 32.1 percent are Assam, Madhya Pradesh, Punjab, Karnataka and Rajasthan. The lowest change is observed in Uttar Pradesh (11.1 %) and Bihar (17.9 %).

Table 2

Table 1
Percent share of elderly in total population: 1961-2001

Sl. No.	State	Male					Female					Total				
		1961	1971	1981	1991	2001	1961	1971	1981	1991	2001	1961	1971	1981	1991	2001
1	Andhra Pradesh	6.1	6.3	6.5	6.6	7.2	6.4	6.4	6.8	6.9	8.0	6.2	6.4	6.7	6.8	7.6
2	Assam	4.6	5.1	—	5.7	5.8	4.0	4.3	—	5.0	5.9	4.3	4.7	—	5.3	5.9
3	Bihar	5.1	5.7	6.8	6.5	6.8	6.1	6.1	6.8	6.0	6.5	5.6	5.9	6.8	6.3	6.6
4	Gujarat	4.5	5.0	5.5	6.0	6.3	5.4	5.6	5.2	6.8	7.8	4.9	5.3	5.3	6.4	6.9
5	Haryana	—	6.5	6.9	7.4	7.0	—	5.0	5.7	8.0	8.1	—	5.8	6.3	7.7	7.5
6	Karnataka	5.6	6.1	6.2	6.8	7.2	5.8	6.1	6.8	7.2	8.2	5.7	6.1	6.5	7.0	7.7
7	Kerala	5.6	6.0	7.2	8.3	9.6	6.0	6.5	7.8	9.3	11.3	5.8	6.2	7.5	8.8	10.5
8	Madhya Pradesh	4.6	5.5	6.1	6.5	6.7	5.7	6.1	6.8	6.8	7.6	5.2	5.8	6.4	6.6	7.1
9	Maharashtra	5.0	5.5	6.1	6.7	7.8	5.5	5.9	6.7	7.3	9.7	5.3	5.7	6.4	7.0	8.7
10	Orissa	5.1	5.8	6.1	7.2	8.1	6.2	6.3	6.7	7.2	8.5	5.7	6.0	6.4	7.2	8.3
11	Punjab	7.3	8.2	8.3	8.1	8.6	5.7	6.6	7.3	7.6	9.5	6.6	7.5	7.8	7.8	9.0
12	Rajasthan	5.0	5.5	5.8	6.1	6.2	5.3	5.5	6.3	6.5	7.3	5.1	5.5	6.0	6.3	6.7
13	Tamil Nadu	5.6	5.8	6.5	7.7	8.7	5.6	5.7	6.3	7.3	8.9	5.6	5.7	6.4	7.5	8.8
14	Uttar Pradesh	6.2	7.0	7.1	7.2	7.1	6.3	6.5	6.6	6.5	7.0	6.3	6.8	6.8	6.9	7.0
15	West Bengal	4.6	5.0	5.3	6.1	6.7	5.4	5.6	5.8	6.2	7.5	5.0	5.3	5.6	6.1	7.1
	India	5.5	5.9	6.4	6.7	7.1	5.8	6.0	6.6	6.8	7.8	5.6	6.0	6.5	6.8	7.4

Source: Census of India, *Socio-cultural Tables*, 1961, 1971, 1981, 1991 and Age Tables 2001

Note: 1. The state of Haryana was not formed in 1961 and census was not conducted in Assam in 1981 due to disturbances in the state.

Percentage change in the aged population from 1961 to 2001

Sl. No.	*State*	*Percentage change during 1961-2001*		
		Male	*Female*	*Total*
1	Andhra Pradesh	18.0	25.0	22.6
2	Assam	26.1	47.5	37.2
3	Bihar	33.3	6.6	17.9
4	Gujarat	40.0	44.4	40.8
5	Haryana*	7.7	62.0	29.3
6	Karnataka	28.6	41.4	35.1
7	Kerala	71.4	88.3	81.0
8	Madhya Pradesh	45.7	33.3	36.5
9	Maharashtra	56.0	76.4	64.2
10	Orissa	58.8	37.1	45.6
11	Punjab	17.8	66.7	36.4
12	Rajasthan	24.0	37.7	31.4
13	Tamil Nadu	55.4	58.9	57.1
14	Uttar Pradesh	14.5	11.1	11.1
15	West Bengal	45.7	38.9	42.0
	India	29.1	34.5	32.1

*Refers to 1971-2001

The sex-wise differential in the tempo of ageing shows that in all the states except Bihar, Madhya Pradesh, Orissa, Uttar Pradesh and West Bengal the speed of ageing is higher among females than males. During the forty years period, more than fifty percent increase in the proportion of the aged among both males and females is observed in Kerala, Maharashtra, Punjab and Tamil Nadu. Kerala stands out with an exceptionally higher pace of ageing among females with 88.3 percent followed by Maharashtra (76.4 %), Punjab (66.7 %) and Tamil Nadu (58.9 %) in that order. Haryana state also had a speed of 62.0 percent among the aged females during 1971-2001.

The changes in the age structure of the Indian population for the years 1961 - 2021 can be seen from the age pyramids given in Fig. 1. The projected age distribution based on the 2001 census age structure made by the Technical Group on Population Projections (Registrar General, 2006), is used for the population pyramids of 2011 and 2021. The change from a very broad base in 1961 to a shrunken base in 2001 indicates a decline in fertility leading to an increase in the proportion of aged population. Note further that twenty years from now, the pyramid is expected to take an entirely

Fig. 1
Age pyramids of India

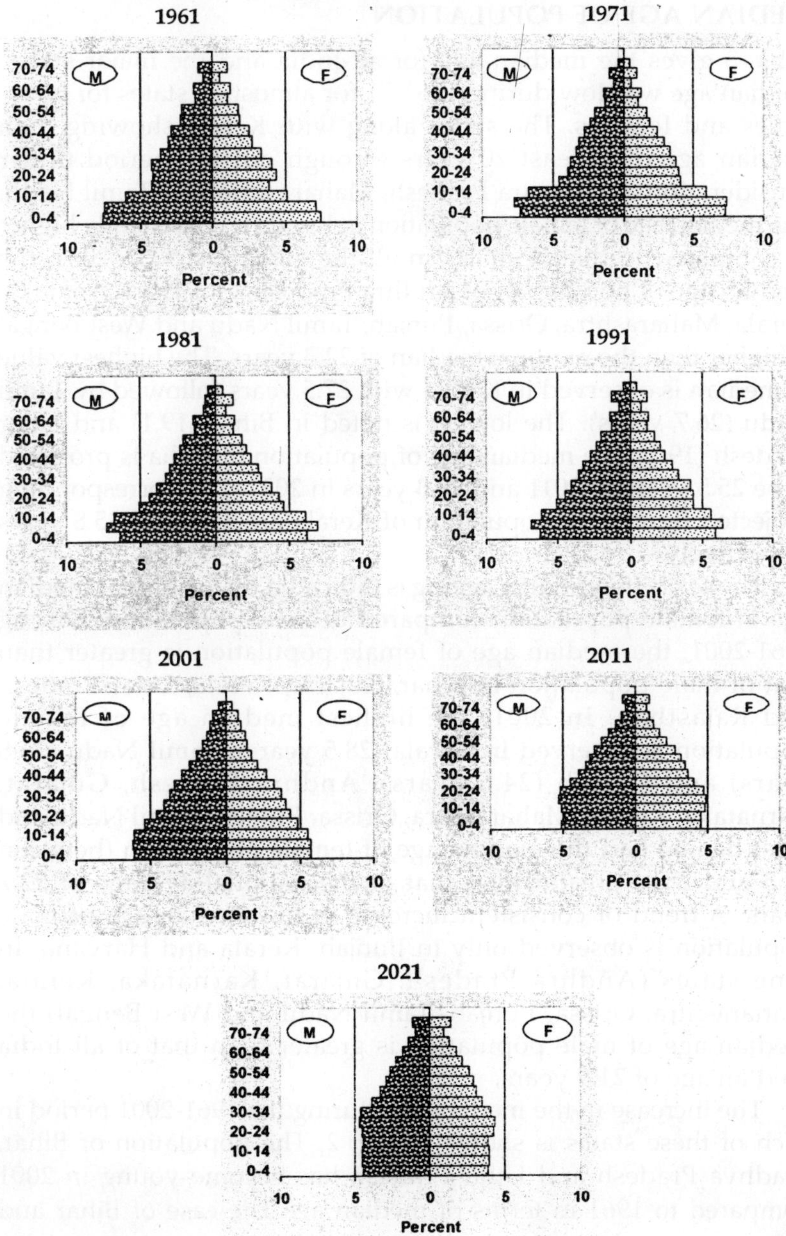

different shape with a larger proportion of population in the adult and older age groups.

MEDIAN AGE OF POPULATION

Table 3 gives the median age for all-India and the major states. Median age was low during 1961-71 for almost all states for both males and females. The states along with Kerala showing high median age of at least 20 years through out the period under consideration are Andhra Pradesh, Maharashtra and Tamil Nadu. The median age of female population in Kerala is consistently higher as compared to that of males in all the given years. In 2001, the median age of population of Andhra Pradesh, Gujarat, Karnataka, Kerala, Maharashtra, Orissa, Punjab, Tamil Nadu and West Bengal is higher than the national median of 22.3 years. The highest value of median is observed in Kerala with 27.5 years followed by Tamil Nadu (26.7 years). The lowest is noted in Bihar (19.1) and Uttar Pradesh (19.2).The median age of population of India is projected to be 25.5 years in 2011 and 29.3 years in 2021. The corresponding projected figures for population of Kerala are 31.8 and 35.8 years respectively.

The sex differential in ageing is indicated by the higher median age of female population compared to male population. During 1961-2001, the median age of female population is greater than that of male population in Bihar, Gujarat, Kerala, Uttar Pradesh and Rajasthan. In 2001, the highest median age of female population is observed in Kerala (28.5 years), Tamil Nadu (26.8 years) and Punjab (24.5 years). Andhra Pradesh, Gujarat, Karnataka, Kerala, Maharashtra, Orissa, Punjab, Tamil Nadu and West Bengal had the median age of female population (between 23.5 and 28.1) greater than that of the national average of 22.7 years. A trend of consistent increase in the median age of male population is observed only in Punjab, Kerala and Haryana. In nine states (Andhra Pradesh, Gujarat, Karnataka, Kerala, Maharashtra, Orissa, Punjab, Tamil Nadu and West Bengal) the median age of male population is greater than that of all India median age of 21.9 years.

The increase in the median age during the 1961-2001 period in each of these states is shown in Fig. 2. The population of Bihar, Madhya Pradesh and Uttar Pradesh has become young in 2001 compared to 1961 in terms of median age.The case of Bihar and

Table 3
Median age of population: 1961-2001

Sl. No.	State	*Male* 1961	1971	1981	1991	2001	*Female* 1961	1971	1981	1991	2001	*Total* 1961	1971	1981	1991	2001
1.	Andhra Pradesh	20.9	20.6	21.4	22.6	23.6	20.7	20.7	21.5	22.7	24.3	20.8	20.7	21.4	22.6	23.9
2.	Assam	19.5	18.1	—	20.6	21.3	16.6	15.1	—	19.2	20.9	18.1	16.8	—	19.9	21.1
3.	Bihar	19.3	19.0	19.4	19.8	18.6	20.7	20.3	20.5	20.5	19.7	20.0	19.7	19.9	20.1	19.1
4.	Gujarat	19.1	18.4	20.1	22.0	22.7	19.9	19.0	20.7	22.3	23.6	19.5	18.7	20.4	22.2	23.1
5.	Haryana	—	17.0	18.8	20.0	20.9	—	16.8	18.8	20.6	22.0	—	16.9	18.8	20.3	21.4
6.	Karnataka	20.1	19.4	20.4	22.2	23.4	19.5	18.9	20.1	22.2	24.2	19.8	19.1	20.2	22.2	23.8
7.	Kerala	18.9	19.2	21.3	24.3	26.7	19.8	19.7	21.8	24.8	28.1	19.3	19.5	21.6	24.6	27.5
8.	Madhya Pradesh	20.9	19.0	19.6	20.8	20.3	21.1	18.5	19.9	21.1	21.1	21.0	18.8	19.7	21.0	20.7
9.	Maharashtra	20.9	20.2	21.2	22.6	23.4	20.4	20.1	21.4	23.0	24.5	20.7	20.1	21.3	22.8	23.9
10.	Orissa	21.6	19.6	20.5	22.8	23.7	21.7	19.8	20.1	22.3	23.7	21.6	19.7	20.3	22.5	23.7
11.	Punjab	18.9	19.2	21.0	22.5	23.2	18.2	19.0	20.8	22.5	24.5	18.6	19.1	20.9	22.5	23.8
12.	Rajasthan	19.5	18.2	18.9	19.6	19.2	19.6	18.7	19.1	20.2	20.3	19.5	18.4	19.0	19.9	19.7
13.	Tamil Nadu	22.2	22.0	22.8	24.9	26.5	23.3	22.1	22.7	24.7	26.8	22.8	22.0	22.7	24.8	26.7
14.	Uttar Pradesh	20.7	19.7	19.3	19.8	18.9	21.1	20.4	20.1	20.3	19.7	20.9	20.0	19.7	20.0	19.2
15.	West Bengal	21.6	19.6	21.0	22.6	23.7	19.2	17.8	19.7	21.6	23.5	20.5	18.8	20.4	22.1	23.6
	India	20.5	19.6	20.2	21.6	21.9	20.4	19.6	20.6	21.8	22.7	20.5	19.6	20.4	21.7	22.3

Source: Computed from Census of India, *Socio-cultural Tables*, 1961, 1971, 1981, 1991 and Age Tables 2001.
Note: The state of Haryana was not formed in 1961 and census was not conducted in Assam in 1981 due to disturbances in the state.

Madhya Pradesh is mainly because of the division of the states which is evident from the positive increase of median age during 1961-91. But in Uttar Pradesh, the population has a "younging" trend. Reduction in the median age is noted for both men and women of Uttar Pradesh during the three decades. For women in Madhya Pradesh there is no change in the median age over the period under consideration. More than three years of increase in median age is observed for male and female population in Gujarat, Haryana Karnataka, Kerala, Punjab and Tamil Nadu.

Fig. 2
Change in median age for males and females during 1961-2001 (years)

Note: Haryana refers to 1971-2001

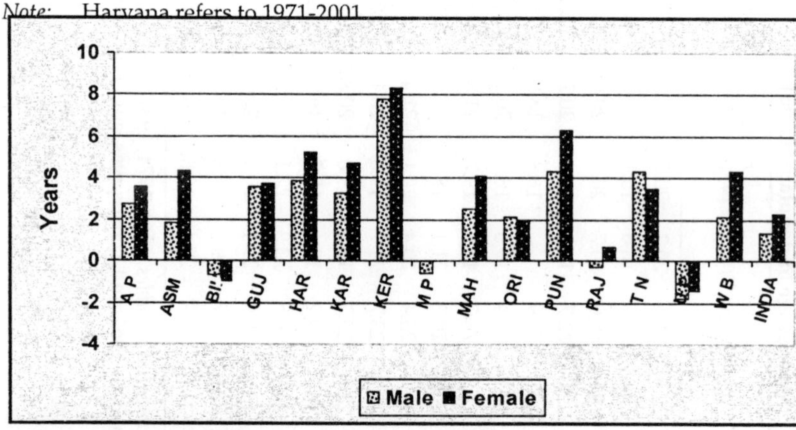

INDEX OF AGEING

This, as stated earlier, is an aged-child ratio expressed as percentage. From Table 4, the changes in age structure are evident during 1961-2001 for the fifteen major states. Kerala has the highest index of ageing in 2001 (40.2) with 35.1 for males and 45.5 for females. The next highest index for males is in Tamil Nadu (33.0) followed by Punjab (28.8). For women also Tamil Nadu (34.1) and Punjab (31.3) followed Kerala in that order.

All the states except Kerala and Tamil Nadu have an intermediate population as indicated by the ageing index. Kerala and Tamil Nadu have an old population as the index is exceeding the value of 30. Decade-wise differences in the pattern of change can also be noticed from Table 2.4. The increase in ageing index is highest during the decade1991-2001 for Andhra Pradesh, Karnataka,

Table 4
Index of ageing: 1961-2001

Sl. No.	*State*	*Male* 1961	1971	1981	1991	2001	*Female* 1961	1971	1981	1991	2001	*Total* 1961	1971	1981	1991	2001
1	Andhra Pradesh	15.4	15.6	16.8	19.9	22.1	16.1	15.8	17.7	19.4	25.4	15.8	15.7	17.2	19.6	23.7
2	Assam	10.7	11.4	—	14.3	15.7	8.4	8.7	—	12.0	15.6	9.6	10.1	—	13.1	15.7
3	Bihar	11.8	13.2	16.1	16.0	16.0	14.8	14.5	16.6	14.6	15.6	13.3	13.9	16.3	15.3	15.8
4	Gujarat	10.6	11.5	14.1	16.7	18.5	13.0	13.1	16.7	19.3	24.0	11.8	12.2	15.4	17.9	21.0
5	Haryana	—	14.1	16.6	19.0	19.3	—	10.7	13.6	20.3	22.8	—	12.5	15.2	19.6	20.9
6	Karnataka	13.6	14.6	15.9	19.0	22.3	13.6	14.1	17.0	19.8	26.0	13.6	14.4	16.4	19.4	24.1
7	Kerala	12.9	14.5	19.9	27.1	35.1	14.5	16.4	23.0	32.3	45.5	13.7	15.4	21.5	29.7	40.2
8	Madhya Pradesh	13.1	12.5	14.8	16.8	17.3	16.9	14.0	16.5	17.3	19.7	14.9	13.2	15.6	17.0	18.4
9	Maharashtra	12.5	13.5	16.0	18.8	24.2	13.5	14.2	17.4	20.4	30.4	13.0	13.8	16.7	19.6	27.2
10	Orissa	13.0	13.6	15.6	20.2	24.1	15.9	14.8	16.7	20.2	25.7	14.5	14.2	16.1	20.2	24.9
11	Punjab	16.9	20.1	22.6	23.3	26.7	12.9	15.9	19.5	21.9	31.3	15.1	18.1	21.1	22.6	28.8
12	Rajasthan	11.8	12.4	13.7	14.9	15.4	12.4	12.5	14.8	16.0	18.6	12.1	12.5	14.2	15.4	16.9
13	Tamil Nadu	14.8	15.3	18.6	24.6	31.9	16.8	15.1	18.1	23.7	34.1	15.7	15.2	18.3	24.2	33.0
14	Uttar Pradesh	15.3	16.6	16.9	18.0	17.2	15.6	15.7	15.9	15.9	17.1	15.4	16.2	16.4	17.0	17.2
15	West Bengal	11.8	12.2	14.1	17.0	20.4	12.7	12.5	14.5	16.4	22.4	12.2	12.4	14.3	16.7	21.4
	India	13.3	14.2	16.0	18.2	19.9	14.1	14.1	16.6	18.1	22.3	13.7	14.2	16.4	18.1	21.1

Source: Computed from census data.

Note: The state of Haryana was not formed in 1961 and census was not conducted in Assam in 1981 due to disturbances in the state.

Kerala, Maharashtra, Orissa, Punjab, Tamil Nadu, West Bengal and at all India level. The highest contribution to the index of ageing in the case of Bihar, Gujarat, Madhya Pradesh, Haryana and Rajasthan was made during the 1971-81 decade.

The increase in the index of ageing during the 1961-2001 period is shown in Fig. 3. In Uttar Pradesh, Madhya Pradesh, Bihar and Orissa the increase in the index of ageing is more among men than women. Noticeable increase in the index of ageing among males over the reference period is observed in Kerala (22.2), Tamil Nadu (17.1), Maharashtra (11.7) and Orissa (11.1). During this 40-year period the lowest increase in the index for men is noted for Uttar Pradesh (1.9) and Rajasthan (3.6). Similarly the lowest increase in the index of ageing for women is noted for Bihar (0.8), followed by Uttar Pradesh (1.5) and Madhya Pradesh (2.8) and the highest increase is in Kerala (31.0) followed by Punjab (18.4), Tamil Nadu (17.3) and Maharashtra (16.9).

Thus, when the entire period of 1961-2001 is considered, the increase in percentage points in the index of ageing is the lowest in Uttar Pradesh (1.8) Bihar (2.5) and Madhya Pradesh (3.5). Kerala is standing out way above all the other states with 26.5 percentage points. Tamil Nadu (17.3) Maharashtra (14.2), Punjab (13.7), Karnataka (10.5) and Orissa (10.4) have also shown a noticeable increase of more than ten points.

Fig. 3
Increase in the index of ageing among males and females during 1961-2001 (Percentage Points)

Note: Haryana relates to 1971-2001

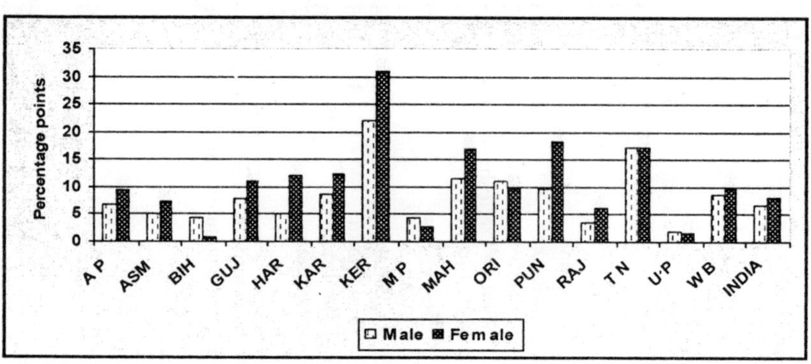

EXPECTATION OF LIFE AT BIRTH

The fourth index considered here is the expectation of life at birth and the required information is given in Table 5.

Generally female life expectancy at birth is found to be higher than that of males in many countries. But in India this type of situation is a recent phenomenon. Among the major states it is only in Andhra Pradesh, Kerala and Maharashtra where the female life expectancy is found to be more than that of males in 1970-75. In all the other states considered here, life expectancy of males is higher. But slowly the situation is changing. In the decade that followed (1981-85) apart from the three already mentioned states, Gujarat, Karnataka, Madhya Pradesh, Punjab, Rajasthan, Tamil Nadu and West Bengal also joined this group with female life expectancy more than that of males. In the next decade Haryana also entered this group. However, in Bihar and Orissa the life expectancy of males is consistently higher than that of females. It should also be mentioned that only Kerala has about 5-6 years difference between male and female life expectancy.

Table 5

Expectation of life at birth: 1970-75 to 1999-2003

Sl. No.	*State*	*Male*				*Female*				*Total*			
		1970-1975	*1981-1985*	*1993-1997*	*1999-2003*	*1970-1975*	*1981-1985*	*1993-1997*	*1999-2003*	*1970-1975*	*1981-1985*	*1993-1997*	*1999-2003*
1	Andhra Pradesh	48.4	57.2	61.2	62.2	49.3	59.8	63.5	64.8	48.8	58.4	62.4	63.7
2	Assam	46.2	52.0	56.6	57.8	44.8	51.9	57.1	58.3	45.5	51.9	56.7	58.0
3	Bihar	—	54.2	60.4	61.6	—	51.5	58.4	59.7	—	52.8	59.6	61.0
4	Gujarat	48.8	55.5	60.9	62.5	48.8	59.3	62.9	64.6	48.8	57.6	61.9	63.5
5	Haryana	59.0	61.5	63.7	65.0	55.6	59.0	69.6	65.6	57.5	60.3	64.1	65.4
6	Karnataka	55.4	59.7	61.6	62.9	55.1	62.0	69.9	66.4	55.2	60.6	63.3	64.6
7	Kerala	60.8	65.4	70.4	70.9	63.3	71.5	75.9	76.0	62.0	68.4	73.3	73.6
8	Madhya Pradesh	47.6	51.5	55.6	57.2	46.3	51.9	55.2	56.9	47.2	51.6	55.5	57.1
9	Mahara-shtra	53.3	59.6	64.1	65.2	54.5	62.1	66.6	67.6	53.8	60.6	65.5	66.4
10	Orissa	46.0	53.1	57.1	58.6	45.3	53.0	57.0	58.7	45.7	53.0	57.2	58.7
11	Punjab	59.0	62.6	66.7	67.6	56.8	63.6	68.8	69.6	57.9	63.1	67.7	68.6
12	Rajasthan	49.2	53.3	59.1	60.7	47.5	53.8	60.1	61.8	48.4	53.5	60.0	61.3
13	Tamil Nadu	49.6	56.5	63.2	64.3	49.5	57.4	65.1	66.5	49.6	56.9	64.1	65.4
14	Uttar Pradesh	45.4	51.4	58.1	59.6	40.5	48.5	56.9	58.7	43.0	50.0	57.6	59.3
15	West Bengal	—	56.8	62.2	63.5	—	58.0	63.6	65.0	—	57.4	62.8	64.1
	India	50.5	55.4	60.4	61.8	49.0	55.7	61.8	63.5	49.7	55.5	61.1	62.7

Source: Registrar General, 1984, 1989, 2000 and 2006.

The increase in life expectancy at birth during 1970-75 to 1999-

2003 is shown in Fig. 4.

Since in Kerala the life expectancy at birth was about 60 years which is higher than that of all India (49 years), even during 1970-75, its increment was not very high during the ensuing decades. The highest increase is noted in Karnataka and Haryana, and that too among the women. However, it is worth noting that in all the states the increase was more for women than for men with degrees of differences.

Fig. 4
Increase in expectation of life at birth for males and females: 1970-75 to 1999-2003 (Years)

Note: Data for Bihar and West Bengal relates to 1981-85 to 1999-03

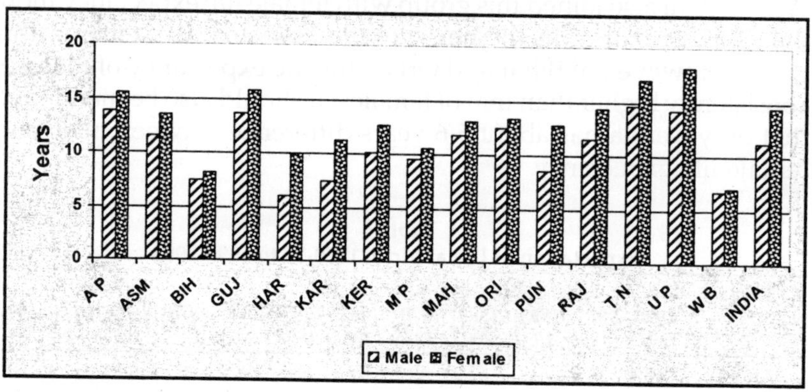

The expectation of life at age 60 is also considered in this section and the information for all the major states is given in Table 6.

Table 6
Expectation of life at age 60: 1970-75 to 1999-2003

Sl. No.	*State*	*Male* 1970-1975	1981-1985	1993-1997	1999-2003	*Female* 1970-1975	1981-1985	1993-1997	1999-2003	*Total* 1970-1975	1981-1985	1993-1997	1999-2003
1	Andhra Pradesh	12.3	14.0	14.9	16.4	13.2	16.2	15.8	17.4	12.8	15.1	15.5	17.1
2	Assam	11.3	13.1	13.8	15	12.0	14.0	15.5	16.1	11.6	13.4	14.5	15.6
3	Bihar	-	15.0	17.0	17.5	-	15.3	17.5	17.2	-	15.1	17.4	17.4
4	Gujarat	12.8	15.0	14.6	15.7	14.7	17.8	16.2	17.4	13.8	16.4	15.4	16.6
5	Haryana	15.7	17.1	17.5	19.5	16.1	17.4	19.7	20.2	16.0	17.2	18.3	19.8
6	Karnataka	15.2	15.7	15.0	16.2	16.5	18.0	17.3	18.5	15.8	16.6	16.4	17.4
7	Kerala	15.0	16.5	18.0	19.0	16.5	19.4	20.7	20.6	15.8	17.9	19.7	19.9
8	Madhya Pradesh	13.3	13.5	14.4	15.3	14.8	15.5	14.6	15.9	14.3	14.4	14.5	15.7

Sl. No.	State	Male 1970-1975	Male 1981-1985	Male 1993-1997	Male 1999-2003	Female 1970-1975	Female 1981-1985	Female 1993-1997	Female 1999-2003	Total 1970-1975	Total 1981-1985	Total 1993-1997	Total 1999-2003
9	Maharashtra	13.7	15.0	16.3	17	14.9	17.7	17.5	17.9	14.3	16.2	17.0	17.5
10	Orissa	11.6	14.1	15.5	16	11.3	14.5	15.7	15.9	11.4	14.3	15.4	16.0
11	Punjab	16.6	16.9	20.6	20.5	16.0	19.3	21.7	21.4	16.3	17.9	21.1	20.9
12	Rajasthan	13.6	13.8	14.9	16	15.7	17.0	15.9	17.5	14.6	15.3	15.9	16.9
13	Tamil Nadu	12.8	14.3	15.2	16.3	12.8	15.0	15.9	16.9	12.8	14.6	15.6	16.6
14	Uttar Pradesh	13.4	14.3	14.8	15.7	14.5	15.3	15.8	16.6	13.6	14.8	15.6	16.2
15	West Bengal	-	14.0	15.3	16.4	-	16.2	16.5	17.5	-	15.0	15.8	16.9
	India	13.4	14.6	15.5	16.3	14.3	16.4	17.5	18.5	13.8	15.4	16.5	17.4

Source: Registrar General, 1984, 1989, 2000 and 2006.

In 1999-2003, the expected number of years of remaining life (residual length of life) after attaining age 60 in Kerala (19.9 years) is second only to Punjab, which has one year more than that of Kerala. Thus, on an average, a 60 year old person is likely to live up to 80 years in Kerala and 81 years in Punjab. The lowest in this case is Assam and Madhya Pradesh with about 15.6 years. Sex-wise differences also showed more or less the same pattern. During the entire period under consideration Punjab added 4 years to the expected life of men and 5.4 years to that of women. The corresponding figures for Kerala are comparatively low with years added being 4.0 and 4.1 for men and women respectively.

AGE DEPENDENCY RATIO

Age dependency ratio is another indicator of analyzing the changes in the age structure of a population, the ratio being expressed as a percentage of population in dependent age group to working age population. Given below in Table 7 is the dependency ratio of young and old population in the 15 major states in India.

Kerala has the lowest young age dependency ratio (41.1) because of the low fertility level achieved by the state and Tamil Nadu is closer by 42.0 percent. The highest young age dependency ratio is prevailing in Bihar (82.2), Uttar Pradesh (79.1), Rajasthan (75.5) and Madhya Pradesh (71.2) which indicates the high fertility level of these states. Old age dependency ratio is the highest in Kerala (16.5) followed by Punjab (15.2). The old age dependency ratio of the country is 13.1 percent and it is projected to attain 16.7 by 2021. The total age dependency ratio of Kerala (57.6) is next only to Tamil Nadu which has the lowest among the major states.

Table 7
Age dependency ratio: 2001

Sl. No.	*States*	*Age Dependency ratio* Young	Old	Total
1	Andhra Pradesh	53.2	12.6	65.8
2	Assam	55.8	11.9	67.8
3	Bihar	82.2	13.0	95.1
4	Gujarat	54.5	11.5	66.0
5	Haryana	63.7	13.3	77.0
6	Karnataka	52.8	12.7	65.6
7	Kerala	41.1	16.5	57.6
8	Madhya Pradesh	71.2	13.1	84.3
9	Maharashtra	54.4	14.8	69.1
10	Orissa	56.8	14.1	70.9
11	Punjab	52.7	15.2	67.9
12	Rajasthan	75.5	12.8	88.2
13	Tamil Nadu	42.0	13.9	55.9
14	Uttar Pradesh	79.1	13.6	92.6
15	West Bengal	55.8	11.9	67.8
	India	62.1	13.1	75.2

AN ASSESSMENT OF THE OVERALL SITUATION

Using four indices of ageing, a summary picture of the ageing in the major states is presented in Table 8. For this purpose only the 2001 situation is taken into account and the all-India situation is used for dividing the states into two groups. As can be seen from the Table, the states are entered in ascending order of values.

The indices of ageing given in the Table shows that Kerala stands out with unique features like the highest proportion of elderly (10.5 percent), highest median age (27.5 years), the highest index of ageing (40.2 percent) and the highest expectation of life at birth (73.6 years) among the 15 major states of the country.

Based on the classification described in the methodology for the indices of ageing, none of the major states in India can be described as having a young population. All states, except Kerala, are in the transitional stage from intermediate population to the old category. Kerala is the only state which satisfies the criterion of an aged population in three measures, viz. the proportion of aged, Index of ageing and expectation of life at birth. The projected population of the state indicates that the median age will reach 31.8 years by 2011.The trend shown in the Table also indicates that Tamil Nadu and Punjab will soon join the category of "old population".

Table 8
Classification of states by indices of ageing: 2001

Percent old, 2001 (India=7.4)		*Median age, 2001 (India=22.3)*		*Index of ageing, 2001 (India = 21.1)*		*Life expectancy at birth, 1999-03 (India = 62.7)*	
< 7.4	*>=7.4*	*< 22.3*	*>=22.3*	*< 21.1*	*>=21.1*	*<62.7*	*>=62.7*
Asm (5.9)	Har (7.5)	Bih (19.1)	Guj (23.1)	Asm (15.7)	WB (21.4)	M P (57.1)	Guj (63.5)
Bih (6.6)	AP (7.6)	U P (19.2)	WB (23.6)	Bih (15.8)	AP (23.7)	Asm (58.0)	AP (63.7)
Raj (6.7)	Kar (7.7)	Raj (19.7)	Ori (23.7)	Raj (16.9)	Kar (24.1)	Ori (58.7)	WB (64.1)
Guj (6.9)	Ori (8.3)	MP (20.7)	Kar (23.8)	UP (17.2)	Ori (24.9)	UP (59.3)	Kar (64.6)
UP (7.0)	Mah (8.7)	Asm (21.1)	Pun (23.8)	MP (18.4)	Mah (27.2)	Bih (61.0)	Har (65.4)
MP (7.1)	TN (8.8)	Har (21.4)	AP (23.9)	Har (20.9)	Pun (28.8)	Raj (61.3)	TN (65.4)
WB (7.1)	Pun (9.0)		Mah (23.9)	Guj (21.0)	TN (33.0)		Mah (66.4)
	Kerala (10.5)		TN (26.7)		*Kerala (40.2)*		Pun (68.6)
			Kerala (27.5)				*Kerala (73.6)*

Note: The states are arranged in ascending order of the value of the index

AGEING AND THE AGED IN KERALA

According to the census of India 2001, Kerala had a population of 31,841,374. Since Kerala's population is ageing faster than that of other states some of the population related aspects in general and selected characteristics of the aged population in particular is presented in this section. Given in Fig. 5 is the growth of total population of Kerala from 1961-2001.

Fig. 5
Total population of Kerala: 1961-2001

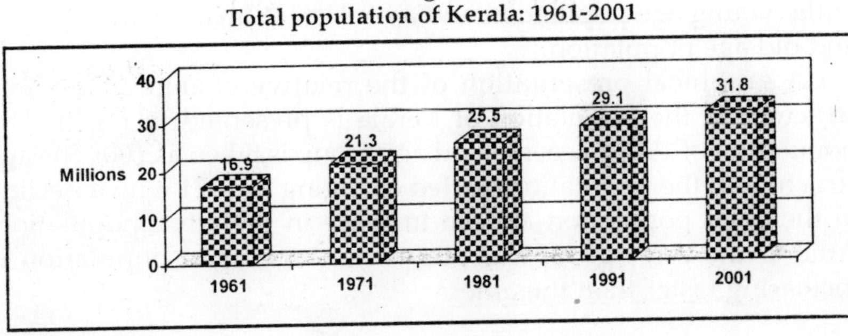

Fig. 6
Percent share of population increase in Kerala by decade: 1961-2001

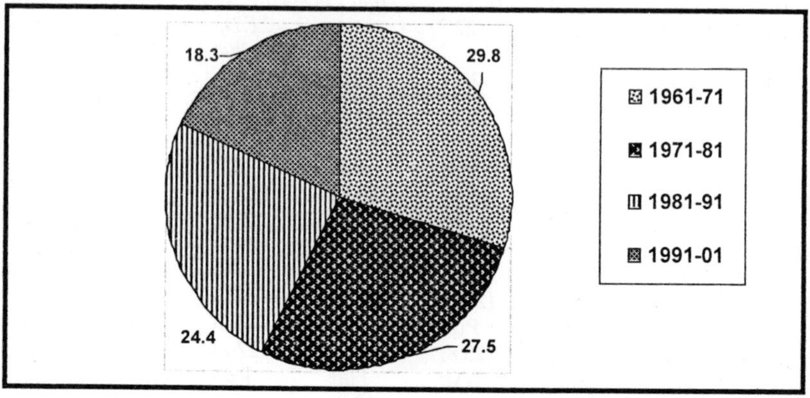

The population of Kerala has been increasing at a slower rate. A total of 14.93 million people had been added to the 1961 population during the 1961-2001 period. The percent share of each decade in this contribution is shown in Fig. 6.

It can be seen that the contribution made to the total population has steadily declined over the four decades. While the decade 1961-71 accounted almost 30 percent of the increase in population, the last decade (1991-2001) accounted only for 18 percent.

Changes in the age composition of the population of Kerala can be seen from Fig. 7. The transition of the age structure from a pyramidal shape with a broad base to a cylindrical shape during 1961-2021 clearly portrays the changing age structure of the population.

For a quick understanding of the age composition of the population Table 9 can be used where distribution of population by broad age groups is given. Note that there is a consistent decline in the young age population and a consistent increase in the adult and old age population.

A graphical presentation of the relative change in the age structure of the population of Kerala is presented in Fig. 8. The population of 1961 in each broad age group is taken as 100. The age structure of the population started changing in 1971 with a decline in the child population and an increase in the adult population. Among the three groups of population, the aged population is increasing faster than the others.

Fig. 7
Population pyramids of Kerala

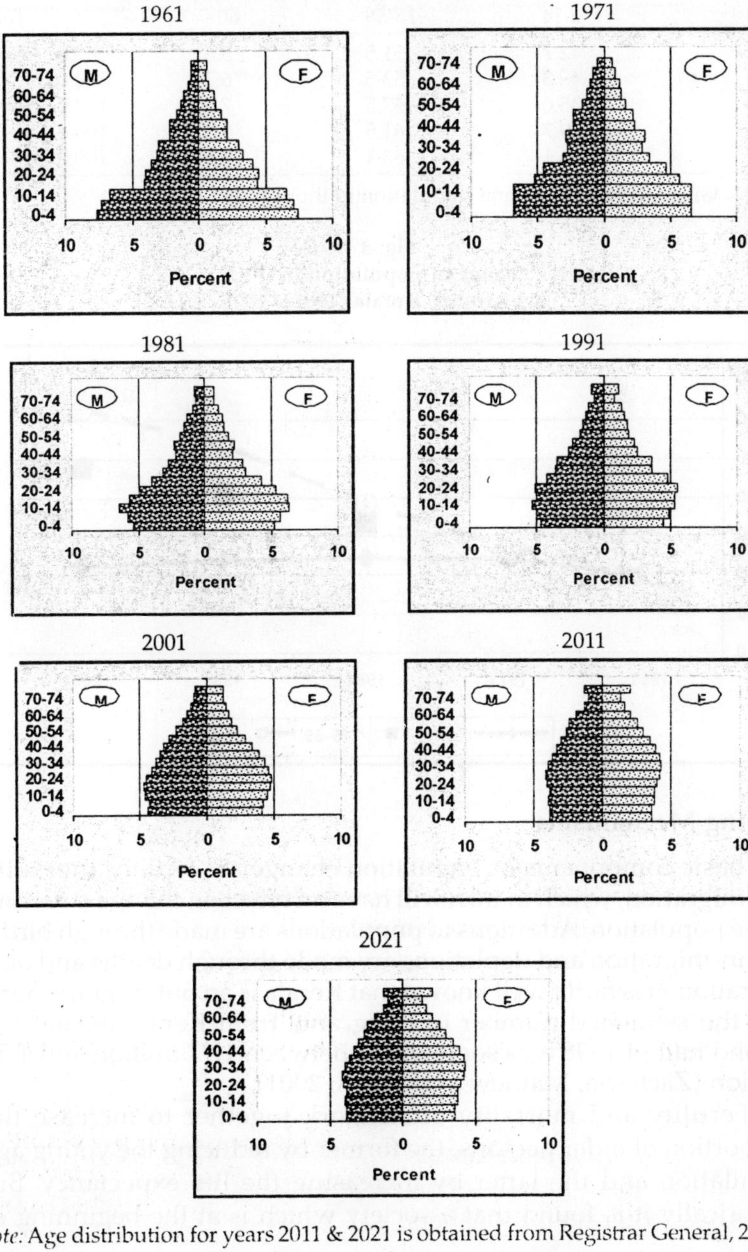

Note: Age distribution for years 2011 & 2021 is obtained from Registrar General, 2006.

Table 9
Percentage distribution of population in Kerala by broad age group

Census Year	0-14	15-59	60+	Total
	Percentage distribution of population			
1961	42.7	51.5	5.8	100.0 (16900)
1971	40.3	53.5	6.2	100.0 (21346)
1981	35.0	57.5	7.5	100.0 (25450)
1991	29.7	61.5	8.8	100.0 (29028)
2001	26.1	63.4	10.5	100.0 (31842)

Note: Given in bracket is total population in thousands

Fig. 8
Relative change of population in three broad age groups, Kerala (1961 = 100)

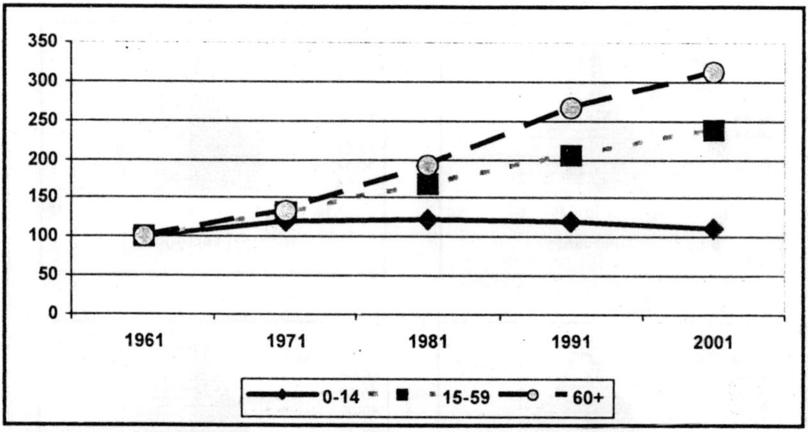

Ageing Mechanisms

The basic components of population change are fertility, mortality and migration, which in turn will have an effect on the age structure of the population. Additions to populations are made through births and in-migration and depletions are made through deaths and out-migration. It is fairly well known that Kerala is an out-migrant state, and the estimated number of emigrants from Kerala during the second half of 1998 was somewhere between 1.17 million and 1.55 million (Zacharia, Mathew and Rajan, 2001).

Fertility and mortality often work together to increase the proportion of older persons, the former by reducing the young age population and the latter by increasing the life expectancy. But historically it is found that a society which is at the beginning of transition, fertility would play a major role than mortality (Lorimer, 1951; Coale, 1956). That is, at the early stages of demographic transition a decline in mortality will have the immediate effect of reducing deaths among infants and children, which will have the same effect as that of high fertility. Such a change will have the effect of slowing down the ageing process rather than accelerating it (Radha Devi, 1998). However, once the mortality and fertility reach a very low level, mortality will start playing a major role in the ageing process by reducing the deaths among the aged persons. However, other things remaining constant, faster and continued decline in mortality will have the effect of increasing the number of persons in all age groups, thereby disallowing any change in the proportion of persons in the different age groups.

The birth, death and infant mortality rates of Kerala are given in Fig. 9. Infant mortality rate is provided mainly because of its effect on fertility. Though decline in mortality will affect all the age groups, the risks of death being comparatively high at infancy and at very old age, both young and the very old will benefit from a decline in mortality at the beginning. However, overall age structure of the population will be affected by the decline in the infant mortality than by the decline in the death rate of very old persons, as the number involved in both the extremes of life are different and that the gains due to decline in mortality could only be moderate for the elderly.

In the 1950s, the infant mortality rate in Kerala was very high (120) and the corresponding birth rate also was fairly high at 39 (Srinivasan, 1995). By 1966 there was a drastic decline in the infant mortality rate (92) due to various measures adopted by the Government to improve the health status of the people. This decline continued fast in the ensuing decades and so did the birth rate. However, Kerala has not yet reached a situation where both the birth and death rates are equal. In 2004, the birth rate of the population of Kerala was 15.2 and death rate was 6.1 as compared to the corresponding rate of India 24.1 and 7.5 respectively (Registrar General India, 2006).

SELECTED FEATURES OF THE AGED POPULATION

Using mostly census data, a few selected characteristics of the aged population are given in this section.

Fig. 9
Birth, death and infant mortality rates in Kerala

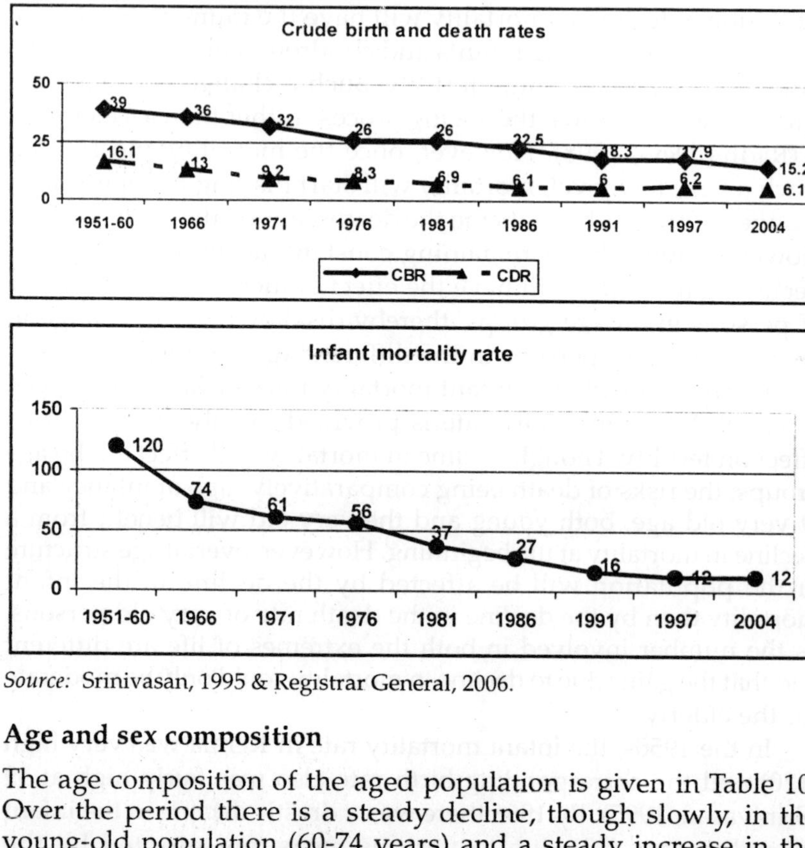

Source: Srinivasan, 1995 & Registrar General, 2006.

Age and sex composition

The age composition of the aged population is given in Table 10. Over the period there is a steady decline, though slowly, in the young-old population (60-74 years) and a steady increase in the old-old population (75 years and above). Eighty one percent of the elderly were aged 60-74 years in 1961 compared to 76 percent in 2001.

Table 10
Age distribution of the aged population of Kerala

Age group (in years)	*Percentage distribution of aged population* 1961	1971	1981	1991	2001
60-64	38.3	36.3	35.6	33.9	30.9
65-69	24.9	26.3	27.2	27.2	27.0
70-74	17.3	17.3	16.8	16.8	18.4
75-79	11.0	10.7	10.8	10.8	12.0
80+	8.5	9.4	9.6	11.3	11.7
Total	100.0 (986383)	100.0 (1327696)	100.0 (1909789)	100.0 (2567365)	100.0 (3335675)

Sex composition is measured in terms of number of males per 1000 females. Unlike in almost all other parts of the country Kerala state has more female population giving a low sex ratio. Table 11 gives the sex ratio of the population in each age group.

Table 11
Sex ratio of the aged population of Kerala by age

Age group (in years)	*Males per 1000 females* 1961	1971	1981	1991	2001
60-64	934	948	947	918	871
65-69	943	901	870	867	796
70-74	895	896	852	859	804
75-79	910	871	823	787	770
80+	840	844	834	796	679
Total	918	908	884	865	802

The number of males per 1000 females for the total population is consistently declining. Perhaps in Kerala, like in many of the more developed countries, more women survive to a higher age group than is the case with men.

Literacy/Education

The level of literacy and the level of education of literate population are given in Table 12 for elderly population of Kerala. Even in 1981, two out of three elderly men in Kerala were literate of whom nearly one-third had at least primary level of education. The share of literates among the total elderly men has increased to 78.7 percent by 1991 and 75 percent had at least primary level of education. Among elderly women, though the proportion was lower than that of elderly men, it still is not too bad – with one-third of the elderly women being literate in 1981 and slightly more than half (52.3%) falling in this category in 1991. The level of education of the literate elderly women shows that those with at least primary level of education have increased from 29.6 percent in 1981 to 48.6 percent in 1991. For both men and women, the increase in the middle school education and above is quite conspicuous.

Marital status

The distribution of elderly by their marital status (Table 13) shows that the proportion never married has reduced to 2.4 for males while it remained 3.3 percent among women during 1991-2001. A higher proportion of elderly men are currently married while a higher proportion of elderly women are currently widowed. The proportion of currently married in 2001 is 87 percent among males

Table 12
Literacy rate and educational level of literate population, Kerala

Literacy rate and level of education	*Male 1981*	*Male 1991*	*Female 1981*	*Female 1991*	*Total 1981*	*Total 1991*
Literacy rate	66.1	78.7	32.9	52.3	48.4	64.6
Percentage distribution of literate population by level of education						
Below primary*	68.2	25.2	60.2	33.9	65.3	30.9
Primary	30.7	48.0	29.6	48.6	30.3	48.3
Middle and above	1.1	26.8	10.2	17.5	4.4	22.8
Total	100.0	100.0	100.0	100.0	100.0	100.0

*Includes non-formal education

as against 37 percent among females. In both men and women the proportion of widowed increased during 1991-2001 as compared to a decreasing trend during 1961-1991. The decline in the proportion of widowed women during the three decades is much higher than the increase in the proportion of currently married elderly men. This could be due to the improvement in health care systems in the state and consequent increase in the life expectancy of men. One in ten elderly males was widowed as compared to 59 percent among women in 2001.

Table 13
Percentage distribution of aged by marital status, Kerala

Sl. No.	*Marital status*	*Male 1961*	*1971*	*1981*	*1991*	*2001*	*Female 1961*	*1971*	*1981*	*1991*	*2001*
1	Never married	1.5	1.9	2.1	3.2	2.4	1	1.5	0.9	3.3	3.3
2	Currently married	79.4	84.2	85.3	87.6	87.4	23.2	27.3	30.1	38	36.6
3	Widowed	17.7	12.8	11.5	8.6	9.7	74.1	69.8	66.1	57.5	58.7
4	Divorced/Separated	1.4	1.1	1.1	0.6	0.5	1.7	1.4	1.5	1.2	1.4
5	Not specified	—	—	—	—	—	—	—	1.4	—	—
6	Total	100	100	100	100	100	100	100	100	1000	100

Work participation

Work participation rate obtained from the census data should be interpreted with caution, as there are frequent changes in the definition of workers and thus changes in the number of workers. In 1971, work was divided into "main work" and "subsidiary work" where subsidiary work information was obtained for both main worker as well as non-workers. Moreover, the data are not classified by age. Since 1981 census, a new category of worker was made on the basis of whether they had been working for 180 days in a year or less than that. The former group is called "main workers" and the latter is called "marginal workers". Nevertheless, the work participation rate of the elderly of the state is presented in Table 14 for the period 1961-2001. In 2001, among elderly persons, about one-fourth was engaged in some economic activities while another two percent of the non-workers were seeking or available for work. Two-fifths of the aged men including 32 percent of main workers and eight percent of marginal workers were engaged in some activity.

Among the female elderly, work participation *per se* is very low. In 2001, their work participation rate was less than 10 percent (8.8%) with 5.5 percent of main workers and 3.3 percent of marginal workers.

Table 14
Work participation rate of elderly in Kerala

	Work participation rate of elderly (%)		
Year	*Male*	*Female*	*Total*
1961	65.6	14.8	39.1
1971	60.1	7.7	32.7
1981	49.1	10.0	28.4
1991	45.6	9.6	26.3
2001	40.5	8.8	22.9

Source: Economic Tables of respective census years

On the whole there is a declining trend for the proportion of workers among the aged population during 1961-2001. However, it should be noted that the *number* of elderly workers have been consistently on the increase as can be seen from Fig. 10 where the relative increase in the number of older workers and population is shown taking 1961 as the base. However, the increase for women workers started only from 1971.

The increase in the number of older persons as well as the workers have taken place particularly after 1971 from which time there was a noticeable decline in the death rate in the population. About fifty six percent of male and female workers were engaged in agriculture related activities in 1991. The non-agricultural workers also have shown some kind of concentration in specific activities as shown in Table 15. The twelve occupational groups together accounts for 62.1 percent of the male and 73.9 percent of the female non-agricultural workers. A noticeable proportion (16%) of the elderly men is found to be working as merchants or shop keepers dealing with wholesale or retail trade.

Table 15
Percentage distribution of elderly main workers in Kerala by major occupational groups (non-agricultural) : 1991

Sl. No.	*Groups*	*Male*	*Female*	*Total*
1	Production and RW, n.e.c.	2.2	15.7	4.4
2	Food and beverage processes	2.3	5.5	2.8
3	Laborers n.e.c.	2.7	2.5	2.7
4	Other farm workers	2.8	1.9	2.6
5	Spinners, weavers etc.	3.0	29.6	7.4
6	Professional workers	3.1	1.3	2.8
7	Hotel and restaurant keepers	4.3	1.1	3.8
8	Salesmen, shop assistants and RW	4.9	4.7	4.8
9	Fishermen and related workers	5.5	0.8	4.7
10	Farmers, fishermen etc.	7.5	2.4	6.7
11	Plantation laborers and RW	8.1	3.8	7.4
12	Merchants/shopkeepers, wholesale and retail trade	16.0	4.9	14.2
13	Other groups	37.9	26.1	35.9
	Total	100.0	100.00	100.00
		141434	28022	169456

Note: n.e.c = not elsewhere classified.

Fig. 10
Relative increase in the number of older population and older workers in Kerala (1961=100)

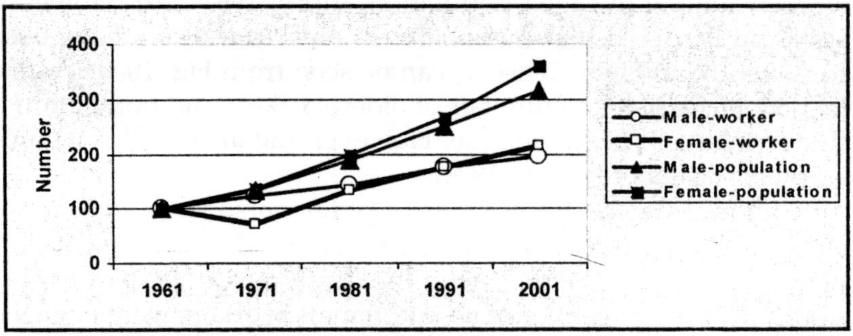

Almost 30 percent of the elderly women are engaged in spinning, weaving and related work. Concentration of women workers in works that are not really classified reflects the type of odd jobs that they will have to do to help themselves and their family. About 16 percent are working as production and related workers, though their nature of work is not specified. Similarly 26.1 percent of the workers are concentrated in the category "other work" indicating that they cannot really be classified into known types of work.

Activity status of non-working elderly

The aged population is not a homogenous group in its activities. Apart from those who are currently engaged in some economic activities, there are retired persons receiving pensions, total dependants, those engaged in household work, beggars/vagrants, inmates of mental and charitable institutions etc. The various censuses of India have collected information for each individual about his/her activity status. The non-working elderly of Kerala are classified on the basis of their activity status and the results are presented in Table 16. There are mainly three activities each for men and women and all the other activities are clubbed together and labeled "others" in the Table.

Table 16
Percentage distribution of elderly non-workers in Kerala by activity status: 1961-2001

Activity status	*1961*	*1971*	*1981*	*1991*	*2001*
Male					
RP/R	20.6	17.2	17	23.3	23.3
HHW	—	8.9	12.2	8.2	9.4
Dependant	74.6	72	68.4	65.5	50.6
Others	4.8	1.9	2.4	3	16.7
Total	100	100	100	100	100
Female					
RP/R	2.5	1.9	2.8	4.1	5.7
HHW	46	43.1	42.2	45.1	42.4
Dependant	50.1	54.5	54.3	50	47.5
Others	1.4	0.5	0.7	0.8	4.4
Total	100	100	100	100	100

Source: Census of India publications
Note: RP/R = retired pensioners/rentiers; HHW = household work

The Table 16 shows that, in 2001, about one-fourth of the non-working men are either retired pensioners/rentiers while half of the aged men are dependents. One in ten aged men has reported that they do household work. On the other hand, half of the elderly women are either engaged in household work or they are dependant. Only about six percent of them receive some kind of service pension. Though small in proportion, a slight increase in the pensioners/rentiers is noted among both men and women. So the sex differential in the activity status of non-workers is also prominent where programmes and policies have to focus on the well being of aged in general and women in particular.

Selected aspects of elder care in Kerala

The National Sample Survey Organization (NSSO) in its 52nd round (Govt. of India, 1998) asked specific questions relating to the economic aspects of the elderly. This information for Kerala is given in Table 17. Majority of the elderly in both rural and urban areas are fully dependent on others and do not enjoy any retirement benefits. Most of them are supported by their own children. The elderly men who enjoy retirement benefits vary from 19 percent in rural to 29.1 percent in urban areas. The corresponding proportion for elderly women is 14.4 percent and 18.4 percent respectively. The economic dependency status shows that 45-50 percent of men are independent, whereas this proportion is very low for women (9.1% to 11.0%). The proportion partially depending on others is more or less the same for both men and women. Three in every four women are fully dependent on others.

Table 17
Percentage distribution of elderly by selected economic characteristics, Kerala

Sl. No.	*Characteristics*	*Male*		*Female*		*Total*	
		Rural	*Urban*	*Rural*	*Urban*	*Rural*	*Urban*
1	*Retirement benefits*						
	Pension only	6.5	7.6	7.9	9.7	7.2	8.3
	Pension with other benefits	7.5	12.1	4.5	4.5	6.0	9.4
	Only other benefits	5.0	9.4	2.0	4.2	3.5	7.6
	No benefits	68.8	35.3	74.2	46.3	71.5	39.2
	No data	12.2	35.6	11.4	35.3	11.8	35.5
2	*Dependency on others (Economic independence)*						
	Not dependent	49.7	44.9	9.2	11.2	27.4	26.3
	Partially dependent	14.8	14.2	13.7	12.0	14.2	13.0
	Fully dependent	32.5	38.1	73.6	76.0	55.2	59.0
	No data	3.0	2.8	3.5	0.8	3.3	1.7
3	*Supporting person*						
	Spouse	7.9	5.7	15.5	11.7	13.1	9.8
	Own children	83.2	83.7	72.9	72.0	76.1	75.8
	Grand children	1.5	2.0	4.0	3.7	3.2	3.2
	Others	4.5	4.2	5.7	11.1	5.4	8.8
	No data	2.9	4.4	1.9	1.5	2.2	2.4

Source: Government of India, 1998

Kerala state has introduced about forty types of social security programmes including pensions for the aged persons of which twenty are financed by the state (Govt. of Kerala, 2007). The pension schemes that cater to a large segment of elderly, viz. widow/destitute pension and agricultural pension form part of the state financed scheme. Pensions to craftsman and sportsmen in indigenous conditions are also financed by the state. Relief and welfare fund for cashew workers, handloom workers, coir workers, *Khadi*[2] workers, construction workers, advocates, clerks and fishermen come under schemes financed with state support. All these welfare schemes are available for retired or disabled workers above 60 years of age of the respective sector. Schemes operated by respective boards include head load worker, *abkari* worker[3], toddy worker, motor workers, artisan, auto-*riksha*[4] workers, agricultural worker, lottery agents and document writers, scribes and stamp vendors. About thirty seven lakhs of persons are benefited by the social security measures with an allotment equal to three percent of the state budget. Some of the pension schemes were introduced way back in 1973 while majority of them have been implemented during 1980-90.The amount of pension ranges from Rs. 100 to Rs. 150 per month. In addition, there exists national old age pension scheme catering to about 131912 elderly persons (in 2006) receiving Rs. 110 per month. A few pension schemes are presented in Table 18 to have a feel of the number of beneficiaries from various social security net work for the year 2003.

It is also of interest here to note that the retirement age for those who are in the service sector is 55 years in Kerala state and the life expectancy at age 55 is 23.2 years in 1991-95 (Registrar General, 1998). Thus it is a matter of great concern for the children of the aged, as this "unproductive group" of persons has to be taken care of for a longer period than it used to be in olden days. Furthermore, the number of children available to take care of parents is also on the decline. The total fertility rate of the state is already below replacement level at 1.8 in 1997 (Registrar General, 1998). The joint family system where the older parents could find some activity to while away their time is also on the decline. In this fast moving society where the children are trying to cope with the increasing needs of their own children and their own life, the elderly end up as burdens which one grudgingly has to endure (United Nations, 1992). This leads to the development of more and more old age homes where the parents are left so that the children and their family can take care of themselves without much concern for the elderly. Ara (1995) reports that Kerala has the largest number of old age homes compared to any other state in India and the largest number of elderly accommodated in these homes. In 2004 there were 164 old age homes in Kerala accommodating 5400 elderly persons (Government of Kerala, 2006). However, the elderly will not get in these Homes what they need in large doses at this stage in their life, namely love and affection from one's own kith and kin.

Table 18
Number of beneficiaries of various pension schemes in Kerala: 2003

Sl. No.	*Schemes*	*No. of persons who received assistance during 2002-03*
1	Kerala *khadi* workers welfare scheme	17
2	Kerala *abkari* workers welfare scheme	97
3	Welfare fund for Cine artist	146
4	Kerala ration dealers welfare scheme	252
5	Welfare fund for journalist	398
6	Kerala Tailoring workers welfare scheme	5450
7	Kerala handloom workers welfare scheme	7407
8	Kerala freedom fighter's pension scheme	8880
9	Kerala toddy workers welfare scheme	14929
10	Kerala fishermen's welfare scheme	28130
11	Kerala construction workers welfare scheme	37969
12	Kerala coir workers welfare scheme	67000
13	National old age pension scheme	134600
14	Widow/destitute pension scheme	208445
15	Agricultural workers pension scheme	527647

Source: Economic Review, 2004, State Planning Board, Government of Kerala, Thiruvananthapuram.

Kerala state is leading in the care and protection of the senior citizens by implementing an old age policy in 2006 (GO.M.S.No.39/2006 dated 5.12.2006) with an objective of empowering the elderly socially and economically for ageing gracefully and with dignity.

NOTES

1. The bifurcation of Bihar, Madhya Pradesh and Uttar Pradesh into two states each took place after 1991 census and thus the 2001 data for the said three states refers to its present form and not the 1991 form which include Chattisgarh in Madhya Pradesh, Jharkhand in Bihar and Uttaranchal (Uttarkhand) in Uttar Pradesh. The new states are not taken into account here as no trend analysis can be done for them.
2. Khadi is Indian handspun and hand-woven cloth.
3. "Abkari Worker" means any person who is employed for wages in connection with the storing, bottling, transport or sale of liquor and who gets his wages directly or indirectly from the employer.
4. A small three wheeled vehicle powered by an engine for 3-4 persons.

APPENDIX

(Age pyramids of selected states)

A P – 1961

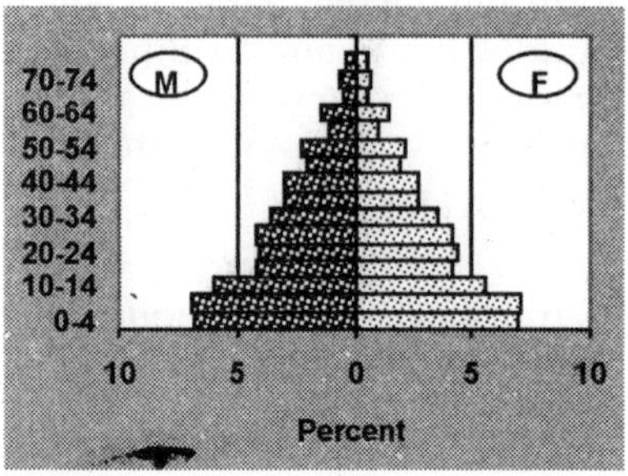

A P – 1971

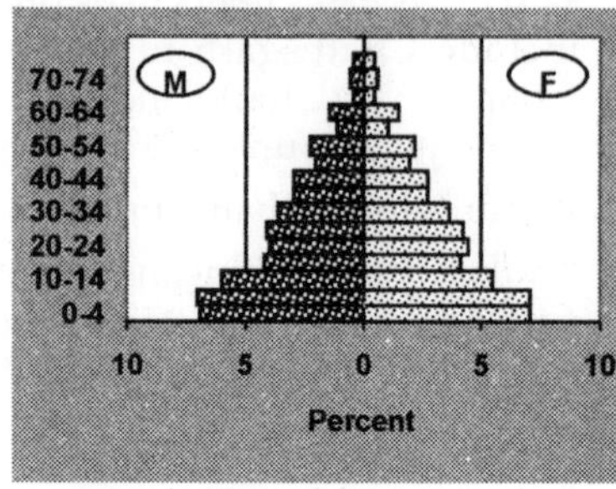

A P – 1981

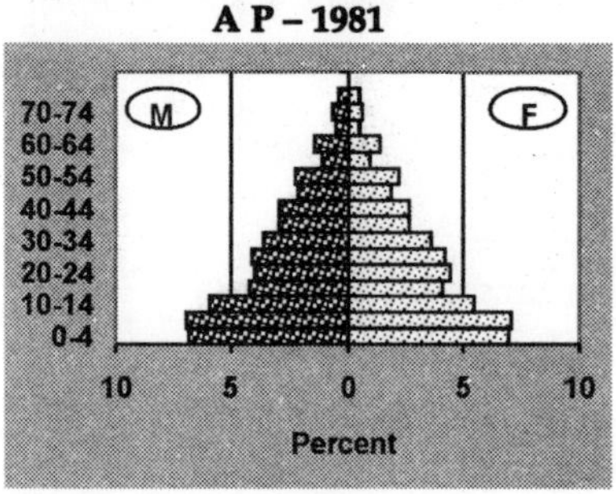

A P – 1991

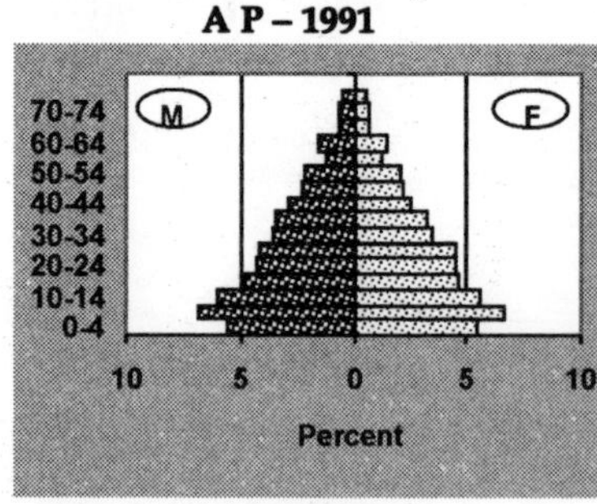

A P – 2001

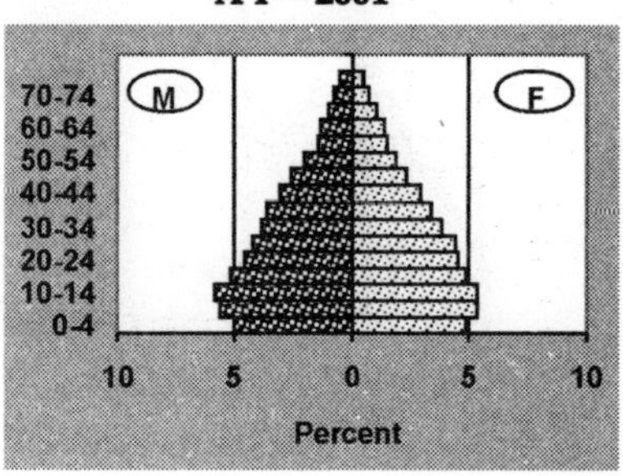

A P – 2011

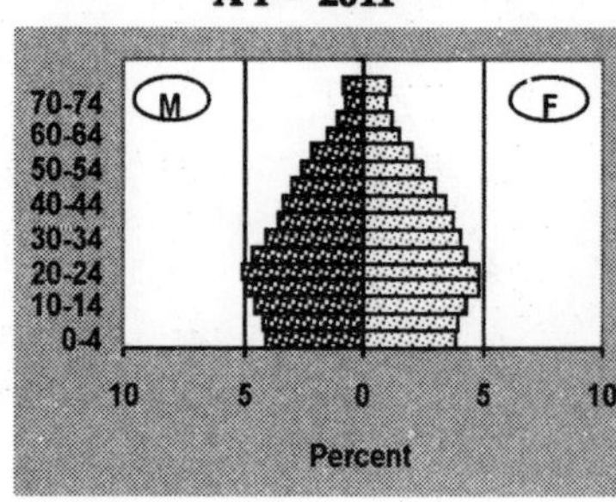

AP – 2021

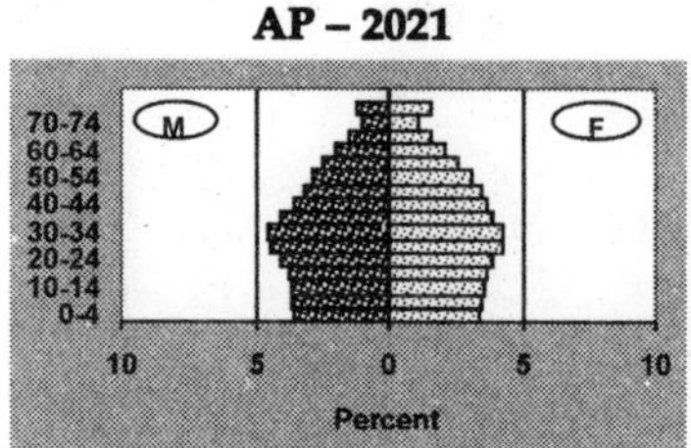

Bihar – 1961

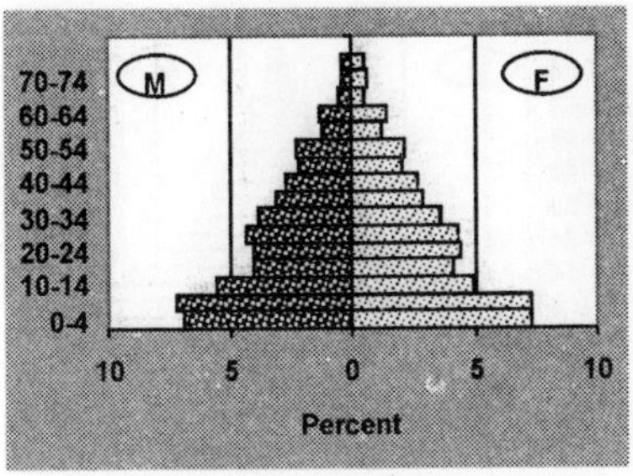

Bihar – 1971

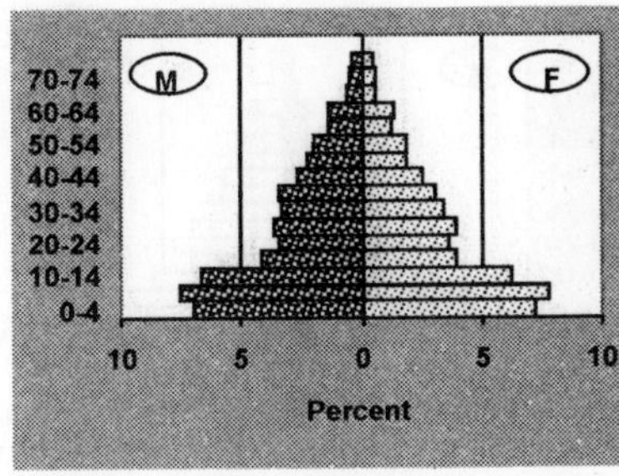

Bihar – 1981

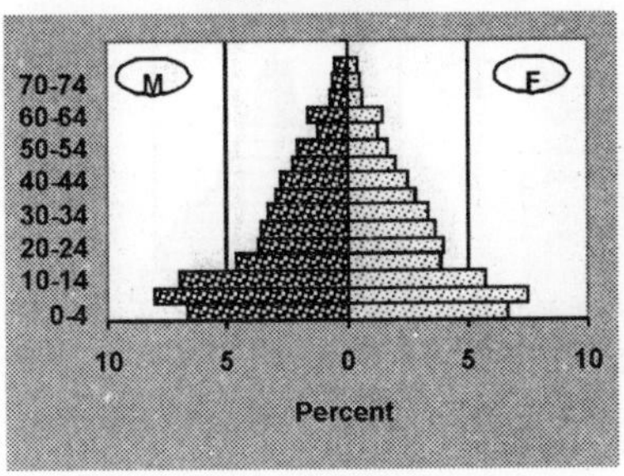

Bihar – 1991

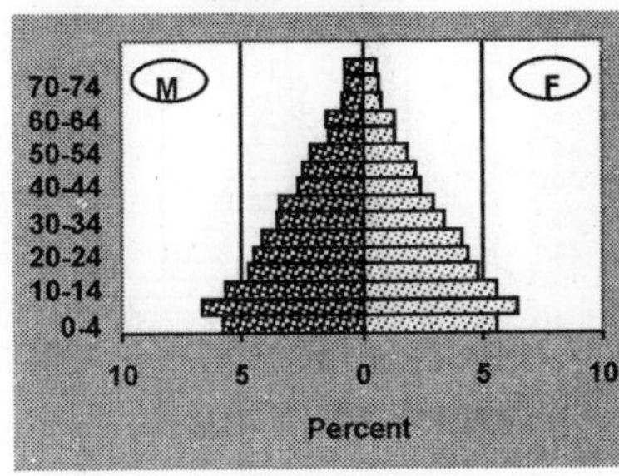

Bihar – 2001

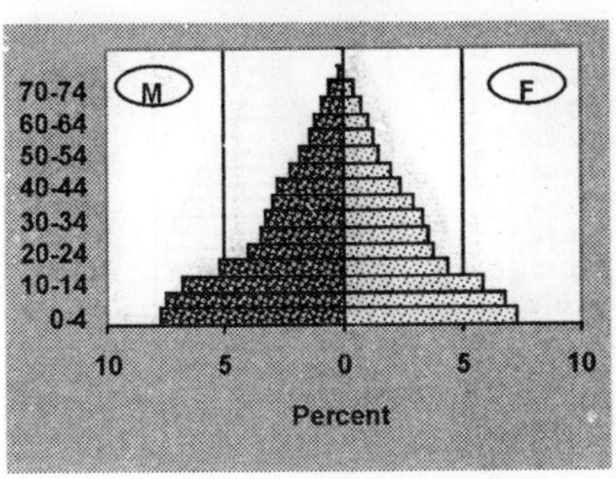

Bihar – 2011

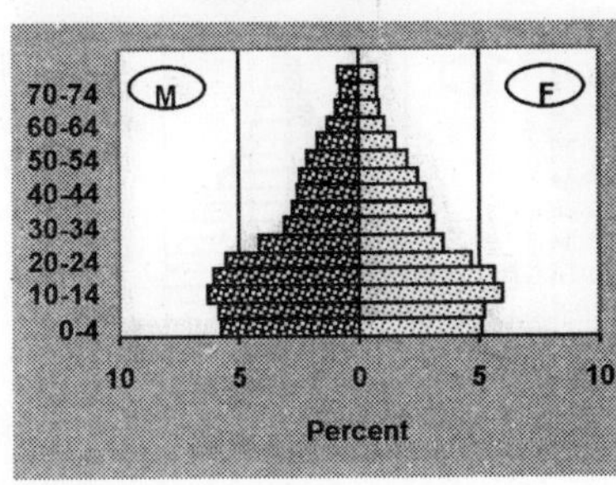

Bihar – 2021

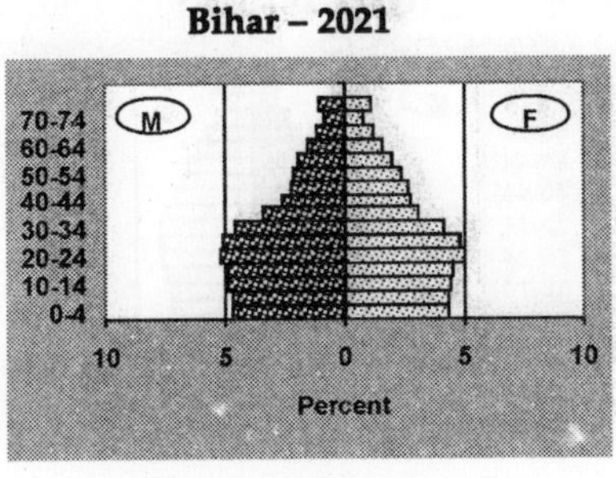

Gujarat – 1961

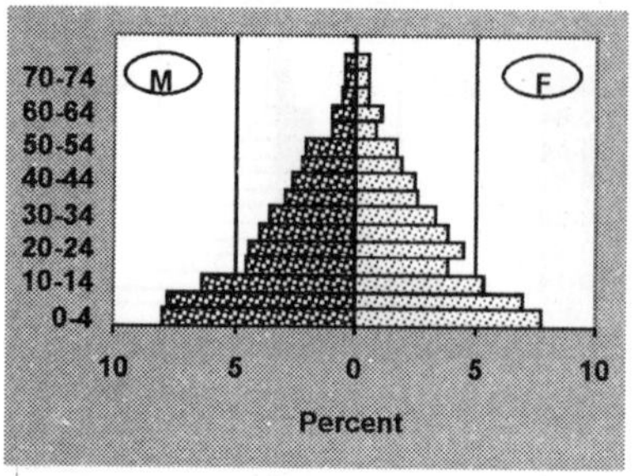

Gujarat – 1971

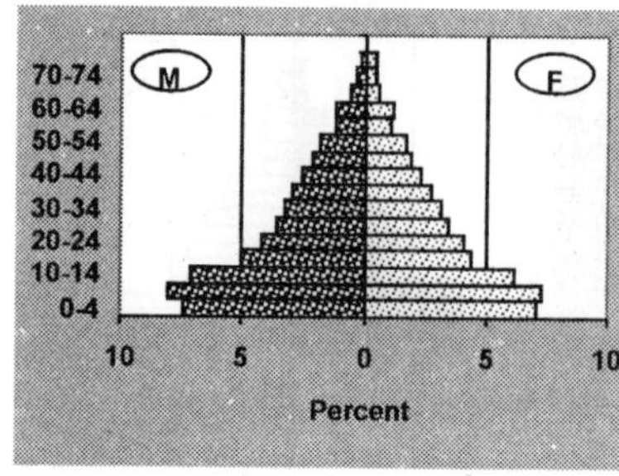

Gujarat – 1981

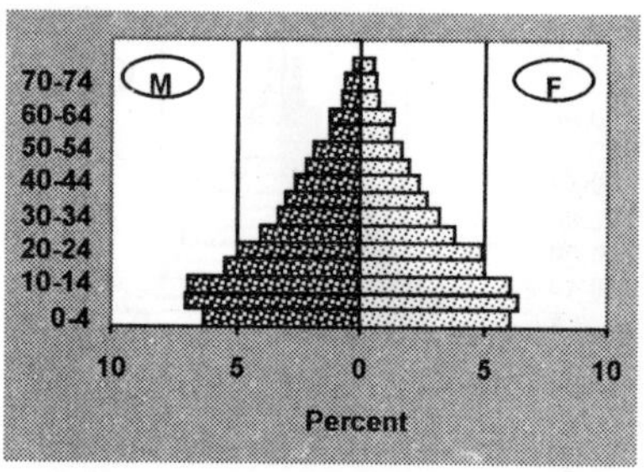

Gujarat – 1991

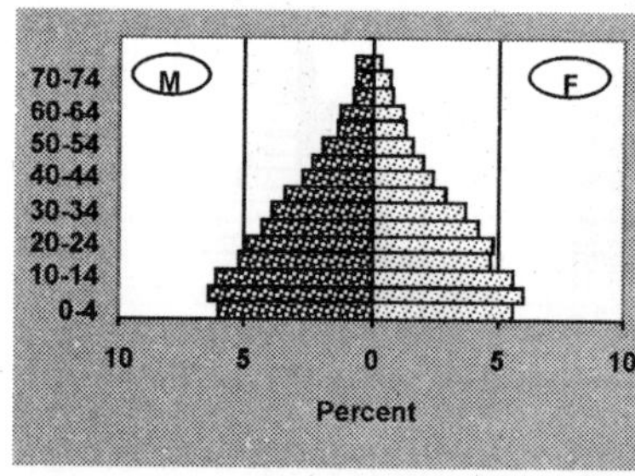

Gujarat – 2001

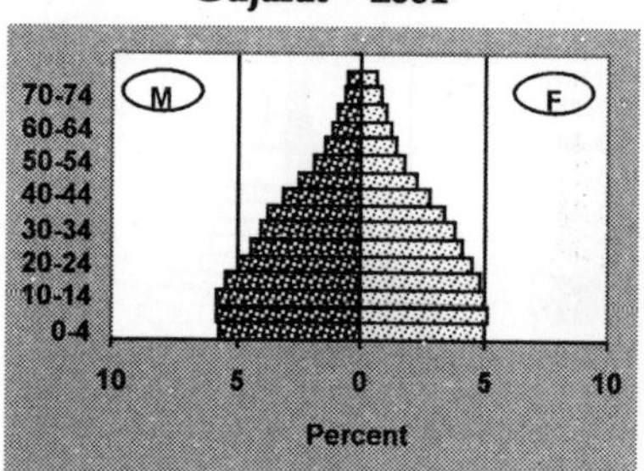

Gujarat – 2011

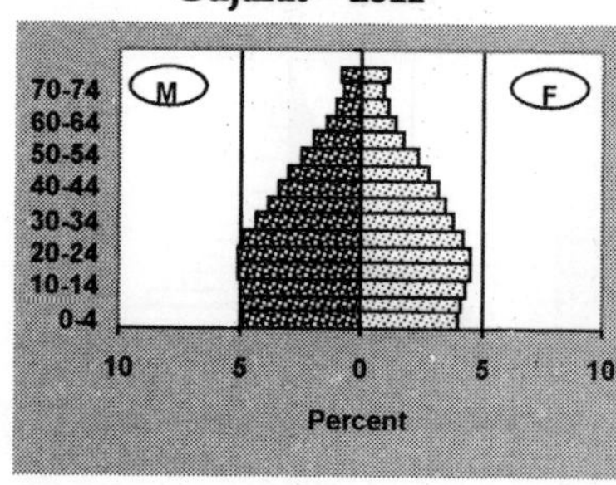

Gujarat – 2021

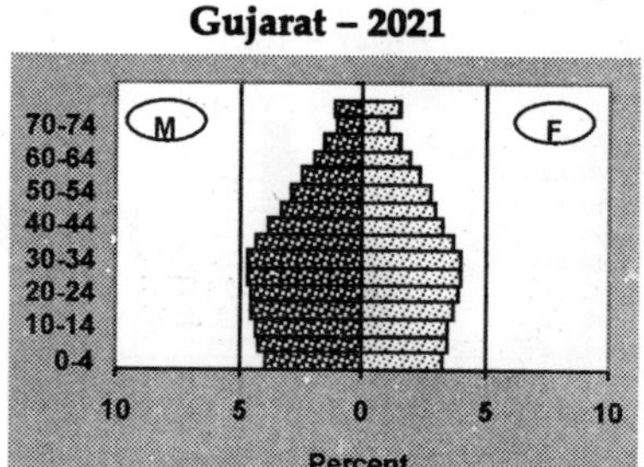

Haryana – 1971

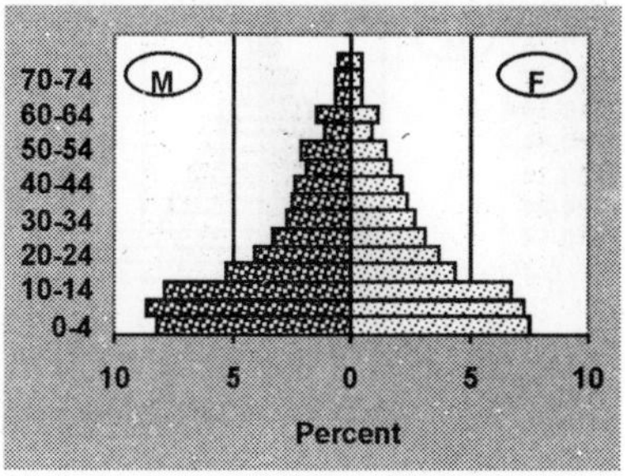

Haryana – 1981

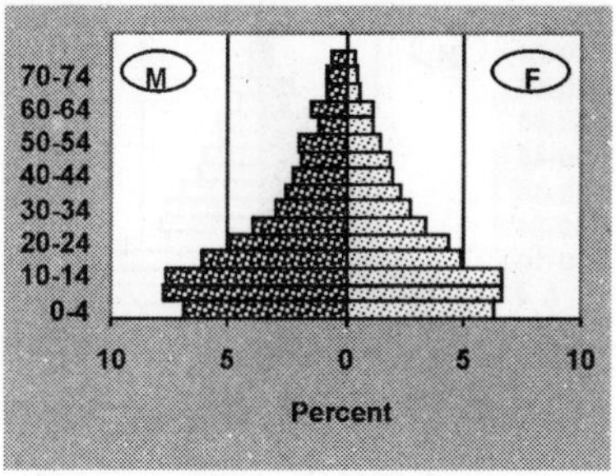

Haryana –1991

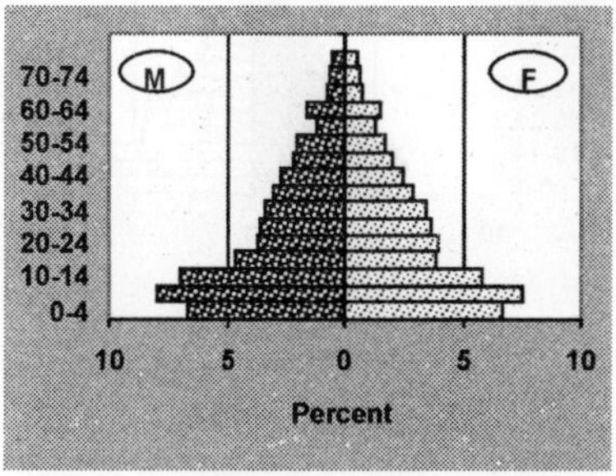

Haryana – 2001

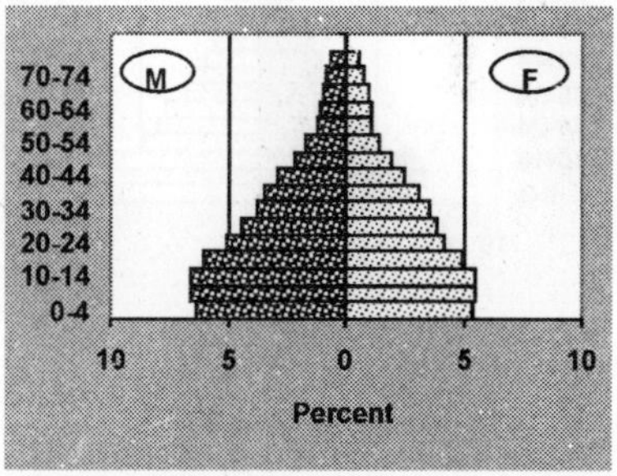

Haryana – 2011

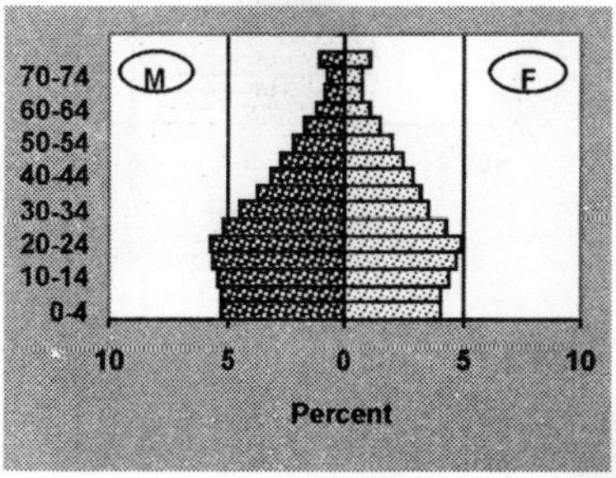

Haryana – 2021

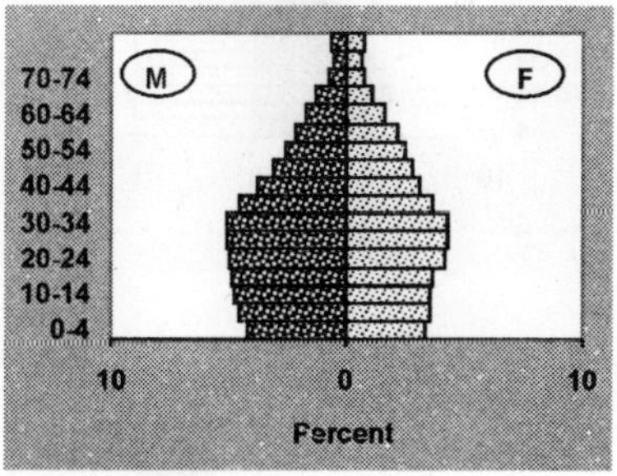

Karnataka – 1961

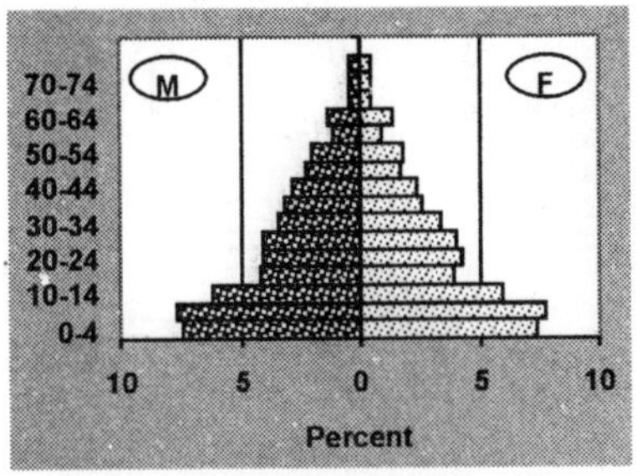

Karnataka – 1971

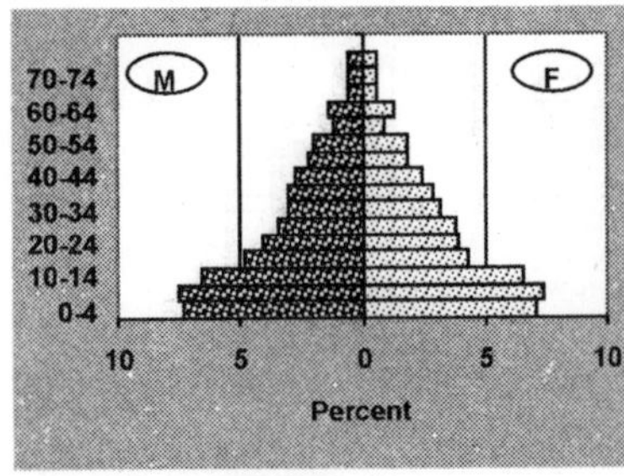

Karnataka – 1981

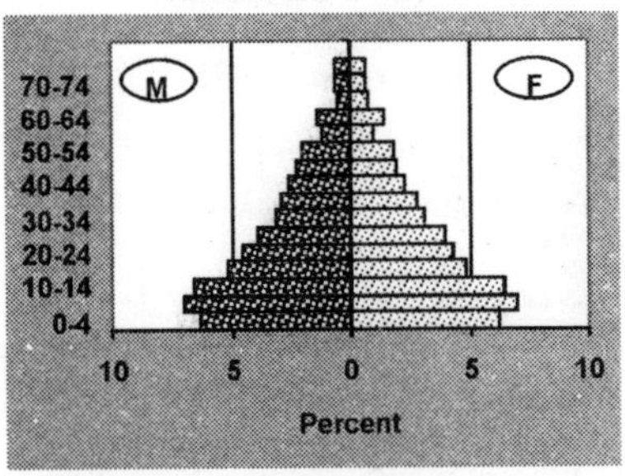

Karnataka – 1991

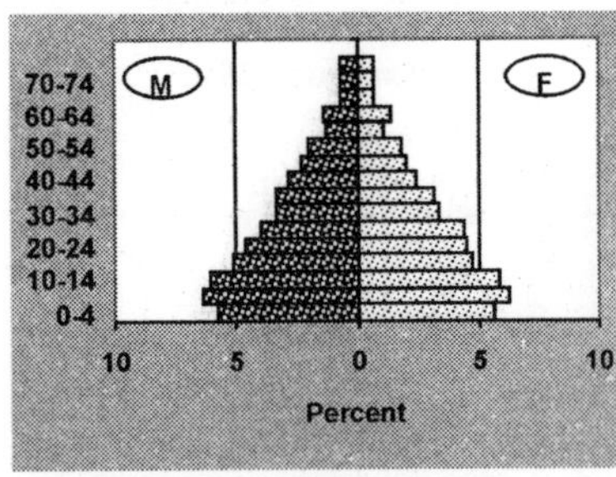

Karnataka – 2001

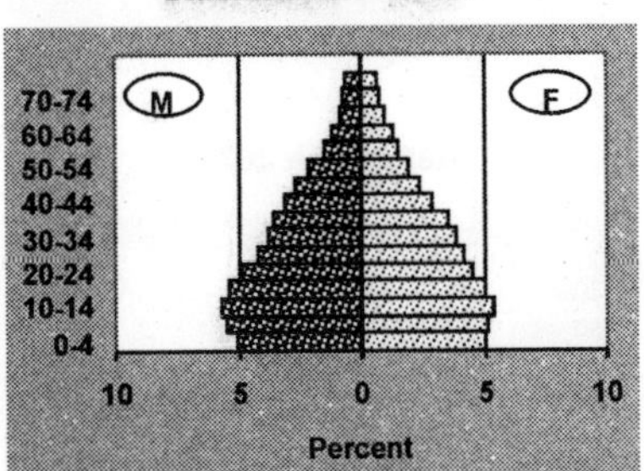

Karnataka – 2011

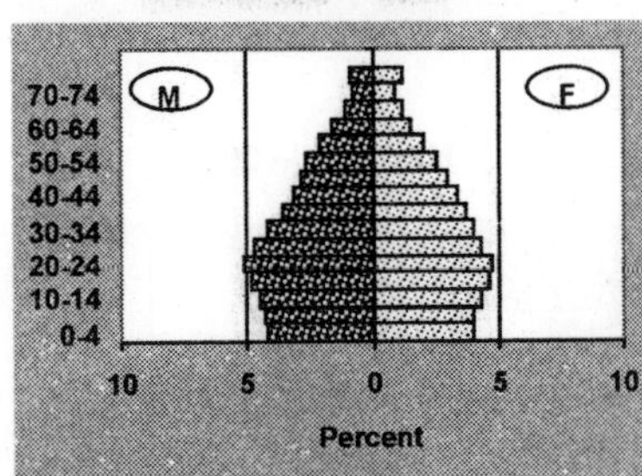

Karnataka – 2021

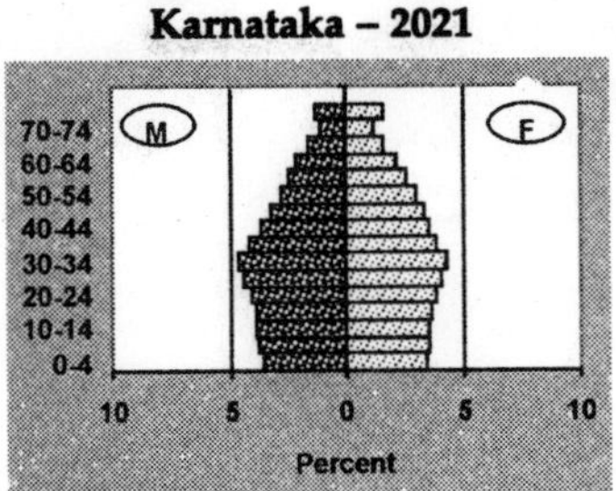

M P – 1961

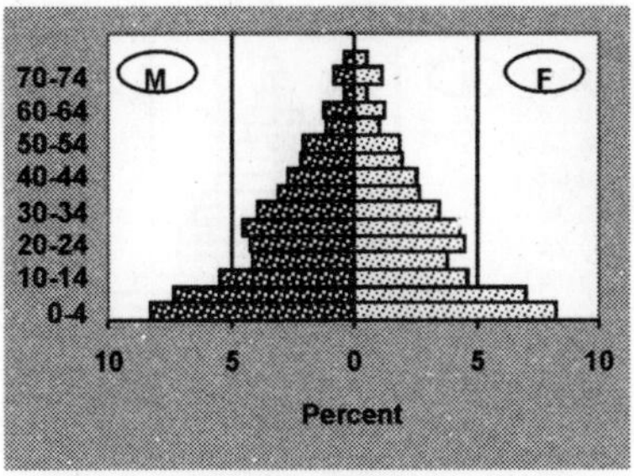

M P – 1971

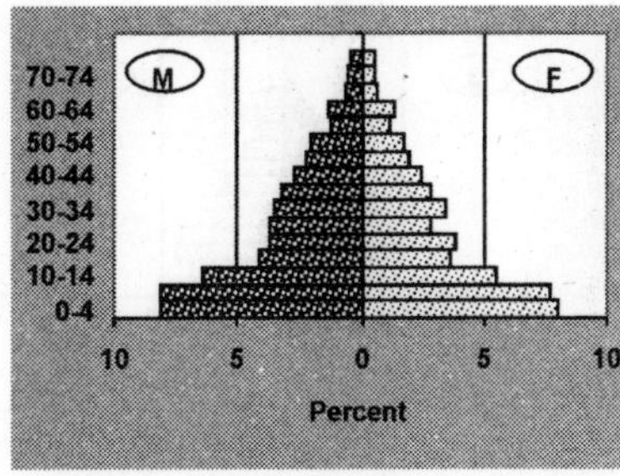

M P – 1981

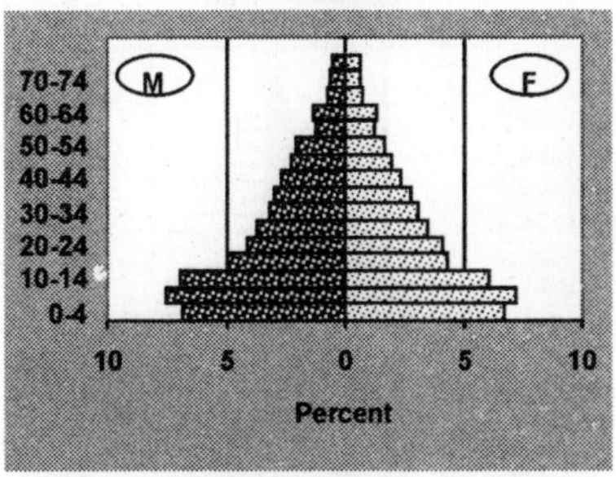

M P – 1991

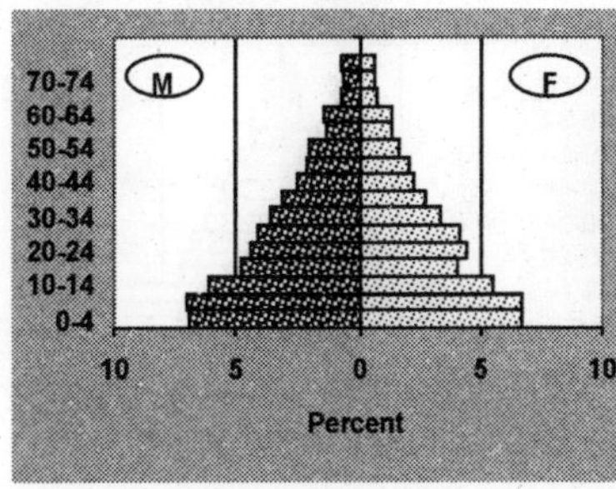

M P – 2001

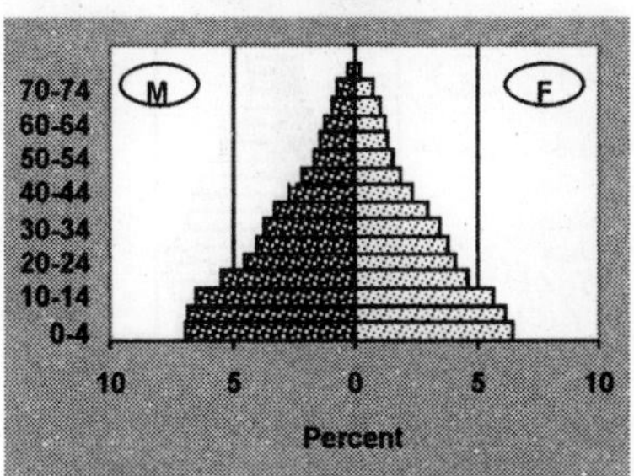

M P – 2011

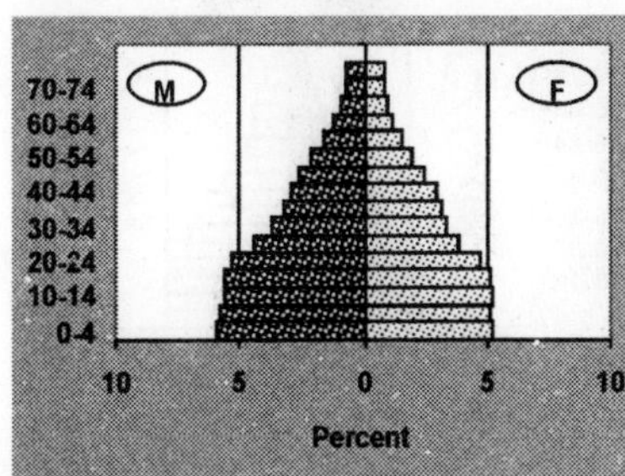

M P – 2021

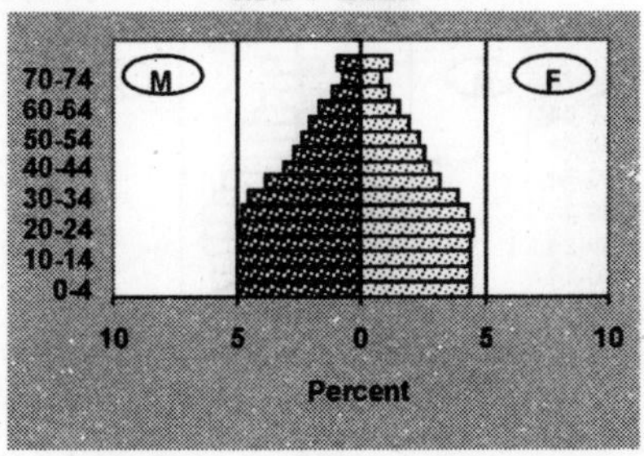

Maharashtra – 1961

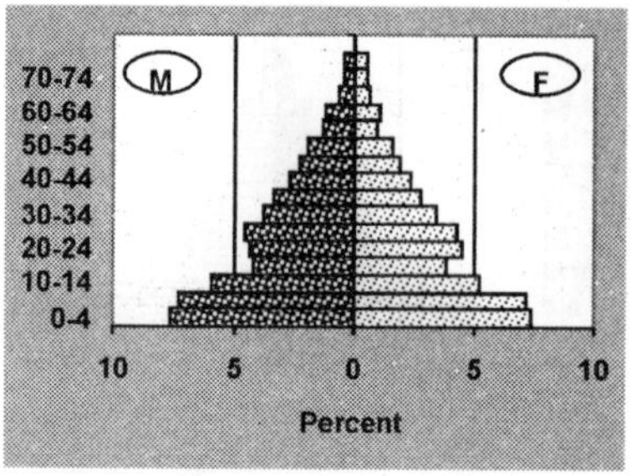

Maharashtra – 1971

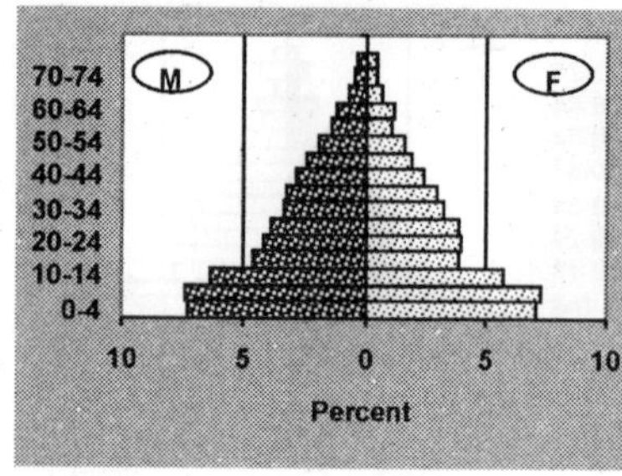

Maharashtra – 1981

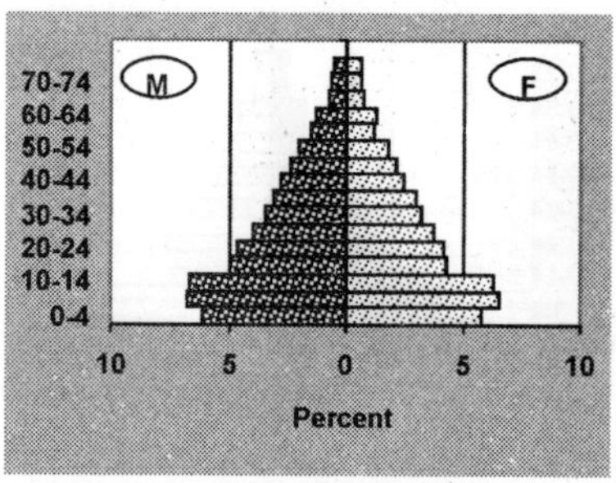

Maharashtra – 1991

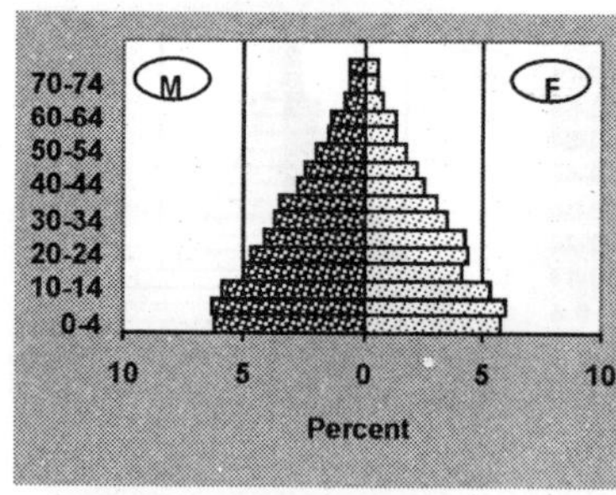

Maharashtra – 2001

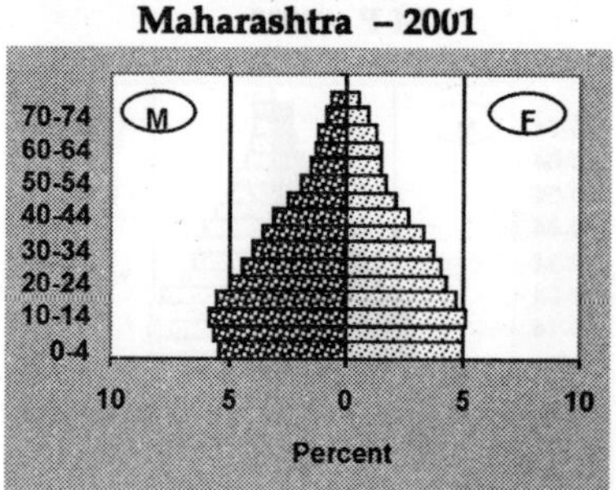

Maharashtra – 2011

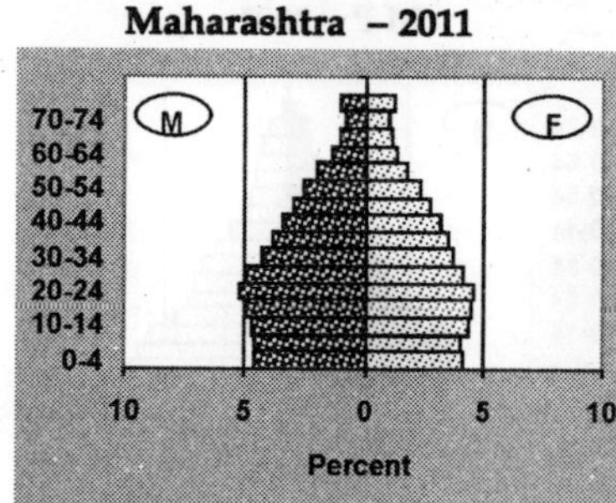

Maharashtra – 2021

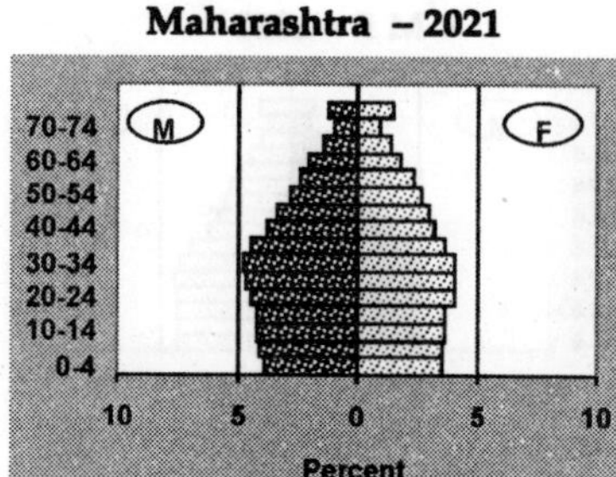

Orissa – 1961

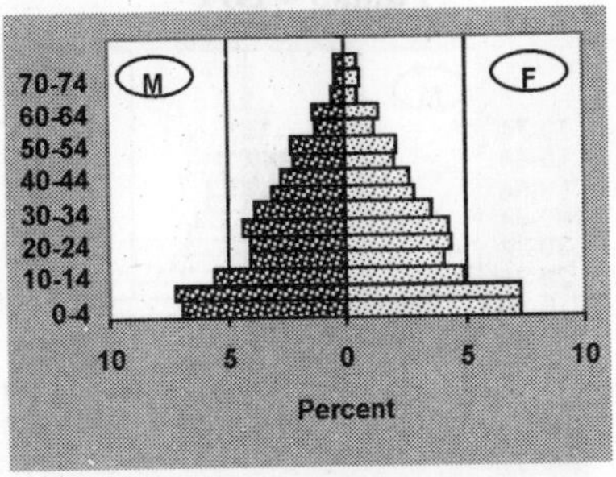

Orissa – 1971

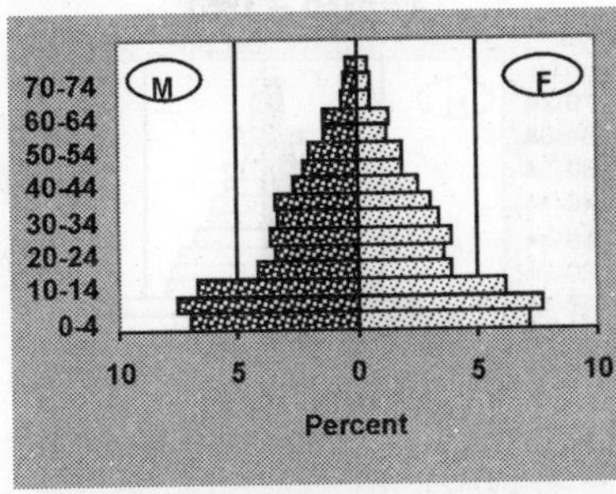

Orissa – 1981

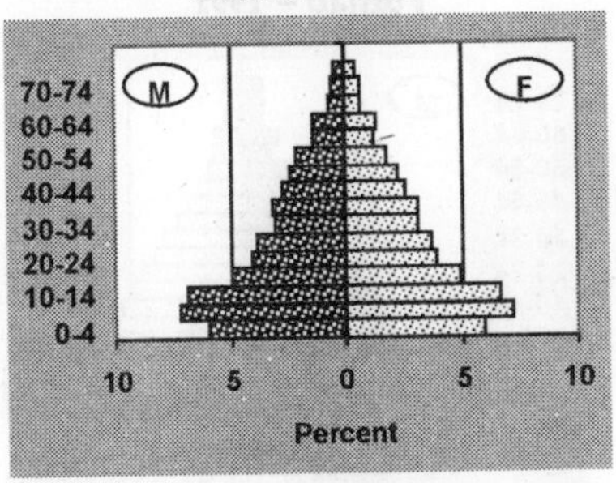

Orissa – 1991

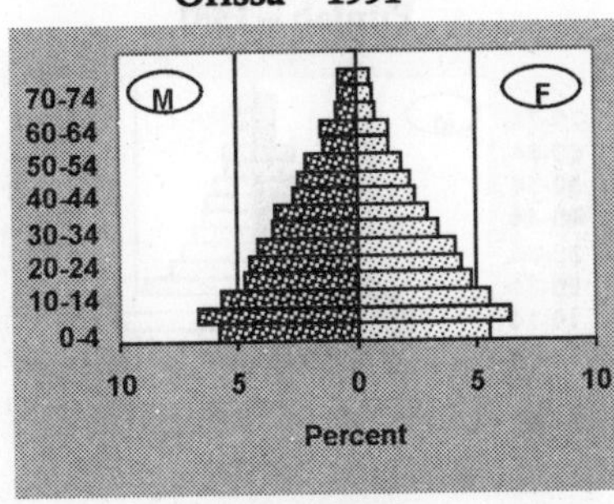

Orissa – 2001

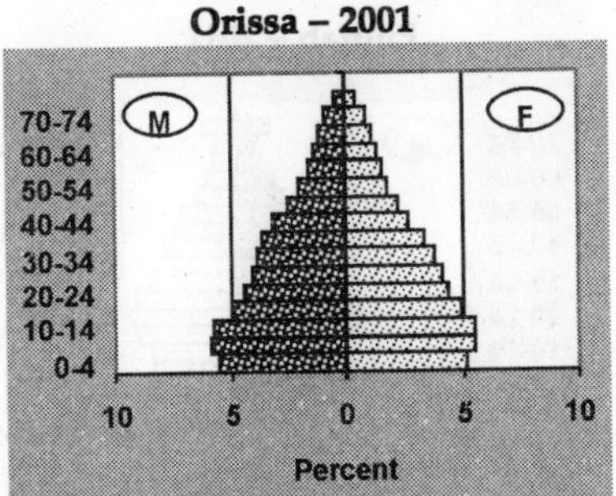

Orissa – 2011

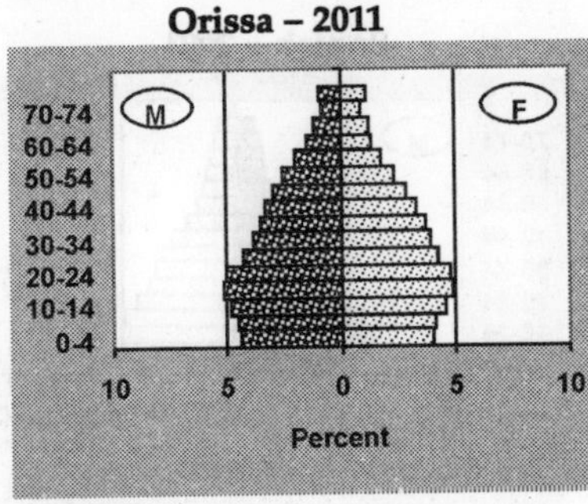

Orissa – 2021

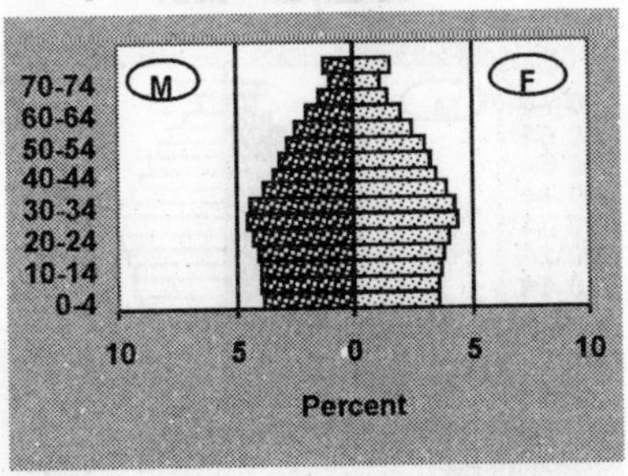

Punjab – 1961

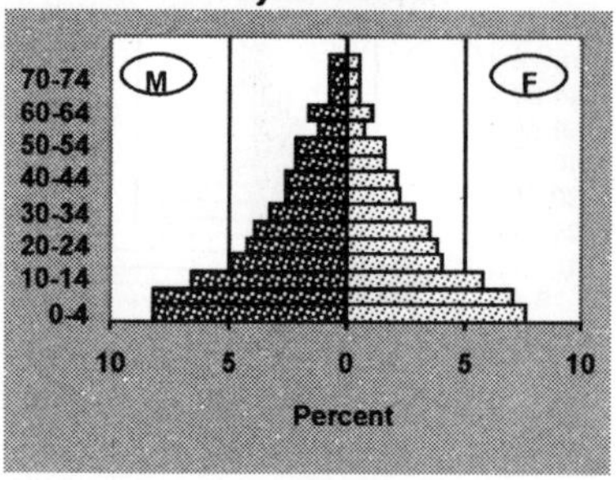

Punjab – 1971

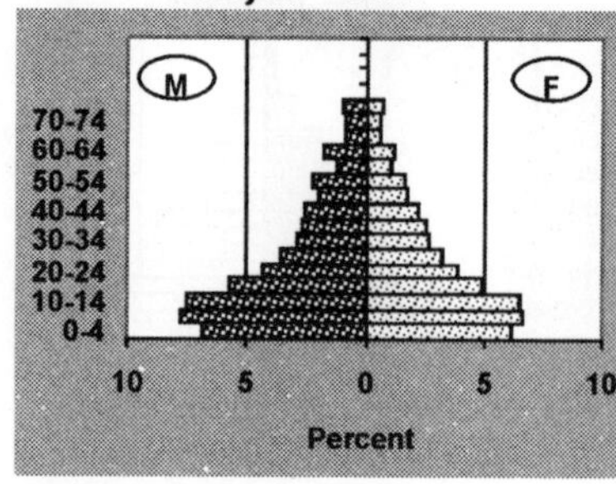

Punjab – 1981

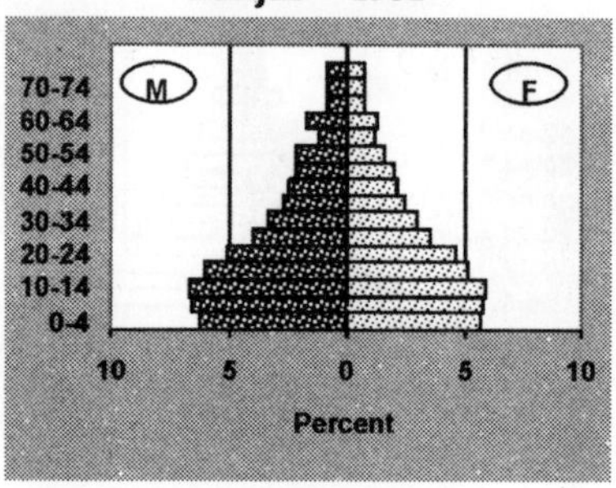

Punjab – 1991

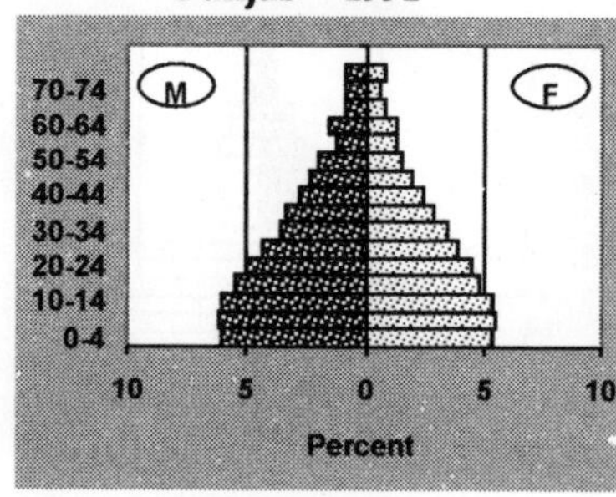

Punjab – 2001

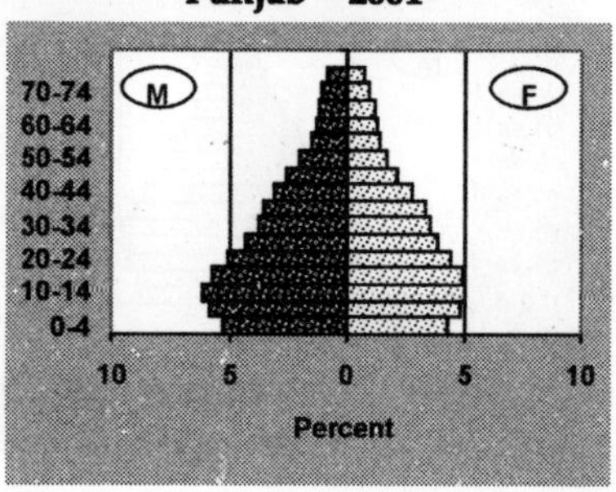

Punjab – 2011

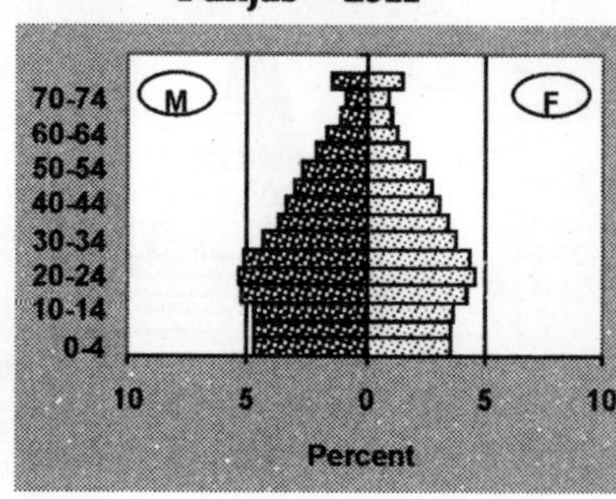

Punjab – 2021

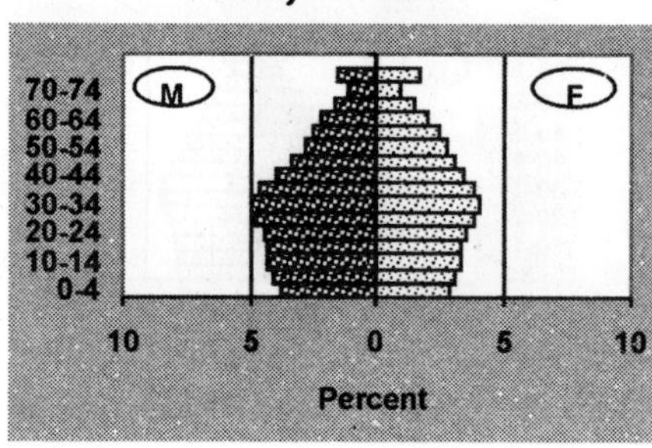

Rajasthan – 1961

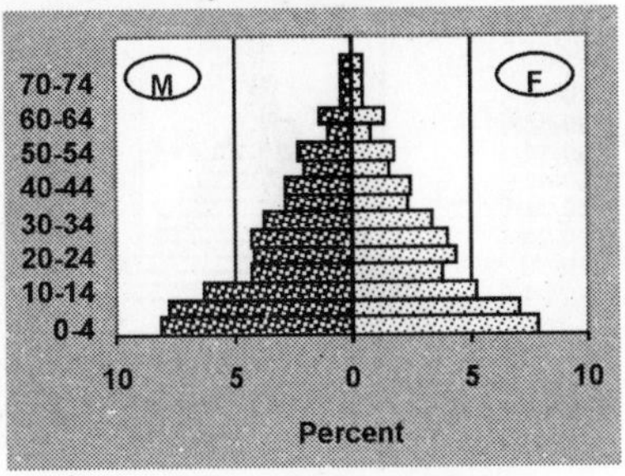

Rajasthan – 1971

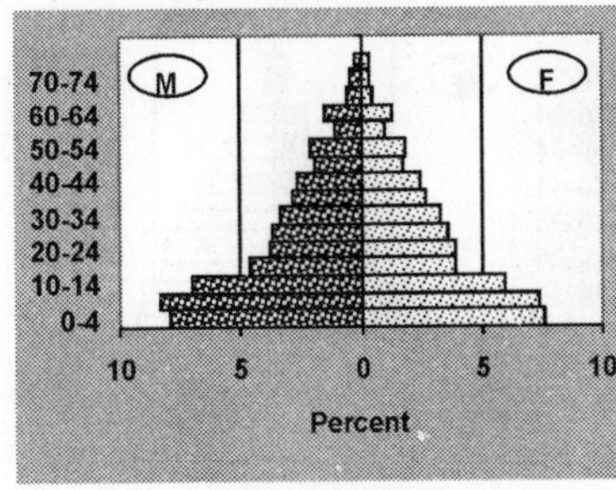

Rajasthan – 1981

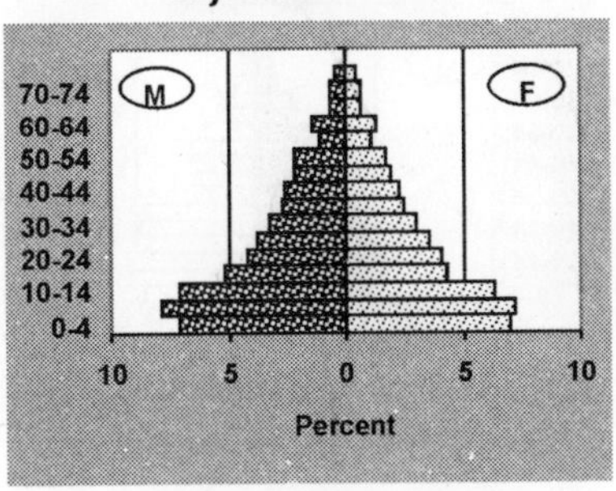

Rajasthan – 1991

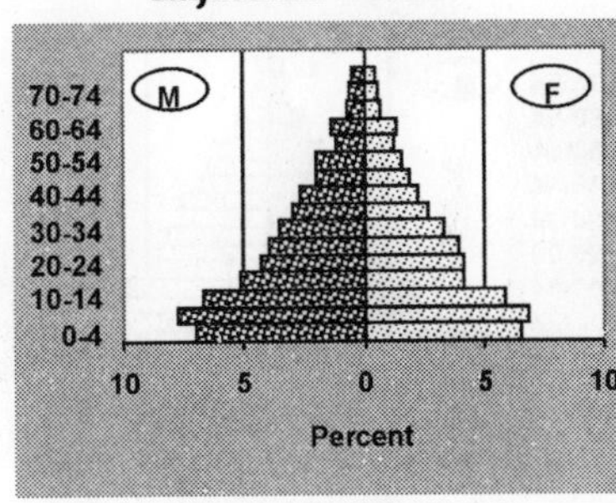

Rajasthan – 2001

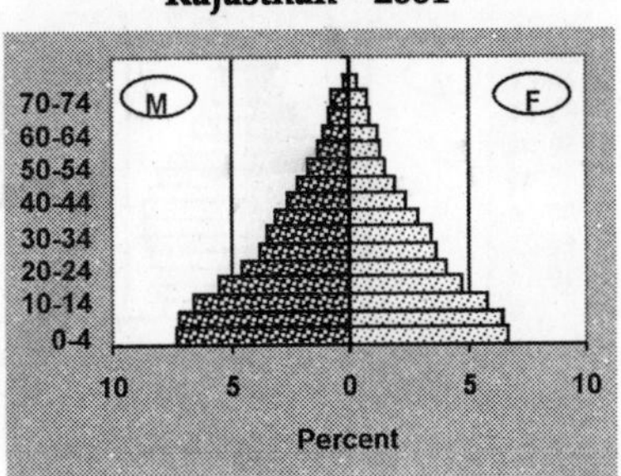

Rajasthan – 2011

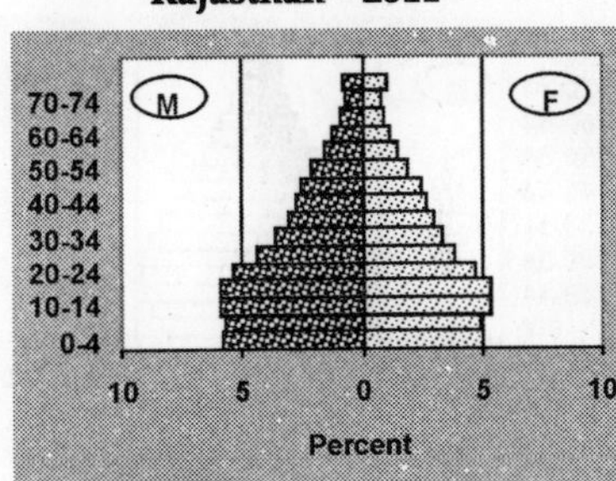

Rajasthan – 2021

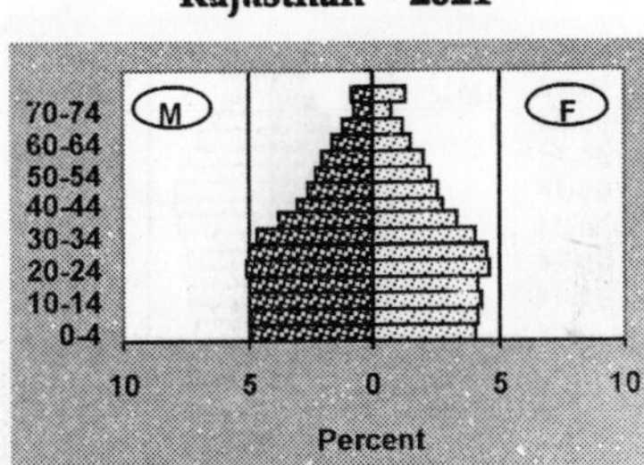

Tamil Nadu – 1961

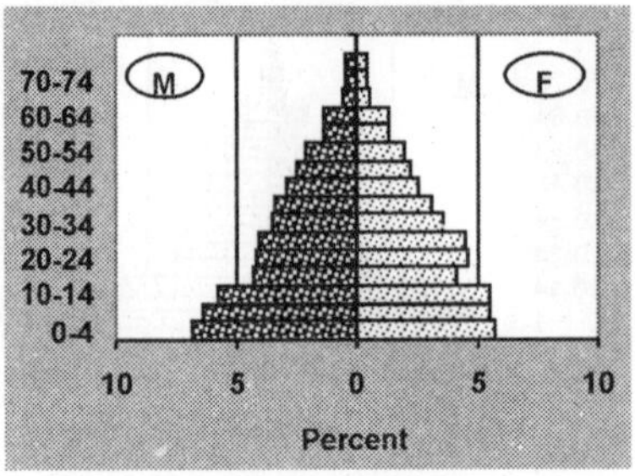

Tamil Nadu – 1971

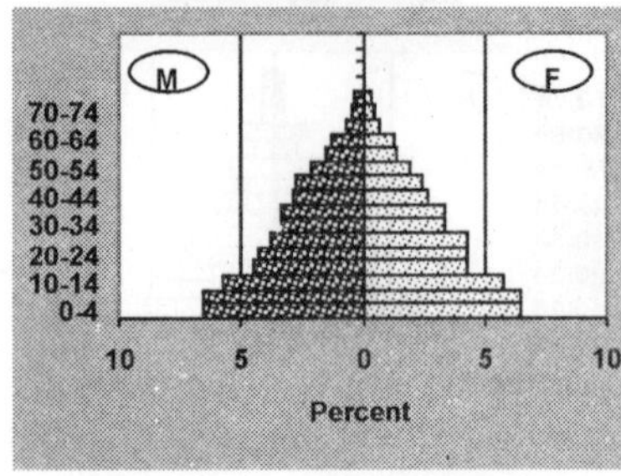

Tamil Nadu – 1981

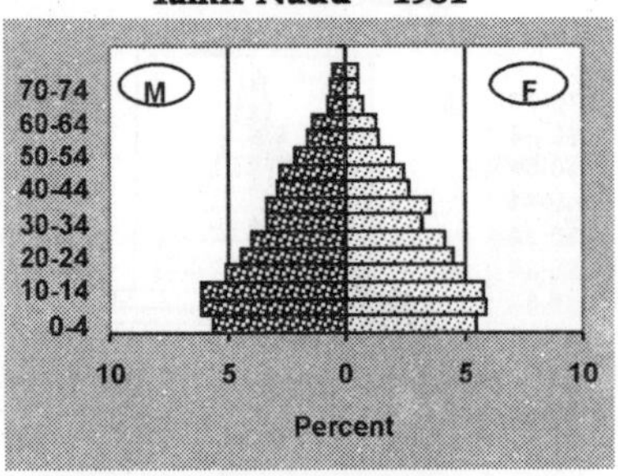

Tamil Nadu – 1991

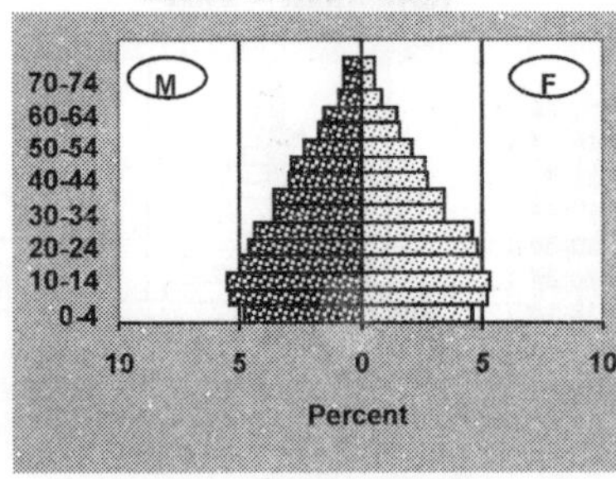

Tamil Nadu – 2001

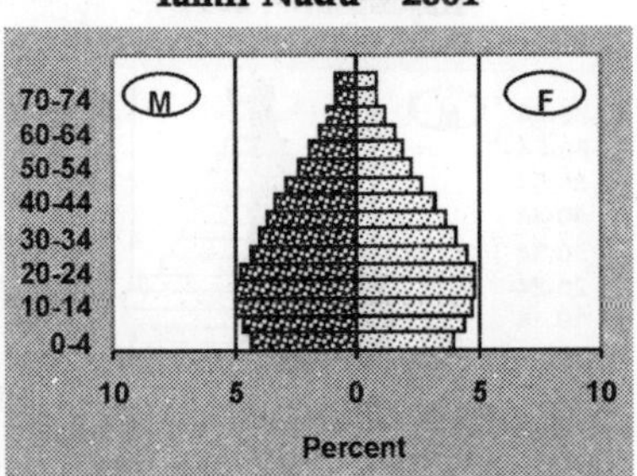

Tamil Nadu – 2011

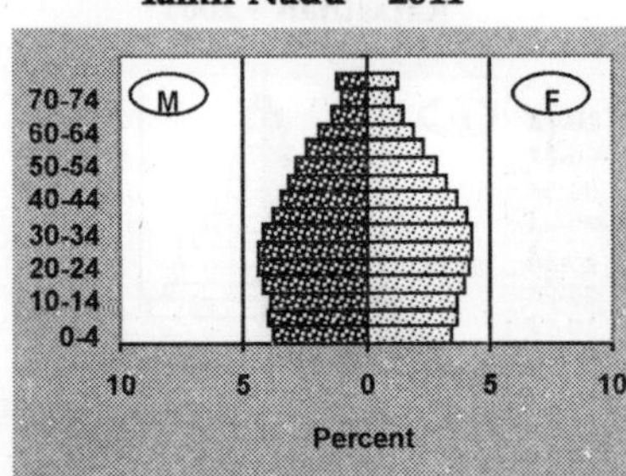

Tamil Nadu – 2021

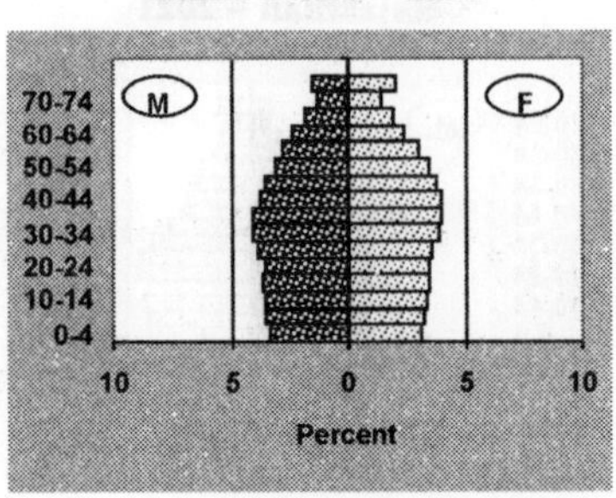

Uttar Pradesh – 1961

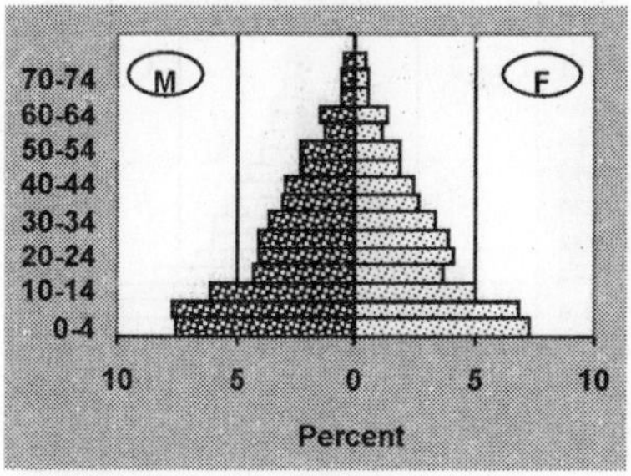

Uttar Pradesh – 1971

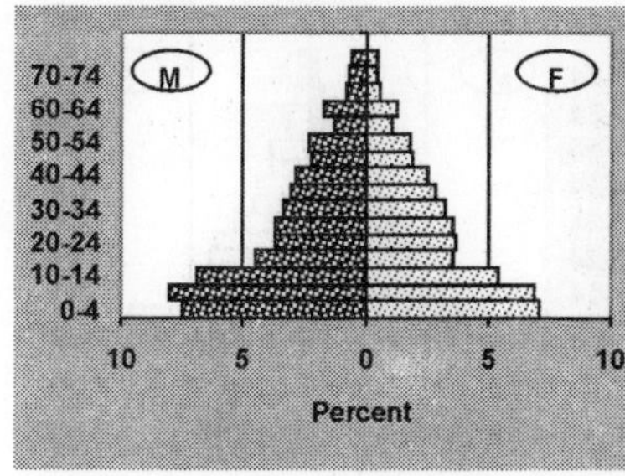

Uttar Pradesh – 1981

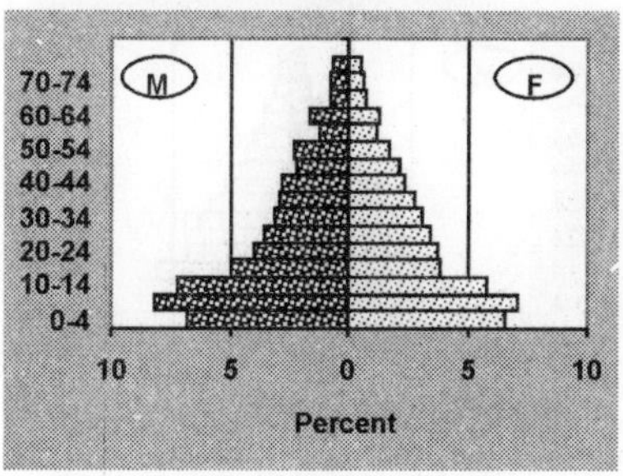

Uttar Pradesh – 1991

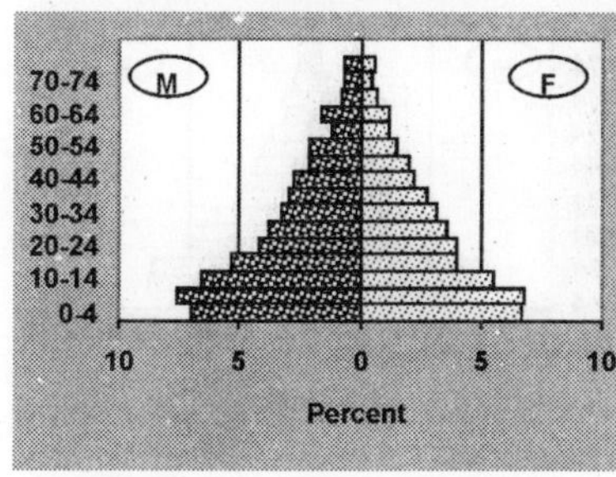

Uttar Pradesh – 2001

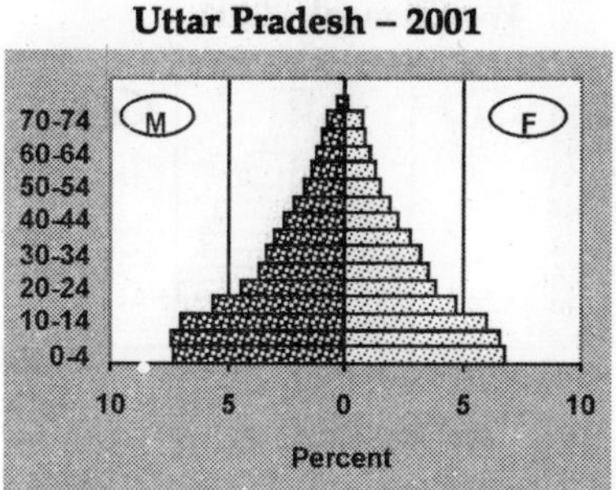

Uttar Pradesh – 2011

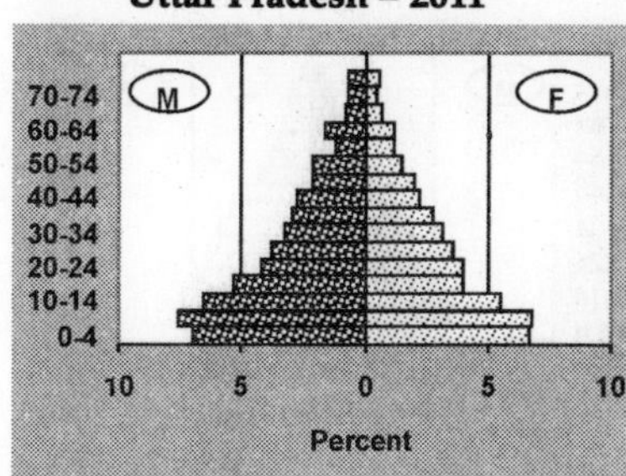

Uttar Pradesh – 2021

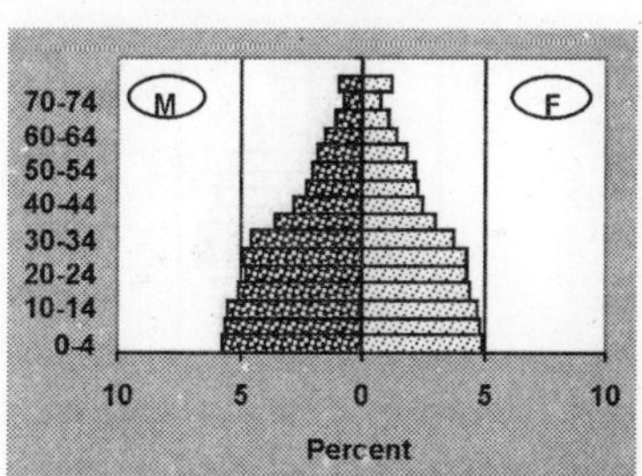

West Bengal – 1961

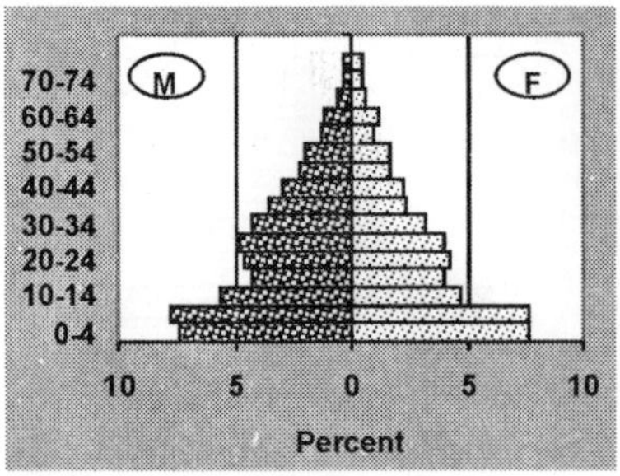

West Bengal – 1971

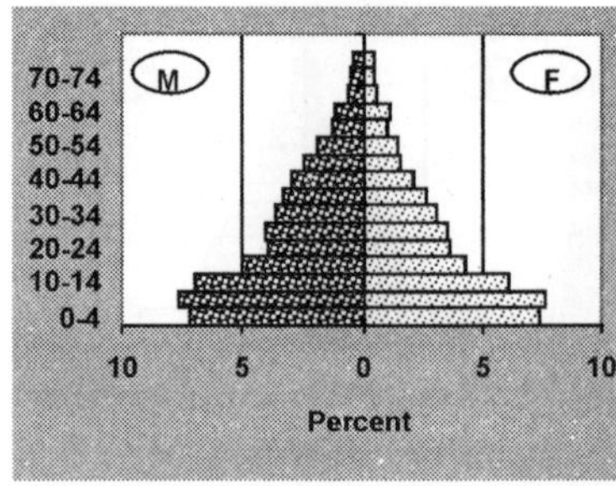

West Bengal – 1981

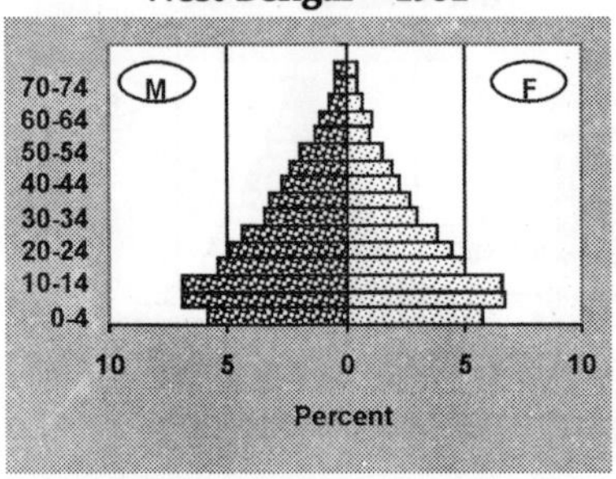

West Bengal – 1991

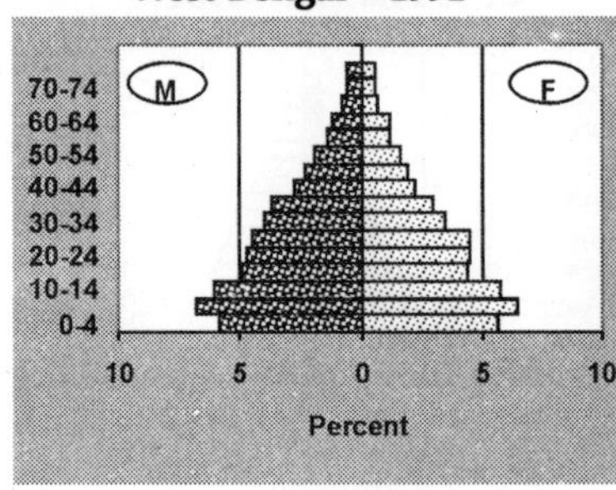

West Bengal – 2001

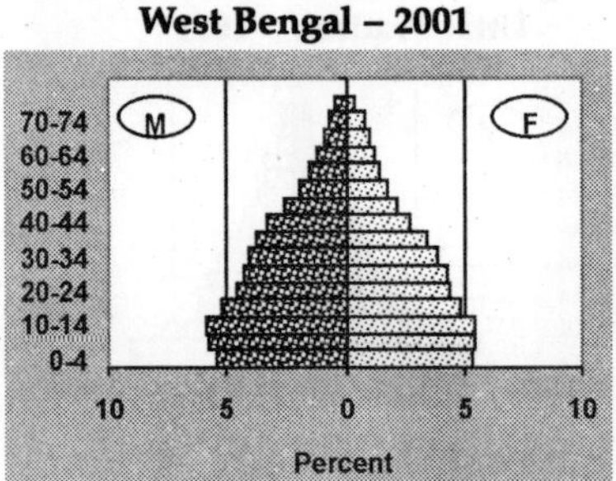

West Bengal – 2011

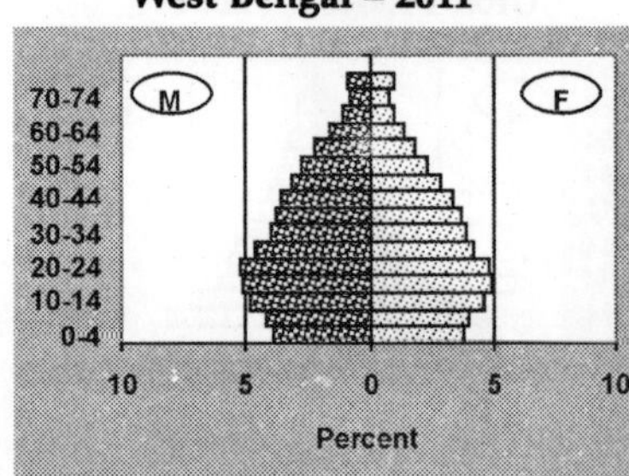

West Bengal – 2021

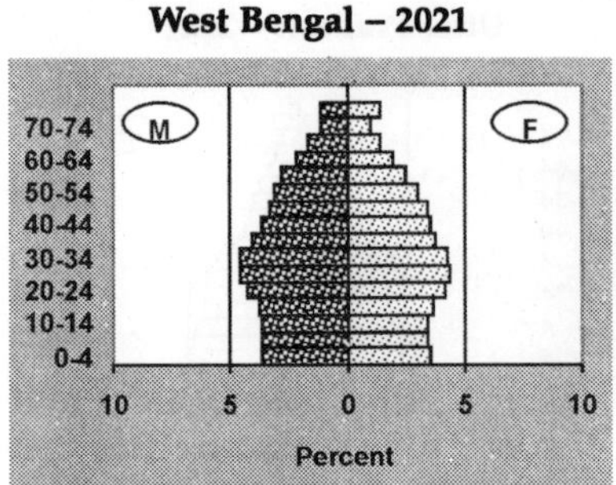

3 METHODS, MATERIALS AND GENERAL BACKGROUND CHARACTERISTICS OF THE STUDY POPULATION

INTRODUCTION

This chapter is divided into two parts. Part I deals with the methods and materials used in the study and Part II contains the background characteristics of the study population. The characteristics are separately analyzed for house/household related aspects, household population and older persons.

I

METHODS AND MATERIALS

Definition of Aged

The term "old" can be associated with physical incapacity, biological deterioration or disabilities or even psychological factors. "A man ages *biologically* as a continuing process, *socially* as perceived by the members of the society, *economically* when retired from the work force and, *chronologically* one grows older with time" (Benyaklef, 1991). However, definitions other than the chronological one are difficult to operationalize, and hence chronological age is the most widely used indicator to define the aged.

Chronological age also is an important indicator of health, functional capacity, labour force participation, life cycle stage and income. But to assign a particular age at which a person becomes aged is a difficult proposition. However, at the World Assembly on Ageing held at Vienna in 1982 (United Nations, 1983), all persons aged 60 years and above were taken as the aged. Similarly, in the United Nations International Conference on Ageing and

Urbanization (United Nations, 1991) the term "elderly" is defined as the population aged 60 years and above. However, this definition of old age ignored the heterogeneous nature of a population group covering a range of at least 25 years. Regrouping this population into smaller age categories, nonetheless, can solve this problem. The most commonly used groups are (i) 60-74 years and (ii) 75 years and over. These two age groups are respectively referred to as "young old" and "old-old".

However, many of the more developed countries classify a person as aged only when he/she reaches the age of 65 years. This cut off age has relation to the longevity of the people. When the life expectancy of the population was 40 years, a person aged 40 years was considered as aged. In the less developed countries of today the expectation of life at birth is hovering around 60 years and hence the 60 year demarcation is accepted for aged. This is true at the all-India level also. But in Kerala where the expectation of life has already crossed 70 years and where the fertility and mortality rates are very low, 60 years is a little too early for classifying a person as aged. Hence, in this empirical study, 65 years was taken as the lowest age to consider a person as aged.

Source of data

The data for the present analysis are taken from an already concluded survey in Kerala (Radha Devi, *et al.*, 2000) which had the necessary data to satisfy the objectives of this study. The survey was conducted in 1996-97 with the specific objectives of understanding the elderly's living arrangements, their health and health care, their financial situation, their actual and expected role in the family, their familial and friendship net work and the general social, economic and demographic condition of the family that accommodates the elderly. The sampling methodology adopted in the survey is described in the following sections.

Selection of districts

Two of the fourteen districts in Kerala (Ernakulam and Kozhikode) were selected at random for the survey and some general characteristics of these districts along with that of the remaining twelve districts of the state as of 1991 are presented in Table 1. Though not the highest by way of total population, these two districts together accounted for 18.7 percent of the total Kerala population in 1991. Further, these two are among the four districts where the density of the population per square kilometer is more than 1000 and barring Kannur, Ernakulam and Kozhikode had the highest percentage of urban population. Among all the districts in Kerala, the selected districts had the lowest proportion of population engaged in agriculture and related activities.

Differences in the religious composition of the two districts are very conspicuous.[1] Ernakulam district had only 48 percent of its population as Hindus (the lowest after Malappuram district) while the corresponding proportion for Kozhikode was 59 percent. Whereas the proportion of Muslim population in Kozhikode (36 percent) was higher than that of Ernakulam (15 percent), the proportion of Christian population was higher in Ernakulam (37 percent) than in Kozhikode (5 percent).

Table 1
Selected characteristics of the districts in Kerala: 1991

Sl. No.	*Districts*	*Population (in '000s)*	*Density (Per sq. km.)*	*Percent of population*				
				Urban	*Hindu*	*Engaged in agriculture Total*	*Male*	*Older persons (60+)*
1	Kasaragod	1072	538	16.4	55.3	37.4	39.8	7.1
2	Kannur	2252	759	50.9	62.9	30.1	25.4	8.4
3	Wayanad	672	315	3.4	50.4	50.9	49.8	6.2
4	Kozhikode	2620	1118	38.3	59.0	19.9	19.4	8.3
5	Malappuram	3096	872	9.1	30.3	47.2	45.2	6.5
6	Palakkad	2382	532	15.7	70.5	57.1	47.4	8.9
7	Thrissur	2737	903	26.3	59.5	32.1	28.6	10.0
8	Ernakulam	2817	1170	48.7	48.0	25.1	23.6	9.4
9	Idukki	1078	215	4.7	51.0	41.7	45.2	6.8
10	Kottayam	1828	830	17.6	48.8	39.5	40.2	10.6
11	Alappuzha	2001	1415	30.5	69.0	32.5	32.2	11.1
12	Pathanamthitta	1188	450	13.0	55.6	53.4	55.6	12.0
13	Kollam	2408	967	18.5	65.3	39.5	44.2	8.9
14	Thiruvananthapuram	2947	1344	33.9	69.8	41.5	44.2	8.5
	Kerala	29098	749	26.4	57.3	37.8	36.6	8.8

Source: Census of India 1991, *General Population Tables and Social and Cultural Tables.*

Selection of villages/urban divisions

Village is a revenue administrative unit. The villages of Kerala are rather unique. It has very little resemblance to its counterparts in the rest of the country. Most part of the state is inhabited and settlement is almost continuous making it difficult to demarcate urban area from rural. The centre of a village is similar to a small town with a high density of population and having educational and other facilities and amenities. However, revenue villages and census villages are slightly different. The total number of revenue villages in Kerala was 1452, as against 1640 census villages in 1991. However, of the 1640 villages 256 were wholly in the urban area giving a total of 1,384 villages in rural area. In 1991, the average population size of a rural village in the state was 15,476 persons.

In Ernakulam district there were 89 rural villages with an average size of 16,225 persons per village. Similarly, Kozhikode had 87 rural villages and the average population size of a village was 18,568 persons.

Six villages from every chosen district were selected using probability proportional to size (PPS) systematic sampling method for the survey. For this, all the villages in rural area of each district were ranked on the basis of the percent of male population engaged

Table 2
Characteristics of the selected villages: 1991

Sl. No.	*Village*	*Taluk to which the village belong*	*Population*	*Density (per sq.km)*	*No. of House holds*	*Sex Ratio (M/F)* 1000*
ERNAKULAM						
1	Njarackal	Kochi	22,978	2672	4350	949
2	Mattur	Aluva	16,299	1552	3269	1008
3	Vazhakulam	Kunnathunadu	12,338	1164	2351	1037
4	Rayamangalam	Kunnathunadu	22,919	767	4795	1012
5	Manjallur	Muvattupuzha	14,200	604	2729	981
6	Tirumarady	Muvattupuzha	16,462	564	3465	1011
KOZHIKODE						
1	Eramala	Vatakara	30,050	1573	5145	911
2	Kavilumpara	Vatakara	17,150	210*	3391	1036
3	Tiruvallur	Vatakara	12,575	1093	2206	957
4	Kozhukallur	Koyilandi	12,865	1005	2351	985
5	Atholi	Koyilandi	24,055	1140	4426	936
6	Peruvayal	Kozhikode	17,682	1126	3234	973

Source: Census of India 1991, *Final Population Totals*
Note: Kavilumpara village is the biggest in area among all the districts, with 82 Sq. Km. but most of its area is mountainous and hence a very low density is observed.

in agricultural sector. The population size of the villages was then cumulated. The first village was randomly selected. The second and subsequent villages were systematically chosen using the sampling method of probability proportional to size. This was done separately for both the districts. To represent the urban area two divisions were selected randomly from the largest Municipal Corporation (Kochi Corporation from Ernakulam district and Kozhikode Corporation from Kozhikode district) of each of the selected districts. Thus, in all, from the two districts 12 villages and 4 urban divisions were selected for this study. Some general characteristics of the selected villages and urban divisions where the survey was conducted are given Table 2.

Selection of households

Since the study was mainly to understand the life patterns of the aged population, only those households that have at least one aged person were selected. From each village and urban divisions, 100 households with elderly were selected with the help of the electoral roll which was updated as on 31 January 1995 for the 1996 election in the state. From the electoral rolls of each selected village/ divisions a separate list was prepared with only those households having at least one person aged 65 or above to form the sampling

Table 3
Total number of households with elderly, households selected and households surveyed in the selected villages

Sl. No.	*Village*	*Number of households*			*Number of completed interviews of elders*
		With elderly	*Selected*	*Surveyed*	
	ERNAKULAM				
1	Njarackal	1,013	100	72	83
2	Mattur	1,130	100	67	84
3	Vazhakkulam	635	100	70	75
4	Rayamangalam	1,465	100	66	76
5	Manjallur	954	100	80	95
6	Tirumarady	1,165	100	82	92
7	Urban: Thevara and Kadavanthra	762	200	98	107
	KOZHIKODE				
1	Eramala	1,752	100	69	77
2	Kavilumpara	980	100	77	83
3	Tiruvallur	659	100	71	74
4	Kozhukallur	600	100	73	80
5	Atholi	1,371	100	82	94
6	Peruvayal	847	100	72	78
7	Urban: Nadakavu and Panniyankara	680	200	88	93
	Total	14,013	1600	1,067	1,191

frame. From this list, 100 households were selected using systematic circular sampling procedure with a random start. All the elderly in each selected household were interviewed provided the elderly is in a position to understand the question and give meaningful answers. Number of households with elderly, number of selected households and number of households surveyed and number of elderly interviewed are presented in Table 3.

Of the 1600 selected households, only 1067 could be surveyed. Forty percent of the remaining 533 were in urban area and most of them have shifted residence permanently since the preparation of the electoral roll. Moreover, some of the elderly expired since the preparation of the electoral roll and hence got excluded. The other major reason for excluding a household from the survey was objection on the part of the household members in interviewing the elderly.

Among the interviewed households there were a total of 1236 elderly persons. However, interviews could be conducted/ completed only for 1191 elderly among whom 554 were males and 637 were females. The reasons for non-interview of the remaining 45 are given in Table 4.

Table 4
Distribution of older persons by reasons for non-interview

Sl. No	*Reasons*	*Male*	*Female*	*Total*
1	Temporarily absent	6	19	25
2	Diminished comprehension	2	8	10
3	Hearing impairment	1	...	1
4	Critically ill	1	...	1
5	Poor mental condition	...	3	3
6	Reduced communication ability	1	1	2
7	Hospitalized	1	1	2
8	Too weak to respond	...	1	1
	Total	12	33	45

Type of data used for the study

The data used for the study from the parent survey mentioned earlier, include education, marital status, children ever born, work participation, work done at the household, status and role including decision making, health status, living arrangement and means of finance for day-to-day expenses. Particulars like age, education, marital status and activity status of all members of the household was used to understand the immediate environment in which the elderly lives.

To understand the financial status of the household, a standard of living index was computed using some of the available information from the original survey. This index has taken into account some of the household related variables and ownership of durable goods with due weightage to house ownership, availability of drinking water within the compound, toilet facilities and electric supply. The durable goods used are radio, cassette player, fan, television, gas stove, refrigerator, washing machine, air conditioner, bicycle and car. The agricultural land and farm implements are also included.

Since this study has its primary focus on financial status of the elderly, only those elderly who explicitly reported their financial status are included in the analysis. There were a total of nine elderly for whom this information was not available. So, the total number of elderly for this study was reduced to 1182 with 553 males (46.8 percent) and 629 females (53.2 percent).

Moreover, gender differentials could be found in many aspects and as such, all analysis will be done separately for men and women and among them for different financial status groups.

Classification of the financial status of the elderly

Since the study is basically to understand how far the financial status of the elderly will affect the various aspects of their life, the financial status of the elderly is assessed using the available data in the following manner. The parent survey had asked a question to all the elderly persons interviewed regarding their financial status. The question was, "Do you have enough money to take care of your day-to-day needs?" No specific amount was given as the needs of the elderly differ from person to person. If the elderly report that they do have enough money, it is accepted as such and they are treated as having liquid asset (cash)[2]. Another question asked related to their asset ownership. All those who have reported as having immovable assets like agricultural land, residential plot, house etc. are grouped into one category labeled as having "immovable asset". There were many having liquid asset and immovable asset and they are included in the liquid asset category as day-to-day needs can be met by liquid asset than by immovable asset. In other words, those grouped as having liquid asset may or may not have property, but those with immovable asset have only property.

The presumption in this classification is that in this materialistic world financial status of the person makes a big difference in his/her life and also in the attitude of others towards him/her. In this study those with liquid assets are considered better than those with immovable asset and they in turn are treated as better than those with no asset. The inclusion of those with only immovable assets as having a better status than those with neither liquid cash nor any other asset is based on the fact that in Kerala property/house is valued very much as everyone would like to have a piece of land and a house of one's own as they can be independent, a feeling which is usually valued very high. In line with this, if the elderly co-residing with them have property/house, household members will have some expectation of getting the asset after the death of the elderly or getting it transferred to their name even before. Hence there is some hope of financial gain sooner or later[3]. This is nothing new as pointed out by Jones (1990) that elderly persons might implicitly trade bequests for care from children or other beneficiaries should it be required or in return for assurance that care would be provided. In Tamil Nadu the importance of property had been brought out very clearly in a study by Sureender, Vaithilingam and Khan (1996) based on focus group discussions where it came out that the elderly were taken care of very well until they transferred their property to the care givers, and some elderly have even suggested that one way of "keeping a hold on the family" is to keep at least some property in one's own name. Pant (1997) also noted the importance of wealth in the form of land to determine the status of the elderly in the family.

The distribution of elderly into these three categories has shown that there are 33.7 percent with no asset, 37.5 percent with liquid assets and the remaining 28.8 percent with only immovable assets. Among those with liquid assets 19 percent had only cash and 81 percent had both cash and property.

Statistical technique used in this study

The determinants of health, involvement in decision-making and involvement in household activities by the elderly are studied with the help of logistic regression analysis. It is a method which is often used to deal with dichotomous dependent variable and is a reformulated multiple regression model in which the predicted variable can take the value of zero and one. Further, the independent variables can be categorical or interval or a combination of the two (Retherford and Choe, 1983; Kamin, 1994). This method has been used in demographic research in topics as diverse as contraceptive use, marital formation and dissolution, premarital sexual experience, premarital pregnancy, childlessness, infant mortality etc[4]. The variables used in the logistic regression and their level of measurement are given in Table 5.

Table 5
Variables used in the Logistic Regression and their Measurement

Sl. No.	*Variable*	*Abbreviation used*	*Measurement*
1	Sex	Sex	0 = Male 1 = Female
2	Age	Age	0 = 75+years 1 = 65-74 years
3	Current marital status	CMS	0 = Disrupted marriage 1 = Currently married
4	Education	Education	0 = Illiterate 1 = Edu.: 1-4 years 2 = Edu.: 5+ years
5	Status at home	SAH	0 = Other than head of the household (HHH) 1 = HHH
6	Financial status of aged	FS	0 = No asset 1 = Liquid asset 2 = Immovable asset
7	Current work status	CWS	0 = Not working 1 = Working
8	Often feel depressed	Depression	0 = Depressed 1 = Not depressed
9	Care giver	Care giver	0 = Other than son 1 = Son
10	Religion	Religion	0 = Hindu 1 = Muslim 2 = Christian
11	Caregiver spent time with aged	CGSTWA	0 = No 1 = Yes
12	Health status	Health	0 = unhealthy 1 = Healthy
13	Involvement in household work	HHW	0 = Not involved 1 = Involved
14	Involvement in decision making	DM	0 = Not involved 1 = Involved
15	Visit to Temple/Church/ Mosque	T-C-M	0 = Do not visit 1 = Visit

These variables are selected keeping in mind their importance in dealing with each of the dependent variable, viz. health, involvement in decision making and involvement in household work.

II

GENERAL BACKGROUND CHARACTERISTICS

Introduction

A total of 1182 elderly were interviewed from 1060 households with a total of 6239 *dejure* population. The average household size works out to be 5.9 with 2.8 males and 3.1 females. In urban areas, the average household size is 6.6 persons (3.1 males and 3.5 females). The corresponding figure for rural areas is 5.7 (2.7 males and 3.0 females).

This part of the chapter has three sections, one each for the household/house related characteristics, characteristics of the household population and characteristics of the elderly persons.

House/Household related characteristics

The enumerated houses are classified into three categories based on the construction materials. The categories are *kachcha, pucca* and semi-*pucca*. Houses made of good construction material for roof, walls and floor are *pucca* houses, and houses made of mud, tin, leafs etc. are *kachcha* houses. Those that fall between these two extremes are termed as semi-*pucca* houses. The *pucca* houses are 23.2 percent and 23.5 percent respectively in urban and rural areas (Table 6). Slightly more *kachcha* houses are found in rural areas and slightly more semi-*pucca* houses are found in urban areas. Most of the houses in both rural and urban areas are semi-*pucca*. One or the other member of the household owns almost all houses.

Electricity is available in 72.3 percent of the houses. But almost a third of the rural households lacked electricity. Similarly, in three out of four houses potable water is available inside the house (piped into the house) or inside the compound in which the house is situated (well water). Twenty nine percent of the rural households had to depend on water sources like ground water or surface water, which mainly is stream water coming from the hills, used by the population of *Kavilumpara* and *Tirumarady* villages.

Flush toilet facilities are available for 73.1 percent of the houses. The proportion of those without any toilet facility is twice as much in rural than in urban areas.

More than half of the houses (56.6percent) have 3-4 rooms and one in every four houses (22.8percent) have five or more rooms. Percent of households having just 1-2 rooms is 17. There is not much difference by place of residence in the proportion of households by number of rooms. The size of room, however, is not known. This data indicates that, other things remaining equal, in majority of the households, older persons have space for some amount of privacy, if they so desire.

Table 6
Selected characteristics of houses/households

Sl. No.	*Characteristics*	*Place of residence*		
		Urban	*Rural*	*Total*
1	*Type of house*			
	Kachcha	25.4	32.7	31.5
	Pucca	23.2	23.5	23.5
	Semi-pucca	51.4	43.8	45.0
2	*House ownership*			
	Own	98.4	99.3	99.2
	Other	1.6	0.7	0.8
3	*Electricity facility*			
	Yes	88.1	68.9	72.3
	No	11.9	31.1	27.7
4	*Water source*			
	Inside*	81.1	71.2	72.9
	Other**	18.9	28.8	27.1
5	*Toilet type*			
	Flush	86.5	70.3	73.1
	Other	8.1	18.1	16.3
	No facility	5.4	11.7	10.6
6	*Number of rooms*			
	1-2	16.2	17.6	17.4
	3-4	59.5	56.0	56.6
	5+	23.2	22.7	22.8
7	*Standard of living*			
	Low	16.2	34.5	31.3
	Middle	47.0	44.9	45.3
	High	36.8	20.6	23.4
8	Total	100.0 (185)	100.0 (875)	100.0 (1060)

Note: In some cases percentages will not add to 100 as the "no data" category is not shown.

* Piped water or well within the compound

** Common pipe/well, bore well, stream water etc.

The standard of living shows that almost half of the selected households belong to the middle level in both urban and rural areas. But place of residence difference is very conspicuous in both low and high standard of living. The proportion of households with low standard of living in rural area is more than double that in urban area. Similarly urban area has more households in high standard of living category.

Characteristics of household population

This section examines selected characteristics of the household population. The characteristics are not differentiated by financial status of the elderly as these are not further utilized in this study. As stated earlier there were a total of 6239 persons in the enumerated household. With 2925 males and 3314 females among the enumerated population, a sex ratio of 883 males per 1000 females is obtained. The urban sex ratio is 893 and that of rural is 880. The age distribution of the population is given in Fig. 1.

Fig. 1
Age distribution of household population

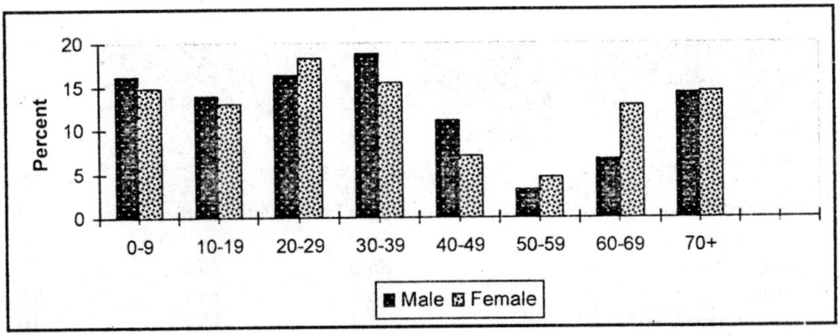

In ages below 20, and age groups 30-39 and 40-49 years there is slightly more males than females while the opposite is true in age group 20-29, 50-59 and 60-69 years. In fact the proportion of women in the age group 60-69 is noticeably higher than that of men. The proportion of those who are aged 70 years and above is almost the same for both men and women.

Proportion of population aged 40-49 and 50-59 years are found relatively lower, which could be because of the selection of houses with at least one elderly person aged 65 years and above. In such households there is less chance of having a large segment of persons from the immediately preceding cohort.

Educational situation is examined at two levels: (i) literacy status and (ii) level of education for the literates measured in terms of years of schooling. It is done only for persons aged 10 years and above on the assumption that at least a few years of schooling is required for a person to become literate. Educational level is classified as: primary (1-4 years), middle (5-7 years), high school (8-10 years) and higher level of education (11 years or more).

Among the total population aged 10 or more years, 88 percent are literate (Fig. 2). Sex-wise difference shows that 82 percent of females and 95 percent of males are literate. Though the proportion of literate is comparatively high for males, the literacy level of females, taken by itself, is also very high compared to the situation prevailing in many of the other states.

Fig. 2
Literacy level of household population aged 10 years and above

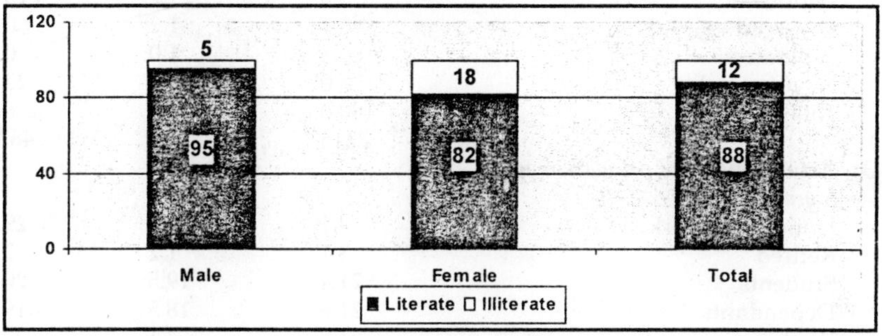

Table 7 gives the percentage distribution of household population by selected characteristics. Among the literate population one in every five had at least 11 years of schooling. Another sixty two percent had 5-9 years and 18 percent had 1-4 years of schooling. The pattern is the same for both males and females.

Marital status distribution is given only for those who are aged 15 years and above. In fact, age at marriage is the highest in this state compared to other, major states in this country. Majority of men and women are currently married and one out of five women are widowed. The comparatively high proportion of widows in the population is due to criteria introduced in the selection of households, i.e. insistence on selecting only those households that have at least one person aged 65 years or more. Thirty percent of males and 18 percent of females are never married. These are mainly boys and girls who are in the 15-19 year age group.

Table 7
Percentage distribution of household population by selected characteristics

Sl. No.	*Characteristics*	*Male*	*Female*	*Total*
1	*Education (Years of schooling of literate population age 10+years)*			
	0*	0.7	0.5	0.6
	1-4	16.0	19.1	17.6
	5-10	63.4	60.4	61.9
	11+	19.9	19.9	19.9
	Total	100.0	100.0	100.0
		2326	2311	4637
2	*Marital status of population age 15 years and above*			
	Currently married	65.4	58.5	61.7
	Widowed	3.8	21.2	13.2
	Divorced	0.2	1.2	0.8
	Separated	0.5	1.0	0.8
	Never married	30.0	18.0	23.5
	Total	100.0	100.0	100.0
		2216	2615	4831
3	*Activity status of population age 5 years and above*			
	Household work	2.1	53.5	29.5
	Retired	3.1	1.2	2.1
	Students	21.4	19.5	20.4
	Dependants	21.6	18.5	19.9
	Working	51.5	7.1	27.8
	No Data	0.3	0.2	0.3
	Total	100.0	100.0	100.0
		2702	3093	5795
4	*Occupation of working persons*			
	Professionals	5.0	22.7	7.4
	Mechanics	5.2	2.3	4.8
	Agricultural workers	9.0	1.8	8.0
	Petty business	18.9	—	17.1
	Peons, attendants, etc	23.7	25.0	23.8
	Non-agri.workers	30.0	23.6	29.1
	Clerical	47.6	9.5	7.9
	Others	0.4	5.9	1.5
	No data	0.3	0.9	0.4
	Total	100.0	100.0	100.0
		1391	220	1611

* Non-formal education.

Activity status is given only for persons aged five years and above on the assumption that those below age five could only be dependents. The Table 7 shows that half of the male population (51.5%) is working and slightly more than half of the female population (53.5%) is doing only household work. Students formed one-fifth of the population and almost equal proportion is found to be dependents. The occupation of working population shows that the households are not really well off with 30 percent of the working men being engaged as non-agricultural labourers, 23.7 percent as peons, attendants, etc. and another 18.9 percent doing petty business. Women are also found to be engaged in the former two activities mentioned above, though there was no woman doing business. But one in every five working women is a professional like teacher, doctor, nurse, etc.

Characteristics of the elderly persons.

This section deals with the characteristics of the elderly in general and that of the elderly by their financial status. Table 8 gives the general characteristics of the elderly. Majority of the elderly belong to the Hindu community (56.5%), followed by Christians (28.8%) and Muslims (14.7%) in that order. Age distribution indicates a slightly higher proportion in the 70-74 year age group for both men and women (36.9% males and 35.8% females). There are more males (19.3%) than females (16.4%) aged 80 years and above, a situation not really expected as the women survive longer than men. However, it should be remembered in this context that of the total women selected for the study 33 could not be interviewed and 8 did not give the required details of their financial status. Thus 41 women were excluded from this analysis as against 13 men. Going by the reasons for non-interview (Table 4) it appears that a good proportion of these aged could be above 80 years. Further, four out of the 8 women who did not give details of their financial status were aged at least 80 years of age. Thus it appears that if all of them were included, this anomaly would not have arisen.

Eighty three percent of males and 55.5 percent of females are literate. It should be noted that the female literacy for women aged 65 years and above being 55 percent is quite an admirable situation as in many of the other states not even the adult women have this high literacy rate. About one percent of men and about two percent of women are reported to be literate but with no formal schooling. It is quite possible in this state where the non-formal education has been given a boost to improve literacy level by the *Kerala Sastra Sahitya Parishad* through their *Saksharatha Yajnam* (literacy mission) and through the efforts of literacy mission of government of Kerala.

Table 8

Percentage distribution of elderly by selected background characteristics

Sl. No.	*Characteristics*	*Male*	*Female*	*Total*
1	*Religion*			
	Hindu	51.5	60.9	56.5
	Muslim	17.5	12.2	14.7
	Christian	30.9	26.9	28.8
2	*Age*			
	65-69	26.4	28.1	27.3
	70-74	36.9	35.8	36.3
	75-79	17.4	19.7	18.6
	80+	19.3	16.4	17.8
3	*Literacy*			
	Illiterate	16.8	44.5	31.6
	Literate	83.0	55.5	68.4
4	*Education (years of schooling) for literates**			
	0	0.9	1.7	1.2
	1-4	52.9	63.9	57.7
	5-9	37.3	29.5	33.9
	10+	8.9	4.9	7.2
5	*Employment*			
	Working	24.4	2.5	12.8
	Not working	76.6	97.5	87.2
6	*Occupation of elderly workers**			
	Modern sector	3.0	18.8	4.6
	Agricultural	45.2	6.3	41.1
	Non-agricultural labour	10.4	50.0	14.6
	Business	14.8	—	13.2
	Other	26.7	25.0	26.5
7	*Marital status*			
	Currently married	83.9	18.3	49.0
	Widowed/Divorced/Separated	14.8	78.7	48.8
	Never Married	1.3	3.0	2.2
8	*No. of children*			
	0	2.9	5.6	4.3
	1-2	11.3	21.2	16.5
	3+	85.8	73.2	79.2
	Total	100.0	100.0	100.0
		553	629	1182

* Denominator is different from what is given at the bottom of the Table as is clear from the item heading

Majority of both men and women are having 1-4 years of schooling. Almost double the proportion of males had at least 10 years of schooling compared to that of women (8.9 percent vs. 4.9 percent). For all further analysis, years of schooling of literate will be grouped into two categories, viz. 1-4 years (which will also include the absolutely negligible 0 years of schooling category) and 5 years or more.

Only a small proportion of the elderly were engaged in economic activities (24.4 percent of men and 2.5 percent of women). Among the working elderly, 45.2 percent of the men were engaged in agricultural and related activities and half the working women were occupied in non-agricultural activities. Petty business accounted for 14.8 percent of men. The miscellaneous category labeled "others" absorbed one-fourth each of the working men and women. Almost 19 percent of the working women were found in the modern sector activities which included teaching, clerical work, administration etc.

Marital status distribution of the elderly shows that 83.9 percent of men are currently married and 78.7 percent of women have disrupted marriage due to widowhood/separation/divorce (widowed form the major chunk of this group). Having a higher proportion of married men and not having a similarly higher proportion of married women is possible in a survey like this where only those aged 65 years and above alone are considered. Many of the wives of the elderly men could be below that age limit. Further, a higher proportion of widows are mainly due to the fact that women live longer than men and also they tend to marry men older than themselves (Goyal, 1997). Also remarriage of widows are not that common in this society.

Even though the current fertility level in this state is very low, that was not the case with earlier generation where comparatively high fertility prevailed. Almost 80 percent of the elderly (79.2 percent) had at least three children. A very small percent (4.3 percent) did not have any living children. This comprised of 16 elderly (4 males and 12 females) who never got married and 35 (12 males and 23 females) who got married but did not have any children.

Since the financial status of the elderly is given a thrust in this study, the distribution of the elderly by financial status is given in

Table 9
Percentage distribution of elderly by selected characteristics and by financial status

Sl. No.	Characteristics	Financially weak		Liquid asset		Immovable asset		Total			
								Percent		Number	
		M	F	M	F	M	F	M	F	M	F
1	*Place of residence*										
	Urban	23.7	49.5	57.0	17.8	19.3	32.7	100.0	100.0	93	107
	Rural	15.4	48.5	52.2	25.1	32.4	26.4	100.0	100.0	460	522
2	*Religion*										
	Hindu	17.9	44.9	46.0	23.8	36.1	31.3	100.0	100.0	285	383
	Muslim	17.5	49.4	49.5	19.5	33.0	31.2	100.0	100.0	97	77
	Christian	14.6	56.8	66.7	26.0	18.7	17.2	100.0	100.0	171	169
3	*Age*										
	65-69	13.7	44.1	54.8	23.2	31.5	32.8	100.0	100.0	146	177
	70-74	8.8	48.9	57.8	24.9	33.3	26.2	100.0	100.0	204	225
	75-79	15.6	46.0	52.1	25.8	32.3	28.2	100.0	100.0	96	124
	80+	37.4	59.2	42.1	20.4	20.6	20.4	100.0	100.0	107	103
4	*Literacy*										
	Illiterate	18.3	52.9	31.2	19.3	50.5	27.9	100.0	100.0	93	280
	Literate	16.3	45.3	57.5	27.5	26.2	27.2	100.0	100.0	459	349

Contd....

Sl. No.	Characteristics	Financially weak		Liquid asset		Immovable asset		Total			
								Percent		Number	
		M	F	M	F	M	F	M	F	M	F
5	*Education (years of schooling)*										
	0	—	—	—	—	—	—	100.0	100.0	4	6
	1-4	18.5	53.4	54.3	22.4	27.2	24.2	100.0	100.0	243	223
	5-9	15.8	33.0	54.4	31.1	29.8	35.9	100.0	100.0	171	103
	10+	4.9	17.6	87.8	76.5	7.3	5.9	100.0	100.0	41	17
6	*Marital status*										
	C - married	13.6	61.7	55.0	17.4	31.5	20.9	100.0	100.0	464	115
	W/D/S	32.9	45.5	43.9	24.4	23.2	31.1	100.0	100.0	82	495
	NM	—	52.6	—	47.4	—	—	100.0	100.0	7	19
7	*No. of children*										
	0	37.5	48.6	50.0	34.3	12.5	17.1	100.0	100.0	16	35
	1-2	16.1	47.4	50.0	26.3	33.9	26.3	100.0	100.0	62	133
	3+	16.3	49.0	53.5	22.0	30.2	29.0	100.0	100.0	473	455
8	Total	16.8	48.6	53.0	23.8	30.2	27.5	100.0	100.0	553	629

Note: Percentages may not add up to 100 in some cases as the "no data" cases are not given M = Male; F = Female; C-Married = Currently married; W/D/S = Widowed/divorced/separated; NM = Never married

Fig. 3. About half of the aged women are observed to be financially weak with no cash or property while more than half of the elderly males are financially sound. Thus there exists a sex differential among the aged favouring the males related to the financial status. The proportion having only immovable asset is more or less the same among both men and women.

Fig. 3
Percentage distribution of elderly by financial status

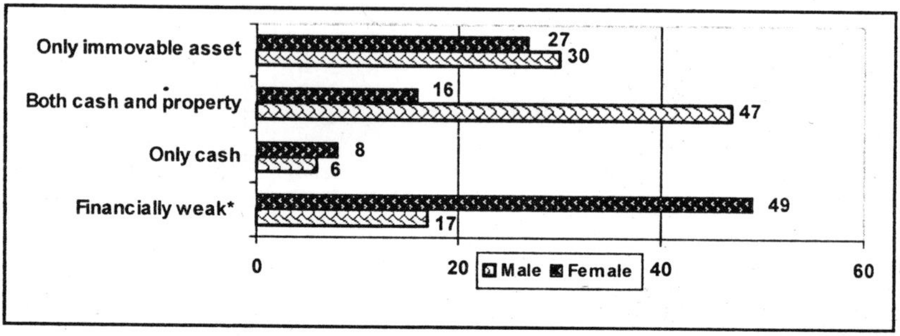

* With neither cash nor property

Table 9 gives the selected characteristics of the elderly by financial status. The place of residence did not make any difference in the case of financially weak women as their proportion in urban (49.5 percent) and rural (48.5 percent) areas remain almost equal. The percent of women with liquid asset is high in rural areas (25.1 percent) compared to urban areas (17.8 percent). It is possible that women in rural areas are comparatively poor. Hence if they are capable of working, some of them may get themselves engaged in any type of work that are available either willingly or forcibly. Conversely it is found that the proportion of women with immovable property is high in the urban areas than in the rural areas.

Between the different religions, almost 57 percent of Christian women have no financial means. In this aspect the lowest proportion is observed among the Hindus with 44.9 percent. In contrast, those men having liquid asset are the highest among Christians (66.7 percent) and lowest among Hindus (46.0 percent). The proportion having immovable asset is the lowest for Christians in the case of both men and women. The financial status of both men and women above the age of eighty years is worse off than their counterparts in the lower age groups. Among those aged 80 years and above 37.4 percent of men and 59.2 percent women are total dependents. Among illiterate men, 50.5 percent have immovable asset and among illiterate women 52.9 percent have no financial means. Almost 58 percent of literate men have liquid asset. Education made a big difference in having liquid asset. Among those with at least 10 years of schooling 87.8 percent of men and 76.5 percent of women have liquid asset. The inference on gender differential in the financial status of the present study is in conformation with Laura Rudkin (1993) who stated that the gender differential is mainly associated with the level of skills like education, job etc.

Financial status of the elderly in each marital status category indicate that all except 13.6 percent of currently married males have some form of asset (55.0 percent liquid and 31.5 percent immovable) while 61.7 percent of currently married women have no financial means. Though the number of women falling into the never married category is few, almost half of them have liquid asset to take care of their day-to-day needs. Financial status and the number of children failed to show any meaningful relationship particularly in the case of women.

NOTES

1. Only the percent of Hindus is shown in the Table. The information is provided for 1991 as the data collection took place in 1996-97.
2. Those who reported that they have money were asked the source of their income which varied from past saving, current earnings, retired pension and other types of pensions given by the government like old age pension, agricultural pension, etc.
3. The importance of having property has been stressed by many elderly in the course of the survey.
4. Several studies are sited regarding the use of this method in demographic research in S.S. Halli and K.V.Rao, Advanced Techniques of Population Analysis, Plenum Press, New York, 1992.

4 FINANCIAL STATUS AND HEALTH OF THE ELDERLY

INTRODUCTION

The major element of individual ageing is a consistent decline in health, though such decline is not uniformly found in all individuals at the same age. As pointed out by Decker (1980) the health situation of the elderly depends upon heredity, life style and nutrition and all individuals must suffer a weakening of physical and psychological capabilities sooner or later. Thus, an increase in the number of such persons will throw up new challenges for the community.

In old age, the financial situation of the elderly has a direct bearing on their health situation in three ways: (i) if one has one's own financial means to take care of one's health problems, the feeling of dependence on health care will be less and this very fact can help to keep the elderly in fairly good health, (ii) the elderly with own finances will seek health care when needed much earlier than the one without any economic means and thus will get back to normal health soon and (iii) if one has to depend on others for one's health care, one's endurance level will be deliberately raised so that the dependency level can be reduced. The last category of persons also may report as healthy. These are only surmises, which needs to be substantiated with the help of data. The economic situation assessed in this study, however, relates only to the availability of financial resources to meet the day-to-day needs. This may also take care of small illnesses one may get once in a while. If, on the other hand, one's illness expenditure needs to be taken care of by others, a person with some economic resources to meet the day-to-day needs may not feel as bad as the one with no resources at all. From that point of view such an examination seems appropriate.

Four approaches are used to assess the health of the elderly in the parent survey: (i) self assessed overall health, (ii) health problems during the last one year prior to the date of survey and treatment seeking pattern, (iii) help needed to perform daily activities and (iv) current health problems, if any. The answer to the question on self-assessed health status is classified into three categories in the data set. They are good, average and bad. Generally, in old age, it appears that, there is a tendency for the elderly to exaggerate their illness status and thus those who report themselves as having average health may actually be having a fairly good health. Keeping this in mind, the first two categories are clubbed together and is labelled as healthy and the last category is kept as such and is labelled as unhealthy.

Another health status indicator considered here is based on current medication status and prolonged health problems even if currently not on medication. That is, a healthy elderly refers to one who is not currently under medication for any health problem and those who are not having any prolonged health problem during the last one year. This health indicator is labelled as "computed" health as against "self-assessed" health.

Fig. 1 shows the health status of the elderly based on these two health status criteria. It shows that the proportion of self-assessed health (62%) is higher than the computed health variable (40%). This difference could be because of the fact that a notable proportion of elderly persons who are under medication have simple and short duration illnesses rather than serious and prolonged ones. Majority of the illnesses reported by the elderly are either uncomplicated (like fever, pain in leg, weakness, etc) or are such that they can be controlled by medication and diet (like blood pressure, diabetes), or rheumatism, the pain of which can be controlled with medicine. In these cases the elderly can still feel healthy. Between males and females a slightly higher proportion of males are found healthy than the elderly women irrespective of the indicator used. Since women does most of the household work in this society, and since majority of them have gone through the process of bearing and rearing of children and the consequent problems associated with it in their adult years, the finding is as one would expect.

Fig. 1
Percentage distribution of elderly by health status

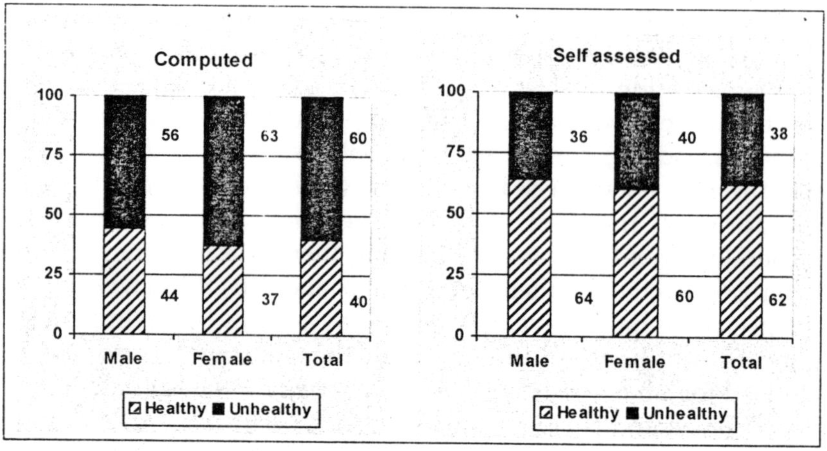

ILLNESSES OF THE ELDERLY DURING THE ONE YEAR PRECEDING THE SURVEY

Of the total 1182 elderly 67 percent (65 percent of men and 68 percent of women) had some illness during the course of the one year preceding the survey. The types of illness suffered by them are given in Table 1. There is no concentration of elderly in any illness category, though rheumatism (13.4%) and blood pressure (10.4%) are the two main illnesses that affected the elderly in Kerala. Some of the elderly who reported themselves as unhealthy are suffering from serious illnesses like diabetes, Asthma, tuberculosis, etc. The source of health care expenditure of the elderly is given in Table 2.

Almost 56 percent of men and 27.9 percent of women with liquid asset used their own financial resources to meet their health expenditure. However, the health care expenditure of the majority was taken care of by the caregiver (son/daughter) of the elderly. In this context the increasing life expectancy of the elderly assumes importance.

HEALTH AND FINANCIAL STATUS OF THE ELDERLY

For the subsequent analysis of this chapter self-assessed health status is taken as the indicator of health for two reasons: (a) most of the diagnosis by doctors are made on the basis of the symptoms/

feelings reported by the elderly, and (b) the behaviour patterns of the elderly will be governed by their feeling of well being which is more important than any clinically diagnosed illness. The financial status of the elderly in relation to their health status is presented in Table 3.

Table 1
Percentage distribution of elderly by nature of illness (suffered during the one year preceding the survey)

Sl. No.	*Nature of illness*	*Male*	*Female*	*Total*
1	Rheumatism	13.0	13.7	13.4
2	Breathing problem	9.1	6.5	7.7
3	Blood pressure	8.0	12.3	10.4
4	Dizziness	5.8	6.7	6.3
5	Heart trouble	5.8	3.0	4.3
6	Diabetes	5.5	2.3	3.8
7	Stomach ailments	5.5	3.9	4.7
8	Asthma	5.3	4.2	4.7
9	Chest pain	5.3	3.2	4.2
10	Fever	5.0	8.1	6.7
11	Leg pain	3.9	5.1	4.5
12	Eye problem	3.6	4.4	4.0
13	Back pain	3.0	4.2	3.7
14	Urinary problem	3.0	1.2	2.0
15	Met with accident	2.8	5.6	4.3
16	Piles	1.9	1.4	1.6
17	Acidity	1.7	...	0.8
18	Ulcer	1.7	...	0.8
19	Tuberculosis	1.1	1.4	1.3
20	Bone disease	1.1	0.7	0.9
21	Weakness	0.3	1.2	0.8
22	Others	6.6	10	8.5
23	No Data	0.8	0.9	0.9
	Total	100	100	100
		361	430	791

* Only the major illness is given though there are cases with multiple illnesses.

Three out of four men having liquid asset is found to be healthy which not the case with others is and this is in tune with our expectation. But having just immovable assets did not make much difference in the case of health status of men. In fact, those without any financial means are found to be slightly better off in their health status than those with only immovable asset.

Table 2
Source of health expenditure of the elderly

Person who met the health care expenditure of	*Financially Weak*	*Liquid. Asset*	*Immovable Asset*	*Total*
Male elderly				
Self	10.9	55.5	12.9	33.0
Care giving child	60.9	22.0	48.4	38.0
Other children	26.6	21.4	37.9	28.0
Others	1.6	1.2	0.8	1.1
Total	100.0	100.0	100.0	100.0
	64	173	124	361
Female elderly				
Self	6.1	27.9	3.9	10.7
Care giving child	58.6	50.0	56.3	55.8
Other children	33.8	22.1	38.3	32.3
Others	1.5	...	1.6	1.2
Total	100.0	100.0	100.0	100.0
	198	104	128	430

Table 3
Percentage distribution of elderly in different financial status group by health status

Health status	*Financial Status*								
	Financially weak			*Liquid asset*			*Immovable asset*		
	Male	*Female*	*Total*	*Male*	*Female*	*Total*	*Male*	*Female*	*Total*
Healthy	54.8	58.5	57.6	75.4	60.0	70.2	49.1	62.4	55.9
Not healthy	45.2	41.5	42.4	24.6	40.0	29.8	50.9	37.6	44.1
Total	100.0	100.0	100.0	100.0	100.0	100.0	100.0	100.0	100.0
	93	306	399	293	150	443	167	173	340

For women, financial status *per se* did not make much of a difference in health status – the proportion of healthy vary from 58.5 percent to 62.4 percent between the different categories.

HEALTH STATUS OF THE ELDERLY BY BACKGROUND CHARACTERISTICS AND FINANCIAL STATUS

Place of residence and health status

Generally the relationship between place of residence and health is studied because of the differential availability and utilization of health care facilities. Urban people will have better health care facilities and will be better informed about them. Further their financial status will also be better than their rural counterparts. All these make one assume that the utilization of health care facilities will also be high in urban areas. But compared to the rural areas, the urban life is rather sedentary and such life style can adversely affect their health status. But rural areas being dominated by non-formal work, the workers, particularly men, may continue to work as long as they are capable of working or there is a need for their contribution to family income. In other words, there are factors that are favourable and unfavourable to healthy life in both rural and urban areas. Fig. 2 indicates that the proportion of healthy men (70%) and women (66%) are high in urban areas compared to their rural counterparts (62 percent of men and 59 percent of women).

Fig. 2
Percent of healthy elderly in rural and urban areas

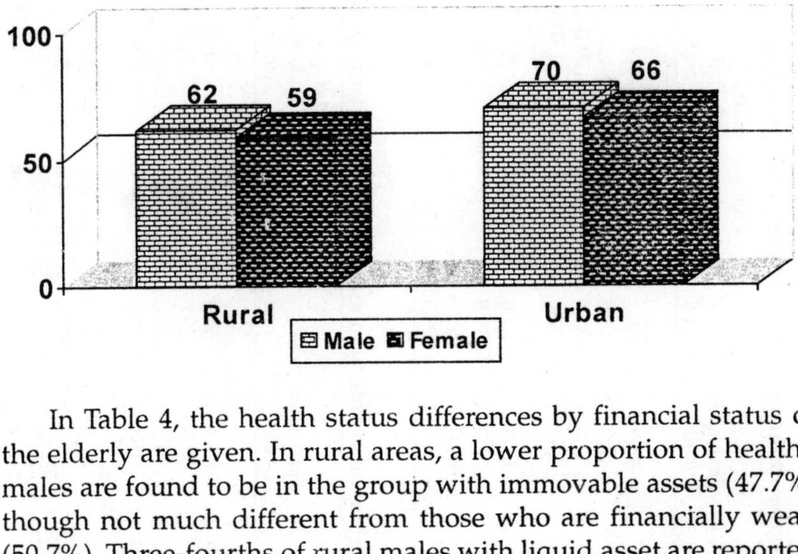

In Table 4, the health status differences by financial status of the elderly are given. In rural areas, a lower proportion of healthy males are found to be in the group with immovable assets (47.7%) though not much different from those who are financially weak (50.7%). Three-fourths of rural males with liquid asset are reported to be healthy. Similar is the situation in urban areas as well.

The health status of rural women failed to show any relation to their financial status. But that is not the case in the urban areas where finance makes a difference. A higher proportion of women with liquid asset (73.7%) and immovable assets (68.6%) are reported to be healthy compared to those who are financially weak (62.3%). It may be indicating two things; first that the urban mentality is

Table 4
Percentage distribution of the aged in different financial status group by health status and place of residence

Place of residence and health	Financially weak Male	Financially weak Female	Financially weak Total	Liquid asset Male	Liquid asset Female	Liquid asset Total	Immovable asset Male	Immovable asset Female	Immovable asset Total
Rural									
Healthy	50.7	57.7	56.2	75.8	58.0	69.5	47.7	60.9	54.0
Not healthy	49.3	42.3	43.8	24.2	42.0	30.5	52.3	39.1	36.0
Total	100.0	100.0	100.0	100.0	100.0	100.0	100.0	100.0	100.0
	71	253	324	240	131	371	149	138	287
Urban									
Healthy	68.2	62.3	64.0	73.6	73.7	73.6	61.1	68.6	66.0
Not healthy	31.8	37.7	36.0	26.4	26.3	26.4	38.9	31.4	34.0
Total	100.0	100.0	100.0	100.0	100.0	100.0	100.0	100.0	100.0
	22	53	75	53	19	72	18	35	53

(Column groups under the heading *Financial Status*.)

Table 5
Percentage distribution of elderly in different financial status group by health status and age of elderly

Age and Health Status	Financially weak Male	Financially weak Female	Financially weak Total	Liquid asset Male	Liquid asset Female	Liquid asset Total	Immovable asset Male	Immovable asset Female	Immovable asset Total
65-74 years									
Healthy	63.2	65.4	65.0	78.8	66.0	74.6	53.5	64.1	58.9
Not healthy	36.8	34.6	35.0	21.2	34.0	25.4	46.5	35.9	41.1
Total	100.0	100.0	100.0	100.0	100.0	100.0	100.0	100.0	100.0
	38	188	226	198	97	295	114	117	231
75+ years									
Healthy	49.1	47.5	48.0	68.4	49.1	61.5	39.6	58.9	49.5
Not healthy	50.9	52.5	52.0	31.6	50.9	38.5	60.4	41.1	50.5
Total	100.0	100.0	100.0	100.0	100.0	100.0	100.0	100.0	100.0
	55	118	173	95	53	148	53	56	109

(Column groups under the heading *Financial Status*.)

such that the care of the elderly women is determined by their own financial status and secondly, those who have money will take care of their health by attending to it in time.

Age and health status

The relationship between ill health and age is expected to be rather direct. In other words, *ceteris paribus,* more young-old persons are expected to be healthier than the old-old persons. Fig. 3 depicts the expected pattern. Among young-old persons 69 percent of males and 65 percent of females reported themselves as healthy compared to 56 percent of males and 51 percent of females among the old-old persons.

Fig. 3
Percent of healthy elderly in each broad age group

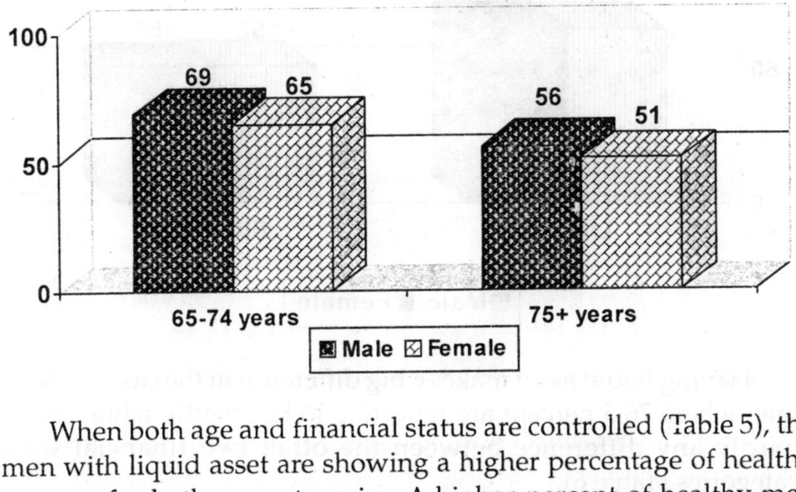

When both age and financial status are controlled (Table 5), the men with liquid asset are showing a higher percentage of healthy persons for both age categories. A higher percent of healthy men are found among financially weak category than among those with immovable assets. For women, on the contrary, financial status did not make any difference among those aged 65-74 years (proportion varying from 64.1 percent for those with immovable asset to 66.0 percent for those with liquid asset). A higher proportion (58.9 %) of the old-old women with immovable asset, reported themselves as healthy compared to the other two groups where the proportion healthy was only 48-49 percent.

Literacy and health status

The relationship between health status and literacy status/education is often found to work through increased knowledge about the health care facilities and the need to take care of one's own health. Besides, literate/educated persons will know the value of personal/environmental hygiene, nutrition etc. which is also very important in health care. Fig. 4 shows that a higher proportion of literate persons are reporting to be healthy compared to their illiterate counterparts, which is expected. However, male-female difference is almost absent.

Fig. 4
Percent of healthy elderly among literates and illiterates

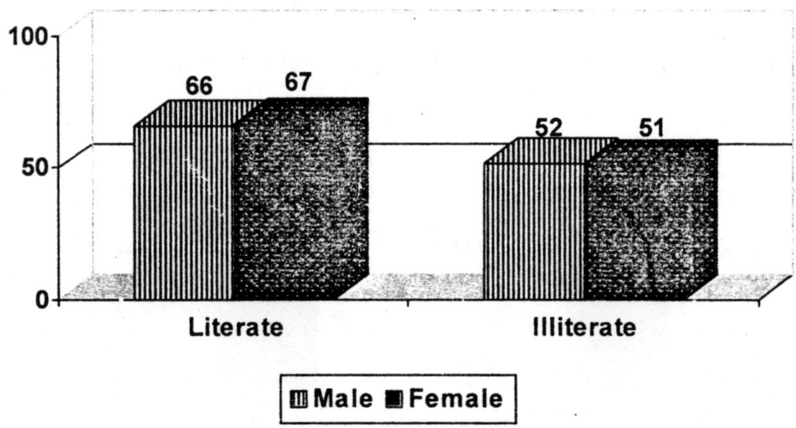

Having liquid asset makes a big difference in the case of literate men where 76.5 percent are reporting to be healthy while there is hardly any difference between the other two financial status categories (Table 6).

The proportion reporting healthy is comparatively low for the illiterate women, particularly those with liquid asset (48.1%) and no asset (47.3%). However 59.0 percent of the women with immovable assets reported themselves as healthy. There is hardly any difference in the proportion reporting healthy among the literate women in the different financial status category though the women with no financial means are reporting a comparatively higher proportion (69.0%) of healthy than those with liquid asset (66.7%) or those with immovable asset (65.3%).

Table 6

Percentage distribution of elderly in different financial status group by health status and literacy status

Literacy and health Status	*Financial Status*								
	Financially weak			*Liquid asset*			*Immovable asset*		
	Male	*Female*	*Total*	*Male*	*Female*	*Total*	*Male*	*Female*	*Total*
Literate									
Healthy	52.0	69.0	63.5	76.5	66.7	73.9	53.3	65.3	58.6
Not healthy	48.0	331.0	36.5	23.5	33.3	26.1	46.7	34.7	41.4
Total	100.0	100.0	100.0	100.0	100.0	100.0	100.0	100.0	100.0
	75	158	233	264	96	360	120	95	215
Illiterate									
Healthy	64.7	47.3	49.1	65.5	48.1	54.2	38.3	59.0	51.2
Not healthy	35.3	52.7	50.9	34.5	51.9	45.8	61.7	41.0	48.8
Total	100.0	100.0	100.0	100.0	100.0	100.0	100.0	100.0	100.0
	18	148	166	29	54	83	47	78	125

Table 7

Percentage distribution of literate elderly in different financial status group by health status and years of schooling

Years of schooling and health status	*Financial Status*								
	Financially weak			*Liquid asset*			*Immovable asset*		
	Male	*Female*	*Total*	*Male*	*Female*	*Total*	*Male*	*Female*	*Total*
1-4 years									
Healthy	56.5	69.4	65.9	73.3	66.7	71.5	47.0	70.2	57.7
Not healthy	43.5	30.6	34.1	26.7	33.3	28.5	53.0	29.8	42.3
Total	100.0	100.0	100.0	100.0	100.0	100.0	100.0	100.0	100.0
	46	121	167	135	51	186	66	57	123
5 + years									
Healthy	44.8	67.6	57.6	79.8	66.7	76.4	61.1	57.9	59.8
Not healthy	55.2	32.4	42.4	20.2	33.3	23.6	38.9	42.1	40.2
Total	100.0	100.0	100.0	100.0	100.0	100.0	100.0	100.0	100.0
	29	37	66	129	45	174	54	38	92

Education and health status

As was described in the literacy section, the expected pattern is to have better health status among those who are more educated than those who are less educated. Education is shown here as in other chapters in two categories based on years of schooling: 1-4 years and 5 years or more. Fig. 5 indicates that among the literates, years of schooling and current health status are directly related only in the case of males.

Fig. 5
Percent of healthy elderly in the two categories of years of schooling

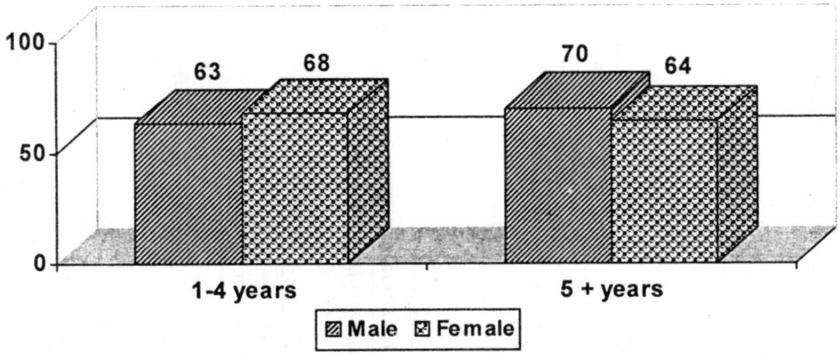

For males without any financial means 56.5 percent of those with 1-4 years of schooling are reported to be healthy compared to 44.8 percent of the next educational category (Table 7) which is not expected. But in the other two financial status categories, the relationship is as expected with four out of five old men reporting themselves as healthy, when they had at least 5 years of schooling compared to 73.3 percent of those with only 1-4 years of schooling. This indicates that the threshold level of education required to have any impact on health status is at least five years of schooling.

Interestingly, the proportion of women reporting themselves as healthy is high (at least equal) in the category having 1-4 years of schooling compared to those with 5 or more years of schooling and not much variations exist over financial status.

Marital status and health status

It is often argued that married persons tend to have better mental health, higher levels of survival, use of health services, social participation and life satisfaction compared to older persons who are not married (Bengtson, Rosenthal and Burtan, 1990). Conversely persons with disrupted marriages tend to view their health negatively compared to those who are in the same age group and currently married (Hobson and Pemberton, 1976). The relationship between marital status and health actually is both psychological and physical. With increasing number of years together, the psychological dependence of husband and wife will increase and thus being in wedlock has the advantage of having some one to share one's happiness and unhappiness and also to discuss their problems, if any. This will be a great relief to persons particularly in old age, as both children and adults, in the present day setup, hardly get time to spend with the elderly. When such a close relative is not available one's own frustrations can lead to physical and other health problems.

Marital status is divided into only two categories in this analysis: currently married and "others". Among "others", nearly 97 percent are widowed persons. As expected a comparatively higher proportion of elderly are found to be healthy among the currently married group than is the case with the other group (Fig. 6). It should also be noticed that in many situations the proportion reporting healthy is higher for men than for women. Among the currently married, a higher proportion of elderly women (70%) reported themselves as healthy compared to their male counterparts (65%). It shows that widowhood and the consequent loneliness and related aspects could be high among women than for men.

Fig. 6

Percent of healthy elderly in the two marital status categories

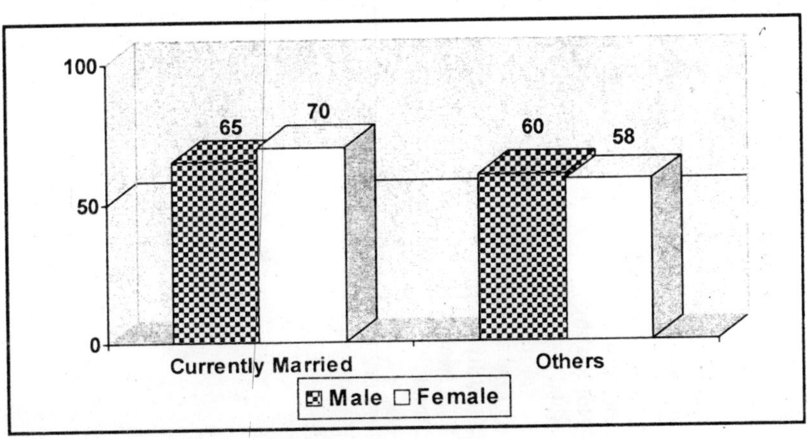

Table 8

Percentage distribution of elderly in different financial status group by health status and marital status

Marital Status and health status	*Financial Status*								
	Financially weak			*Liquid asset*			*Immovable asset*		
	Male	*Female*	*Total*	*Male*	*Female*	*Total*	*Male*	*Female*	*Total*
Currently married									
Healthy	50.8	69.0	60.4	77.3	65.0	76.4	49.3	79.2	53.5
Not healthy	49.2	31.0	39.6	22.7	35.0	23.6	50.7	20.8	46.5
Total	100.0	100.0	100.0	100.0	100.0	100.0	100.0	100.0	100.0
	63	71	134	255	20	275	146	24	170
Others									
Healthy	63.3	55.3	56.2	63.2	59.2	60.1	47.6	59.7	58.2
Not healthy	36.7	44.7	43.2	36.8	40.8	39.9	52.4	40.3	41.8
Total	100.0	100.0	100.0	100.0	100.0	100.0	100.0	100.0	100.0
	30	235	265	38	130	168	21	149	170

Table 8 shows the health situation differentiated by marital status within each financial status category.

Except in the case of financially weak men the proportion of healthy is high among the currently married group. And as in most of the other cases, those with liquid asset reported a higher proportion of healthy persons. The highest proportion of healthy men (77.3%) is found among those who are currently married and have liquid assets.

Women showed a different pattern. Among the currently married women the highest proportion reporting healthy is found among those with immovable assets (79.2 %). Among women with disrupted marriages/never married, a lesser proportion reported themselves as healthy in the financially weak group (55.3%) as compared to those in liquid asset category (59.2%) or those with immovable asset (59.7%).

Religion and health status

Religion is the social attitudes of individuals and communities towards the power or powers, which they conceive as having ultimate control over their interest and destinies (Pratt, 1959). Religion manifests itself in the belief in God, which in turn fulfills a psychological need of the individual. Most religious people visit temple/church/mosque as the case may be to have a peaceful communion with God. Thus it is assumed that those who visit these

Fig. 7
Percent of healthy elderly in each religious group

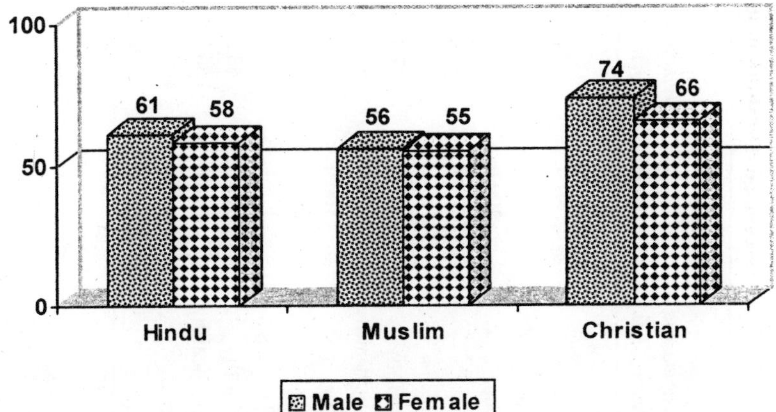

Table 9

Percentage distribution of elderly in different financial status group by health status and religion

Religion and Health Status	Financial Status								
	Financially weak			*Liquid asset*			*Immovable asset*		
	Male	*Female*	*Total*	*Male*	*Female*	*Total*	*Male*	*Female*	*Total*
Hindu									
Healthy	52.9	58.1	57.0	74.8	56.0	67.1	46.6	60.0	53.8
Not healthy	47.1	41.9	43.0	25.2	44.0	32.9	53.4	40.0	46.2
Total	100.0	100.0	100.0	100.0	100.0	100.0	100.0	100.0	100.0
	51	172	223	131	91	222	103	120	223
Muslim									
Healthy	47.1	47.4	47.3	64.6	66.7	65.1	46.9	58.3	51.8
Not healthy	52.9	52.6	52.7	35.4	33.3	34.9	53.1	41.7	48.2
Total	100.0	100.0	100.0	100.0	100.0	100.0	100.0	100.0	100.0
	17	38	55	48	15	63	32	24	56
Christians									
Healthy	64.0	63.5	63.6	80.7	65.9	76.6	59.4	75.9	67.2
Not healthy	36.0	36.5	36.4	19.3	34.1	23.4	40.6	24.1	32.8
Total	100.0	100.0	100.0	100.0	100.0	100.0	100.0	100.0	100.0
	25	96	121	114	44	158	32	29	61

religious places will have better perceived health as they have mental peace. The attitude towards the elderly, taking care of them in every aspect (in this case taking care of their health) is also part of socialization. In general, though the prescriptions relating to the attitude and other behaviour patterns towards the elderly do not differ much across religions, the actual situation could be somewhat different due to many reasons, the most important of which could be the economic status. Fig. 7 shows that the highest proportion reporting healthy is found among the Christians (74% males and 66% females). Between Hindus and Muslims, the proportion healthy is slightly higher among Hindus.

Among all the religious groups, financial status made a big difference particularly for the men (Table 9). The highest proportion (80.7%) of healthy men is found among Christians with liquid asset closely followed by Hindu men (74.8%) in the same financial status category. It is the same category, which has the highest percentage among Muslims as well, but with a comparatively lesser percentage (64.6).

For women, there is hardly any difference in the proportion of healthy women among Hindus by their financial status (the percentage range between 56.0 for liquid asset to 60.0 for those with immovable asset). For Muslim women, having liquid asset is found important with two-thirds reporting themselves as healthy. The corresponding proportion for the other two categories works out to be 47 and 59 percent. A higher proportion (75.9%) of Christian women with immovable assets is found healthy as compared to those with no asset (63.5%) or having liquid asset (65.9%).

Status at Home and Health Status

As has already been shown, the status at home is divided into head of the household and "others". The expectation is that the heads of household, by virtue of their status, may be taken care of even if they are nominal heads and further, for those with financial means the situation could even be better. The health status of the elderly by status at home is given in Fig. 8. The expectation of a significantly higher proportion of heads of household being healthy is not born out by this data in the case of men. The proportion of healthy men showed hardly any difference by status at home while that of women are higher among those who are not head of the households (61%) compared to head of households (55%). A possible explanation for the observed situation could be that the head of the household feel the responsibility of the whole household members and may be giving the least priority to their own health, particularly those with no asset of their own.

Fig. 8
Percent of healthy elderly among head of households and others

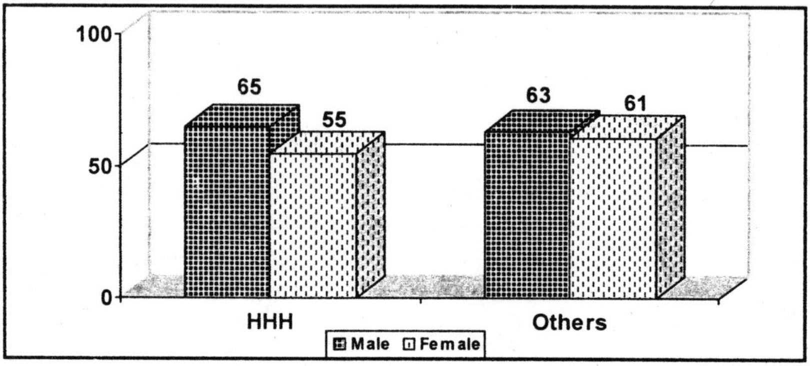

The financial status does make a difference in this situation (Table 10).

Among those men with liquid asset 75.8 percent of head of the households and 75.0 percent of others are found to be healthy while for those with no asset, the proportion of healthy is higher among non-head of the households (56.7%) compared to head of the households (51.5%). For men, invariably it is found that a lower percentage is reporting themselves as healthy among those with only immovable assets.

In the case of women head of the households who are financially weak only 47.9 percent reported themselves as healthy. Correspondingly, among those who are not head of households and those who have only immovable asset almost two-out of three are reported to be healthy.

Relation with caregiver and health status

Other things remaining the same, the care given to the elderly by son/daughter-in-law or daughter/son-in-law or by persons other than one's own children are likely to differ. How this will work cannot be very clear even though it is often said that daughters-in-law are not that careful in taking care of the in-laws. In this study

Table 10

Percentage distribution of elderly in different financial status group by health status and status at home

Status at Home	*Financial Status*								
	Financially weak			*Liquid asset*			*Immovable asset*		
and Health Status	*Male*	*Female*	*Total*	*Male*	*Female*	*Total*	*Male*	*Female*	*Total*
Head of the Household (HHH)									
Healthy	51.5	47.9	49.4	75.8	59.4	73.1	50.5	58.0	53.1
Not healthy	48.5	52.1	50.6	24.2	40.6	26.9	49.5	42.0	46.9
Total	100.0	100.0	100.0	100.0	100.0	100.0	100.0	100.0	100.0
	33	48	81	165	32	197	93	50	143
Other than HHH									
Healthy	56.7	60.5	59.7	75.0	60.2	67.9	47.3	64.2	57.9
Not healthy	43.3	39.5	40.3	25.0	39.8	32.1	52.7	35.8	42.1
Total	100.0	100.0	100.0	100.0	100.0	100.0	100.0	100.0	100.0
	60	258	318	128	118	246	74	123	197

the relevant information is plotted in Fig. 9. It shows that two-thirds of the male elderly who are living with their sons are reported to be healthy as compared to 59 percent living with daughters and 60 percent living with other relatives and non-relatives. This appears to be contradicting the theory that daughters-in-law are half-hearted in taking care of the parents-in-law. The proportion of healthy women does not differ by relation with caregiver.

Fig. 9
Percent of healthy elderly in each category of caregiver

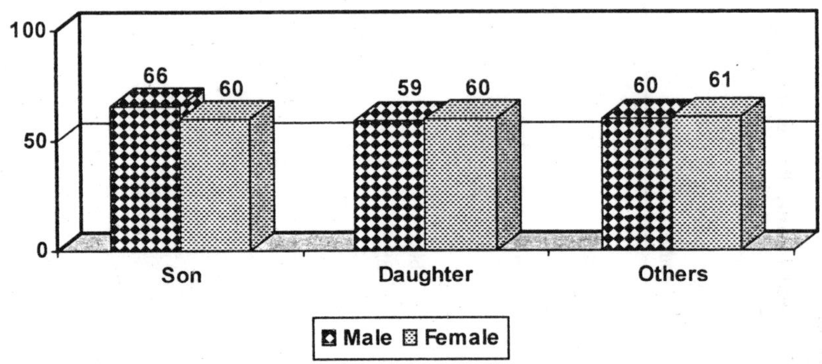

Table 11 gives the proportion of healthy in each financial status category controlling for relation to caregiver. It is found that a higher proportion of elderly males with liquid asset is healthy among all categories of care giver compared to those in other financial status categories.

The lowest proportion of healthy men were found among those who are staying with persons other than their children and are financially weak or have only immovable assets. Women who are staying with persons other than their own children and with immovable asset show the highest proportion reporting as healthy (70.8%) and the lowest proportion is for those who are staying with their daughters in the same financial status category (43.8%).

Standard of living and health status

Standard of living refers to the standard of living of the household in which the elderly is staying. Generally if the standard of living is better, the chances of having better care in the form of good diet, medical care and other facilities will be high which in turn will

Table 11

Percentage distribution of elderly in different financial status group by health status and relation with caregiver

Relation with caregiver and health status	*Financially weak*			*Liquid asset*			*Immovable asset*		
	Male	*Female*	*Total*	*Male*	*Female*	*Total*	*Male*	*Female*	*Total*
Son									
Healthy	61.5	58.4	59.1	76.8	58.3	71.5	50.0	63.2	56.5
Not healthy	38.5	41.6	40.9	23.2	41.7	28.5	50.0	36.8	43.5
Total	100.0	100.0	100.0	100.0	100.0	100.0	100.0	100.0	100.0
	65	221	286	211	84	295	136	133	269
Daughter									
Healthy	—	61.9	56.6	73.1	65.4	69.2	—	43.8	46.4
Not healthy	—	38.1	43.4	29.6	34.6	30.8	—	56.2	53.6
Total	100.0	100.0	100.0	100.0	100.0	100.0	100.0	100.0	100.0
	11	42	53	26	26	52	12	16	28
Others									
Healthy	41.2	55.8	51.7	71.4	60.0	66.7	42.1	70.8	58.1
Not healthy	58.8	44.2	48.3	28.6	40.0	33.9	57.9	29.1	41.9
Total	100.0	100.0	100.0	100.0	100.0	100.0	100.0	100.0	100.0
	17	44	60	56	40	96	19	24	43

Note: Percentages are not calculated if the number of cases is less than 15

improve the health of the elderly. The findings from this survey support this hypothesis (Fig. 10).

Fig. 10
Percent of healthy elderly in each category of standard of living

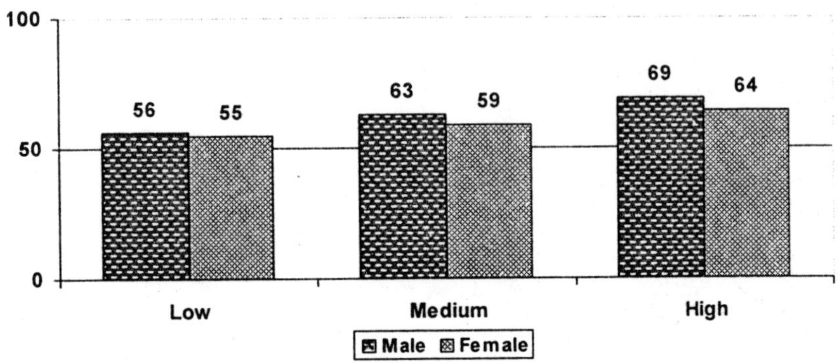

Table 12 shows the percentage distribution of elderly in different financial status groups by health status of the elderly controlling for standard of living of the household. For persons with liquid asset this hypothesis is again born out with a greater jump (particularly in the case of women) from the low to the medium category. The proportion of healthy males with low standard of living and financially weak is almost equal to that of low/medium standard of living with immovable asset (around 47-48 %).

For women with no financial means the difference in the proportion of healthy between the medium and high is quite remarkable (51.6% to 61.1%), but the proportion in low and high standard of living is almost the same. In other words there is no particular pattern visible for the elderly who are financially weak. The increase in the proportion of healthy among those possessing liquid asset from low standard of living (43.6%) to high standard of living (70.7%) is quite noteworthy.

Service contribution made by elderly and health status

Service contribution refers to the type of help given by the elderly towards the household activities which can be grouped into four categories: viz. only household work, only child-care, both household work and child-care, and no work. However, in this

Table 12

Percentage distribution of elderly in different financial status group by health status and standard of living of the household

Standard of living and health status	*Financial Status*								
	Financially weak			*Liquid asset*			*Immovable asset*		
	Male	*Female*	*Total*	*Male*	*Female*	*Total*	*Male*	*Female*	*Total*
Low									
Healthy	47.6	58.9	56.9	68.3	43.6	56.8	47.3	58.5	52.0
Not healthy	52.4	41.1	43.1	31.7	56.4	43.2	52.7	41.5	48.0
Total	100.0	100.0	100.0	100.0	100.0	100.0	100.0	100.0	100.0
	21	95	116	63	55	118	74	53	127
Medium									
Healthy	57.7	51.6	53.4	74.2	65.0	72.0	48.7	65.2	57.6
Not healthy	42.3	48.4	46.6	25.8	35.0	28.0	51.3	34.8	42.4
Total	100.0	100.0	100.0	100.0	100.0	100.0	100.0	100.0	100.0
	26	62	88	62	20	82	39	46	85
High									
Healthy	56.5	61.1	60.0	78.6	70.7	76.1	51.9	63.5	58.6
Not healthy	43.5	38.9	40.0	21.4	29.3	23.9	48.1	36.5	41.4
Total	100.0	100.0	100.0	100.0	100.0	100.0	100.0	100.0	100.0
	46	149	195	168	75	243	54	74	128

chapter the health status of the elderly are classified only into two categories, viz. those who do some work and those who are not engaged in any household activity at all. It is expected that the proportion of healthy persons among those who do some work will be more than among those who do no work at all. The data presented in Fig. 11 supports this expectation.

Fig. 11
Percent of healthy elderly among those who participate in household work and others

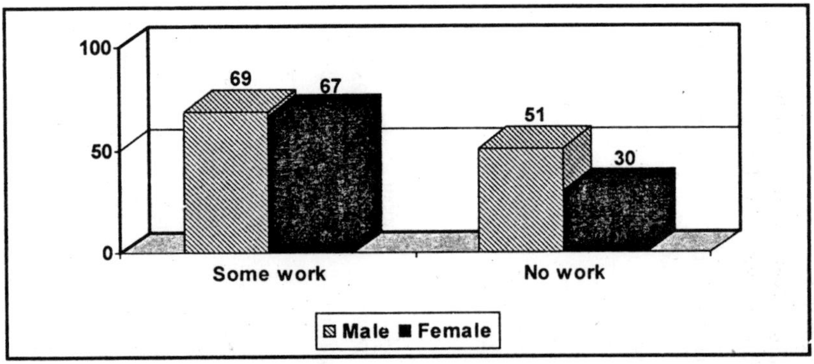

Though not shown in the Figure 11, it is found that among the healthy persons only 21 percent of males and 10 percent of females are not doing any work. Similarly among those who reported themselves as not healthy 37 percent of males and 33 percent of females are engaged in some household activity.

Table 13 gives the health status of elderly controlling for financial status and service contribution.

Majority of those who are not involved in household work among those who are financially weak reported themselves as unhealthy and the reverse is true for those are engaged in some household activity in this financial status category. This is true for both males and females. The pattern is the same for those men and women with only immovable asset and women with even liquid asset. But for males with liquid asset, irrespective of their involvement in household work, majority reported themselves to be healthy.

Table 13

Percentage distribution of elderly in different financial status group by health status and involvement in household work

Service contribution and health status	*Financial Status* — *Financially weak* — *Male*	*Female*	*Total*	*Liquid asset* — *Male*	*Female*	*Total*	*Immovable asset* — *Male*	*Female*	*Total*
Some household work (HHW)									
Healthy	67.2	67.4	67.3	78.2	65.9	73.8	52.1	67.4	60.5
Not healthy	32.8	32.6	32.7	21.8	34.1	26.2	47.9	32.6	39.5
Total	100.0	100.0	100.0	100.0	100.0	100.0	100.0	100.0	100.0
	61	242	303	225	126	351	117	141	258
No work									
Healthy	31.3	25.0	27.1	66.2	29.2	56.5	42.0	40.6	41.5
Not healthy	68.8	75.0	72.9	33.8	70.8	43.5	58.0	59.4	58.5
Total	100.0	100.0	100.0	100.0	100.0	100.0	100.0	100.0	100.0
	32	64	96	68	24	92	50	32	82

DETERMINANTS OF HEALTH OF ELDERLY

Using logistic regression an attempt is made to find the factors that affect the health of the older persons. Two separate logistic regressions are run one each for the elderly men and women. The variables used are financial status of the elderly, relation with caregiver, involvement of elderly in household work, current marital status, education, whether the caregiver spends time with the elderly or not and visit to temple/church/mosque as the case may be. For elderly men one more variable is introduced namely their current work status. This is not included for women as the proportion of working women is very negligible. Age, which is an important health related variable is not included in the model as it is strongly related with most of the other variables. The relationship between the selected variables and health has already been pointed out in the relevant sections earlier. The variable measurement is given in the chapter on methodology (Chapter III).

The results of the logistic regression analysis are presented in Tables 14 and 15 respectively for elderly men and elderly women. Table 14 shows that of the eight variables introduced, all except current marital status of the elderly are significantly related to the health of the elderly. The level of significance is considered up to ten percent. Current work status and visit to religious places have very high significance level. That is, elderly males who are engaged in some economic activity tend to be healthier by a factor of 4.4 compared to those who are not working. But it is not clear whether they participate in work because they are healthy or they are healthy because they are active in some activity. In other words, the cause-effect relation cannot be decided from this analysis. The chance of being healthy increases by a factor of 3.1 when one moves from the state of not visiting religious places like temple/church/mosque to a state of visiting such places.

The relationship between education and health shows that when one moves from the stage of illiteracy to at least five years of schooling the odds of the elderly men becoming healthy increases by a factor of 1.99. This is to be expected as education increases the knowledge of various health care needs and the desire to act on it when required. The person with whom the elderly stays is also important. Those men who are staying with their sons are likely to be healthier than those who are staying with daughters or others.

In the case of the most important variable of concern in this study, viz. the financial status of the elderly, the relation shows that compared to those who are not having any asset those with liquid asset are likely to be healthier by a factor of 1.67 and the relation is significant. However, compared to those who have no asset, those with immovable asset is less likely to be healthy though the relation is not significant.

Table 14
Determinants of health (Male): Results of logistic regression

Variable	*B*	*Sig.*	*Exp(B)*	*Reference category*
FS (Liquid Asset)	0.5139	0.0678	1.6717	No asset
FS (Immovable Asset)	-0.1498	0.6074	0.8609	No asset
Caregiver (Son)	0.5132	0.0333	1.6705	Other than son
HHW (Involved)	0.6028	0.0105	1.8272	Not involved
CMS (Currently Married)	-0.0874	0.7497	0.9163	Disrupted marriage
Education (1-4 years)	0.2633	0.3557	1.3012	Illiterate
Education (5+ years)	0.6896	0.0199	1.9928	Illiterate
CGSTWA (Spend Some Time)	0.4612	0.0964	1.5859	Spend No Time
CWS (Currently Working)	1.4728	0.0000	4.3616	Not working
T-C-M (Visit)	1.1336	0.0000	3.1068	Do not visit
Constant	-1.9064	0.0000	0.1486	

Note: The variable measurement is given in the chapter on methodology(Chapter III) FS = Financial Status; HHW = Household work; CMS = Current Marital Status; CGSTWA = Caregiver Spending Time With Aged Persons; CWS = Current Work Status; T-C-M = Temple/Church/ Mosque

For the mental satisfaction of the elderly and to have a feeling of one-ness with the family, it will be a great help if the caregiver with whom they co-reside spends some time with the elderly on a day-to-day basis. Table 14 shows that compared to those who are not lucky to have the company of the caregiver at least for some time a day, those who get their time are likely to be healthier than others by a factor of 1.59. The next important significant variable is involvement in household work. Those who are involved tend to be healthier than those who are not involved in household work but the cause-effect relation is not clear, as is the case with participation in economic activity.

Current marital status of the elderly is a variable, which was expected to have a significant impact on the perceived health of the elderly. Generally those who are currently in wedlock are expected to be healthy compared to those with disrupted marriage simply because of the presence of a partner to share one's happiness and sorrows. But the current analysis does not support the hypothesis on marital status.

For elderly women Table 15, the most important variables affecting their health is involvement in household work and visit to a place of worship. That is, those who are engaged in some household work are three times more likely to be healthy than their inactive counterparts. As stated earlier, this relationship could work in two ways that those who are healthy are working, or because they are engaged in some activity, they are healthy.

Table 15

Determinants of health (Female): Results of logistic regression

Variable	*B*	*Sig.*	*Exp(B)*	*Reference category*
FS (Liquid Asset)	-0.0668	0.7709	0.9353	No asset
FS (Immovable Asset)	0.1832	0.4004	1.2011	No asset
Caregiver (Son)	-0.1710	0.3985	0.8428	Other than son
HHW (Involved)	1.1314	0.0000	3.0999	Not involved
CMS (Currently Married)	0.3586	0.1399	1.4313	Disrupted marriage
Education (1-4 years)	0.5341	0.0078	1.7058	Illiterate
Education (5+ years)	0.3454	0.1717	1.4126	Illiterate
CGSTWA (Spend Some Time)	-0.1611	0.4744	0.8512	No time
T-C-M (Visit)	1.1196	0.0000	3.0636	Do not visit
Constant	-1.2800	0.0000	0.2780	

Note: The variable measurement is given in the chapter on methodology(Chapter III) FS = Financial Status; HHW = Household work; CMS = Current Marital Status; CGSTWA = Caregiver Spending Time With Aged Persons; T-C-M = Temple/Church/Mosque

The aged women who visit worship places like temple/church/mosque have a chance of being three times healthier than others. Education also is a significantly important factor deciding the health of elderly women. The logistic regression results show that some education compared to illiteracy works in favour of being healthy. None of the other variables introduced in the model for women are statistically significant.

The sex differential in the determinants of the health of the aged is visible from the logistic regression analysis. The financial status of the elderly women did not have a statistically significant relation with their perceived health unlike in the case of elderly men. Another observed difference between the factors associated with the health of men and women related to level of education. A statistically significant relation was observed in the case of men when they had at least 5 years of schooling while for women 1-4 years of schooling was sufficient to have a significant relationship. Further, any increase in the level of education for women did not make any difference. Similar is the case with the variable relating to caregiver spending time with the elderly. Though it has a significant relation with the health of elderly men, it is not so in the case of elderly women. Similarly, when engaging themselves in some household activity tend to increase the chances of being healthy among women, it turned out to be a statistically non-significant variable for men.

But for both men and women visit to religious places increases the chance of being healthy. It is common practice in this state for older persons to get involved in religious/worship related activities in their neighborhood. It gives them opportunity to interact with similar persons/friends giving them psychological satisfaction which in turn to the perception of physical health.

5 FINANCIAL STATUS OF THE ELDERLY AND THEIR INVOLVEMENT IN DECISION-MAKING

INTRODUCTION

Family is a social structure and is the basic unit of a society. Its functioning is specific to the peculiar environment prevailing in each country. In all societies there are socially assigned status and role for each members of the family. But the status and roles of each member of a family are not the same in different cultures under different economic and social conditions and for the same person over a period of time. Involvement in decision making results from the status of an individual in the household and the role played by him/her. The concepts of status and role are inseparable such that there is no status without role and no role without status (Rosow, 1976). They are fundamental to the social structure and informally are even treated as synonymous and interchangeable. But basically they are different concepts. Status is a position in the social structure, which refers to *who* a person is (e.g., head of the household). That is, to the rights and duties or the relative superiority or inferiority fixed by custom which can be evaluated by examining the prestige, honour and respect they receive at home from other members of the family (Seligman and Johnson, 1959).

Role, on the other hand, is the pattern of activity intrinsic to a status; that is *what each person is expected to do* (e.g., the head of the household is expected to look after the welfare of the members of the household). However, roles are not sharply defined. It is not that every individual will have only one status and associated roles. An individual will have different status with respect to different patterns of relationship. For instance, a man can be a father to his children, husband to his wife, grand father to his grand children and so on. He can also be a brother, nephew, friend, or any number of positions in relation to the web of inter-personal relations. And the role expectations from these different statuses are, indeed, different.

To assign a role is easy at the early stages of life where the role expectations can be fulfilled without much complication. In old age it is difficult to have an orderly pattern in the life path, as old age is a time for more and more adjustments. As noted by Phillips, in old age (1957) one will have to retire from job, relinquish household management, withdraw from active community life, become widow/widower due to the death of one's mate, lose independent household, depend on others for physical and/or financial support and the like. In consequence individuals will have to hand over the reign of administration of the household to adult offspring or other relatives. With this, they cease to be the primary decision makers and become subordinate to one's own adult children/relatives. These are changes that are not easy to accept though one eventually has to.

As far as decision making is concerned, it is related to status and roles as well as other socio-economic position of a person in the household. There appears to be three stages that an elderly has to go through with respect to decision making. At the initial stages, the elderly will be consulted on all matters relating to the household, as they are experienced in these activities. But slowly the consultation stops when the children become adept in these matters. Then starts the second stage in which they may be informed of the decisions taken in the household mainly to save their feelings of being left out rather than getting their views on it. In the last and third stage, even that will end. They become absolute dependents with no role to play in the household matters.

In the parent survey from where the data were obtained, there was a question on their direct participation in issues related to the decisions taken in household matters. The term used in this case being whether they were "consulted" in taking decisions. It is assumed that when one is 65 years or more unilateral decision making will be very negligible unless one is staying alone. The term `consulted' here indicates discussion of any household related matter, irrespective of who initiated it. In this chapter all those elderly who were consulted before taking any final decision on any matter relating to household (such as household expenditure on various items, education of children, marriages of children, etc.), is taken as involvement in decision making. All the other elderly are grouped into one category indicating "not involved" in decision making.

Nevertheless, it should be remembered that Kerala is a fast changing society, where many of the situations are different from what it was before. The elderly, thus, may not be in a position to make any meaningful suggestion even if consulted. For example, in deciding on the education of a child the elderly may not be in a position to help the child or his/her parents in deciding, say, whether to go for electronic engineering or for mechanical engineering. It is a decision that is beyond the knowledge of the present cohort of elderly. Under such circumstances, non-consultation should not be seen as disrespect to the elderly or ignoring them for want of love and affection. These are cases where they may be informed about the decision. This aspect should be kept in mind while drawing conclusions from this data. However, involvement in this survey included not only serious matters like children's education but also day-to-day household matters like cooking, shopping etc.

In this chapter, of the 1182 elderly 40 are excluded as 20 elderly are staying in single member households where the entire household related decisions are taken by themselves and another 20 elderly have not given information on their involvement in decision making.

In this materialistic world, it has always been an unspoken reality that most often one's own status in the family and thereby the role results from one's own financial status. A person with no money or asset may not have a say in decisions that are taken in the household merely because of his/her financial dependency. Between those who have liquid asset and immovable assets, it seems to be logical to assume that those with liquid asset will have some say in the matters discussed in the household than those with only immovable assets and those with immovable asset will have a say in the household matters than those with no asset at all.

The involvement of elderly in decision making is given in Fig. 1, which shows that the involvement in general is fairly high for both male and female elderly with 91 percent and 70 percent respectively. However, there is more than 20 percentage points difference in the involvement between male and female elderly.

Fig. 1
Percentage distribution of elderly by involvement in household decision making

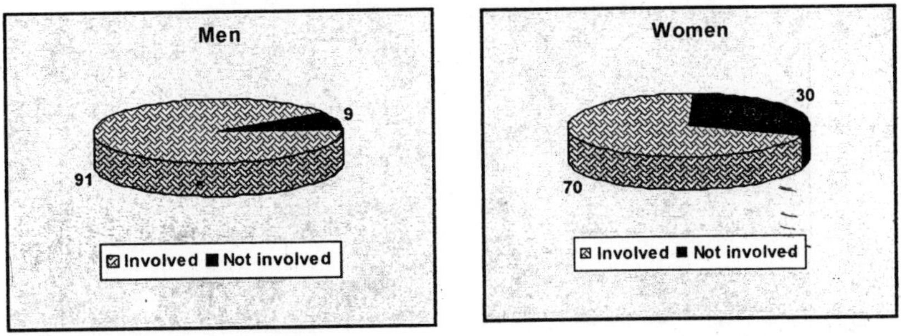

It is satisfying to note that a large segment of the elderly persons (67.3%) who are not having any finance is also being consulted in making decisions Table 1.

The difference in the proportion involved in decision making is conspicuously different from one financial category to the other. While 92.9 percent of those with liquid asset are involved in decision making, the corresponding percent for those with only immovable asset is 79.4 and for those who are financially weak is 67.3.

A higher proportion of both men and women elderly with liquid asset are consulted – 96.8 percent for males and 84.7 percent for females. In every financial status category the proportion consulted is higher for males compared to that for females.

INVOLVEMENT IN DECISION MAKING BY BACKGROUND CHARACTERISTICS

It is assumed that the above relationship may vary depending on changes in the background characteristics of the elderly which include social, demographic and economic aspects. An examination of the relationship between their involvement in decision making and some selected background characteristics is made by controlling the financial status of the elderly and the results are presented in the subsequent sections.

Place of residence and involvement in decision making

Generally the rural-urban set-up is found to be rather different such that the rural set-up is expected to be more traditional and hence

Table 1
Percentage distribution of elderly in different financial status group by involvement in household decision making

Involvement in Decision making	Financial Status								
	Financially weak			*Liquid asset*			*Immovable asset*		
	Male	*Female*	*Total*	*Male*	*Female*	*Total*	*Male*	*Female*	*Total*
Involved	77.8	64.1	67.3	96.8	84.7	92.9	89.6	69.5	79.4
Not involved	22.2	35.9	32.7	3.2	15.3	7.1	10.4	30.5	20.6
Total	100.0	100.0	100.0	100.0	100.0	100.0	100.0	100.0	100.0
	90	301	391	284	137	421	163	167	330

one would expect a comparatively higher involvement of elderly in decision making. But the analysis failed to substantiate this view Fig. 2. In Kerala, however, a rural-urban differential in any general demographic aspect is found to be negligible.

Fig. 2
Percent of elderly involved in decision making in rural and urban areas

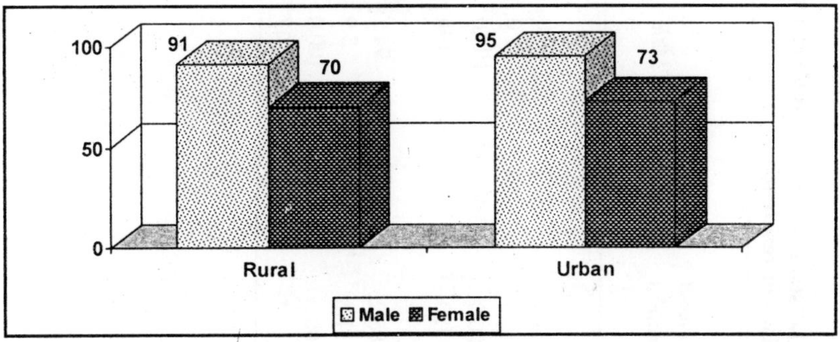

The involvement of elderly differs vastly by sex, not only in the proportion involved but also in the pattern when differentiated by place of residence and financial status (Table 2). Almost all male elderly with liquid asset are consulted in decision making in both rural and urban areas with a slightly lesser proportion among rural elderly with no financial means (70.4%). Though not as high as that of males a significantly higher proportion of female elderly are also consulted in decision making irrespective of their place of residence. Another aspect to be noted here is that almost all urban elderly males are involved in decision making irrespective of their financial status. In general, more elderly males are consulted in urban than in rural areas, the only deviation being males with liquid asset where the proportion is almost the same in rural (97.0%) and urban (95.8%) areas.

Age and Involvement in Decision-Making

Generally, age is an indication of the ability to think properly and to contribute meaningfully to any decision making process. Fig. 3 shows that 91 percent of those males aged 65-74 years is involved in decision making compared to 73 percent of females in the same

Table 2

Percentage distribution of elderly in different financial status group by involvement in household decision making and place of residence

Place of residence and involvement in Decision-making	*Financial Status*								
	Financially weak			*Liquid asset*			*Immovable asset*		
	Male	*Female*	*Total*	*Male*	*Female*	*Total*	*Male*	*Female*	*Total*
Rural									
Involved	70.4	63.7	65.6	97.0	84.2	92.7	89.0	67.4	78.8
Not involved	27.5	36.3	34.4	3.0	15.8	7.3	11.0	32.6	21.2
Total	100.0	100.0	100.0	100.0	100.0	100.0	100.0	100.0	100.0
	69	248	317	236	120	356	146	132	278
Urban									
Involved	95.2	66.0	74.3	95.8	88.2	93.8	94.1	77.1	82.7
Not involved	4.8	34.0	25.7	4.2	11.8	6.2	5.9	22.9	17.3
Total	100.0	100.0	100.0	100.0	100.0	100.0	100.0	100.0	100.0
	21	53	74	48	17	65	17	35	52

age group. This percentage decreased with increase in age though the percent *per se* is not very small.

Fig. 3
Percent of elderly involved in decision making in the two broad age groups

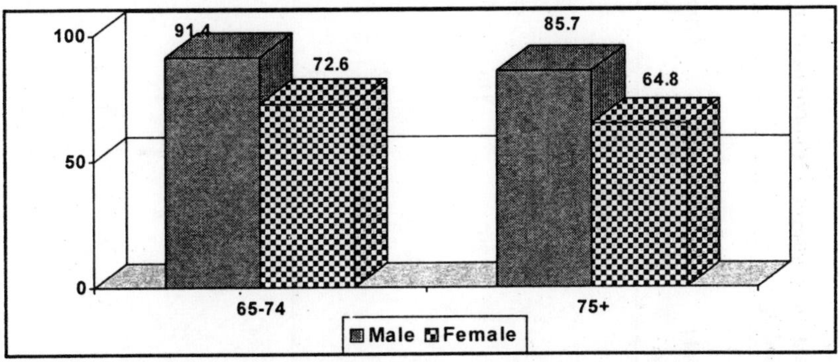

Table 3 shows that participation of males in the age group 65-74 years in decision making varies from 88 percent for those with immovable asset to 94 percent for those with liquid asset. In general with advance in age their participation in household decision making declined, the only exception being males with liquid asset. The involvement in decision making for the aged females depends on their financial status in both the age groups.

Literacy and involvement in decision making

In any society, it is only natural to consult the literate more than the illiterate as they are expected to have a better grasp of things, which would help to guide the next generation in making household decisions. Keeping this in view the literacy status and involvement in decision making has been examined and the overall situation is shown in Fig. 4.

The pattern is as expected though the literacy does not make as much difference in the involvement of elderly males as it does in the case of elderly females. The proportion consulted among women is found to be 75 percent for literates as against 64 percent for the illiterate women. This suggests that basically consulting men whether they are literate or illiterate is acceptable while consulting an illiterate woman is not considered essential. The overall difference between the literate and illiterate women in

Table 3

Percentage distribution of elderly in different financial status group by involvement in household decision making and age

Age and Involvement in Decision-making	*Financial Status* *Financially weak* *Male*	*Female*	*Total*	*Liquid asset* *Male*	*Female*	*Total*	*Immovable asset* *Male*	*Female*	*Total*
65-74 years									
Involved	89.5	66.0	69.9	93.9	86.6	91.5	87.7	71.8	79.7
Not involved	10.5	34.0	30.1	6.1	13.4	8.5	12.3	28.2	20.3
Total	100.0	100.0	100.0	100.0	100.0	100.0	100.0	100.	100.0
	38	188	226	198	97	295	114	117	231
75+ years									
Involved	67.3	61.0	63.0	95.8	73.6	87.8	86.8	64.3	75.2
Not involved	32.7	39.0	37.0	4.2	26.4	12.2	13.2	35.7	24.8
Total	100.0	100.0	100.0	100.0	100.0	100.0	100.0	100.0	100.0
	55	118	173	95	53	148	53	56	109

decision making is 11 percentage points, unfavourable to illiterate women.

Fig. 4
Percent of literate and illiterate elderly involved in decision-making

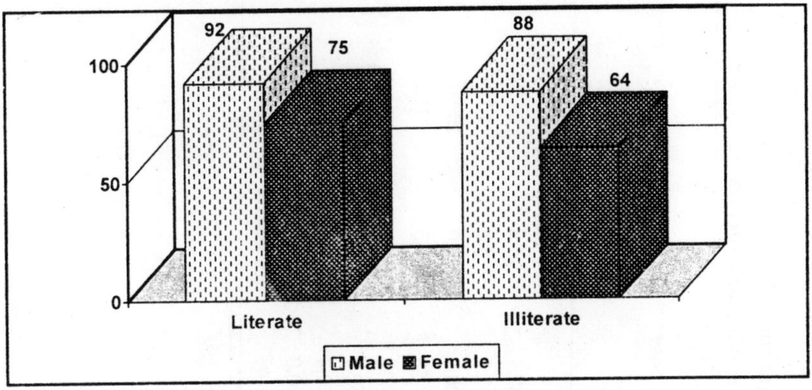

Among the financially weak literate women 71.2 percent were consulted (Table 4). Of illiterate women in the same financial status category only 56.6 percent is found involved in decision making.

Literacy status failed to play any role in any financial status group for men. For women, both literate and illiterate, the financial status also plays a role in involvement in decision making. The highest proportion of 87.5 is found among literate women with liquid asset and the lowest proportion of 56.6 percent is found among illiterate women with no financial capability. As far as decision making is concerned having no asset and being illiterate are found to be double curse for women. The effect of literacy on decision making involvement of the aged seems to be nullified by their financial status. That is, financial status can change the role of elderly in decision making irrespective of the literacy level.

Education and involvement in decision making

It is also of importance to see whether education measured in terms of years of schooling of the literate persons make a difference in being involved in the decisions taken in the Fig. 5 gives the involvement in decision making by level of education for the literate elderly. The Figure shows that education does make a difference for both men and women in their involvement in

Table 4
Percentage distribution of elderly in different financial status group by involvement in household decision making and literacy

Literacy and Involvement in Decision-making	*Financial Status*								
	Financially weak			*Liquid asset*			*Immovable asset*		
	Male	*Female*	*Total*	*Male*	*Female*	*Total*	*Male*	*Female*	*Total*
Literate									
Involved	79.2	71.2	73.7	97.3	87.5	94.8	89.7	69.9	80.9
Not involved	20.8	28.8	26.3	2.7	12.5	5.2	10.3	30.1	19.1
Total	100.0	100.0	100.0	100.0	100.0	100.0	100.0	100.0	100.0
	72	156	228	255	88	343	116	93	209
Illiterate									
Involved	76.5	56.6	58.6	93.1	79.6	84.6	89.4	68.9	76.9
Not involved	23.5	43.4	41.4	6.9	20.4	15.4	10.6	31.1	23.1
Total	100.0	100.0	100.0	100.0	100.0	100.0	100.0	100.0	100.0
	17	145	162	29	49	78	47	74	121

decision making. For men having at least 5 years of schooling the proportion consulted increased by 5 percentage points compared to those with less than 5 years of schooling, whereas the increase is only 3 percentage points for women.

Fig. 5
Percent of literate elderly involved in decision making in the two categories of years of schooling

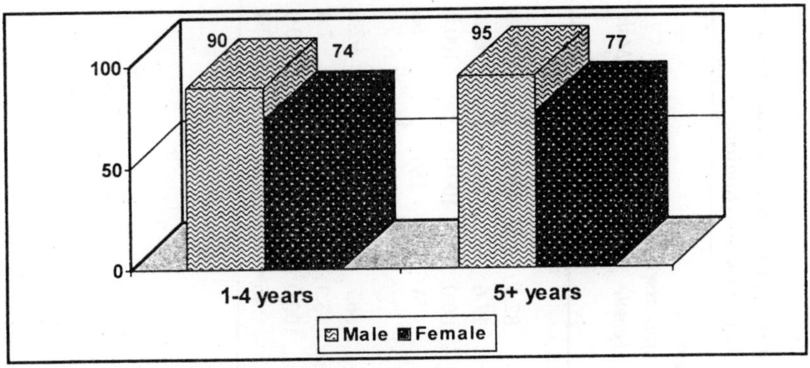

Table 5 shows the distribution for 808 elderly who are literates by financial status and involvement in decision making. The findings indicate that with increase in education, involvement in decision making also increases. The single exception is that of women with immovable assets where a slight decline is noted from 73.7 percent among those with 1-4 years of schooling to 65.8 percent among those with at least 5 years of schooling. When the financial status and the level of education is controlled more than 90 percent of the male elderly with liquid asset are consulted irrespective of their educational status.

Marital status and involvement in decision making

The generally used categories of marital status are: currently married, widowed, separated, divorced and never married. In this survey it is found that only a negligible percentage is accounted by separated/divorced/never married persons. Hence, for analysis purpose two categories are made: currently married and others. A higher percent of currently married elderly men are involved in decision making compared to the other category Fig. 6.

Table 5

Percentage distribution of literate elderly in different financial status group by involvement in decision making and years of schooling

Education and Involvement in Decision-making	Financial Status								
	Financially weak			Liquid asset			Immovable asset		
	Male	Female	Total	Male	Female	Total	Male	Female	Total
1-4 years									
Involved	76.1	71.1	72.5	92.6	82.4	89.8	81.8	73.7	78.0
Not involved	23.9	28.9	27.5	7.4	17.6	10.2	18.2	26.3	22.0
Total	100.0	100.0	100.0	100.0	100.0	100.0	100.0	100.0	100.0
	46	121	157	135	51	186	66	57	123
5 + years									
Involved	79.3	73.0	75.8	96.9	86.7	94.3	92.6	65.8	81.5
Not involved	20.7	27.0	24.2	3.1	13.3	5.7	7.4	34.2	18.5
Total	100.0	100.0	100.0	100.0	100.0	100.0	100.0	100.0	100.0
	29	37	66	129	45	174	54	38	92

Fig. 6
Percent of elderly involved in decision making in the two marital status category

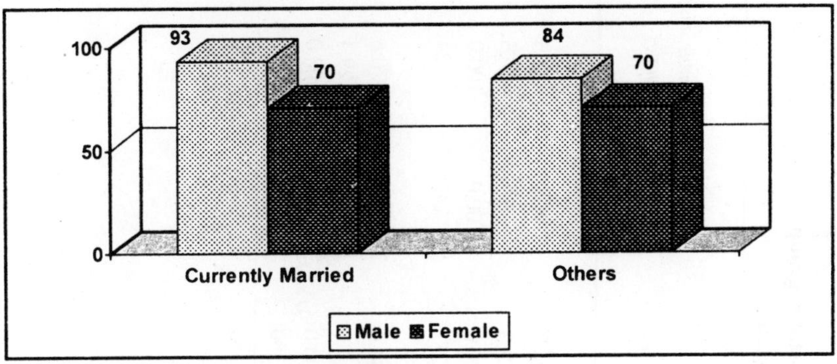

Among the elderly women marital status *per se* made no difference in their participation in household decision making with 70 percent participating in both categories.

Among the currently married men, the difference in all the three categories varies from almost 80.0 percent among those with no financial means to 96.8 percent for those with liquid asset (Table 6). In the case of women, the combination of financial status and marital status plays an important role in their involvement in decision making. Almost all the currently married women (95%) with liquid asset are involved in decision making. Further, involvement is fairly high (82.9%) even among women who are not currently married when they have liquid asset.

Between the elderly women belonging to the other two financial status categories, the difference is not much among the currently married, though it is not so for the "other" marital status category. Those who are not currently married but have immovable assets, the proportion consulted is 70.6 percent compared to 63.6 percent for those who have no asset at all. Interestingly the proportion of women with immovable asset consulted is high among those who are not currently married (70.6%) compared to those who are currently married (62.5%). Going by the argument of having a separate category of persons with immovable assets, it appears that a married woman may not be taking a unilateral decision as to the transfer of property to any one's name even if the property is in her name. But for those who are unmarried/having disrupted

Table 6

Percentage distribution of elderly in different financial status group by involvement in decision making and marital status

Marital status and involvement in decision making	*Financial Status*								
	Financially weak			*Liquid asset*			*Immovable asset*		
	Male	*Female*	*Total*	*Male*	*Female*	*Total*	*Male*	*Female*	*Total*
Currently married									
Involved	80.0	65.7	72.3	96.8	95.0	96.7	90.9	62.5	86.8
Not involved	20.0	34.3	27.7	3.2	5.0	3.3	9.1	37.5	13.2
Total	100.0	100.0	100.0	100.0	100.0	100.0	100.0	100.0	100.0
	60	70	130	251	20	271	143	24	167
Others									
Involved	73.3	63.6	64.8	97.0	82.9	86.0	80.0	70.6	71.8
Not involved	26.7	36.7	35.2	3.0	17.1	14.0	20.0	29.4	28.2
Total	100.0	100.0	100.0	100.0	100.0	100.0	100.0	100.0	100.0
	30	231	261	33	117	150	20	143	163

marriage, the decision in all probability will solely rest with her. Perhaps the desire to get the property may make the care givers involve these women in decisions taken in the household.

Religion and involvement in decision making

The norms and behaviour patterns prescribed by different religions could be different such that it may also affect the involvement of the elderly in household decision making. It is found that among the elderly men, a higher proportion (94%) of the Muslims are involved in household decision making compared to 91 percent of Hindus and 90 percent of Christians (Fig. 7). Among women, however, the pattern is different. A higher proportion of Christian women (77%) were consulted compared to Muslims (73%) and Hindus (67%).

Fig. 7
Percent of elderly involved in decision making in each religious group

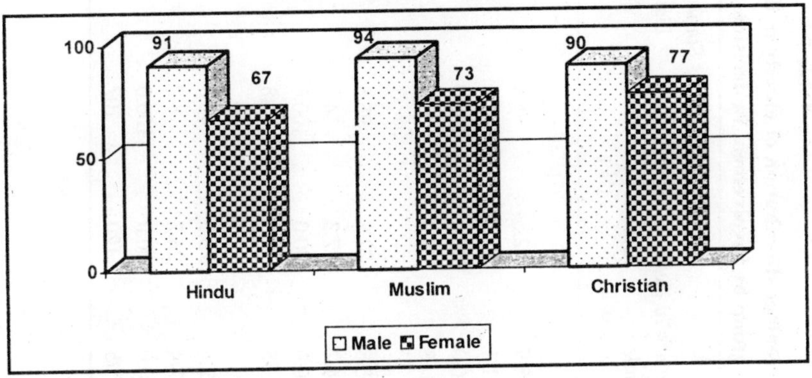

The percentage distribution of elderly in different financial status groups by religion and involvement in household decision making is given in Table 7.

Among the financially weak category the proportion of men involved in decision making is the highest among Muslims (88.4%) and lowest among Hindus (75.0%). In the case of financially weak women, the difference in the three religions is quite prominent. Whereas the proportion of Christian elderly women involved in the household decision making is 72.6 percent, the corresponding percent for Muslim women is 65.8 percent and for Hindu women is 58.9 percent. The pattern is the same for those with liquid asset

Table 7

Percentage distribution of elderly in different financial status group by involvement in decision making and religion

Religion and involvement in decision making	*Financial Status*								
	Financially weak			*Liquid asset*			*Immovable asset*		
	Male	*Female*	*Total*	*Male*	*Female*	*Total*	*Male*	*Female*	*Total*
Hindu									
Involved	75.0	58.9	62.5	98.4	79.8	91.1	90.0	68.4	78.3
Not involved	25.0	41.1	37.5	1.6	20.2	8.9	10.0	31.6	21.7
Total	100.0	100.0	100.0	100.0	100.0	100.0	100.0	100.0	100.0
	48	168	223	129	84	213	100	117	217
Muslim									
Involved	88.2	65.8	72.7	95.8	91.7	95.0	93.8	75.0	85.7
Not involved	11.8	34.2	27.3	4.2	8.3	5.0	6.3	25.0	14.3
Total	100.0	100.0	100.0	100.0	100.0	100.0	100.0	100.0	100.0
	17	38	55	48	12	60	32	24	56
Christians									
Involved	76.0	72.6	73.3	95.3	92.7	94.6	83.9	69.2	77.2
Not involved	24.0	27.4	26.7	4.7	7.3	5.4	16.1	30.8	22.8
Total	100.0	100.0	100.0	100.0	100.0	100.0	100.0	100.0	100.0
	25	95	120	107	41	148	31	26	57

with the proportion ranging from 79.8 percent for Hindus to 91.7 percent for Muslims to 92.7 percent for Christians. When it comes to immovable asset the highest proportion of 75.0 percent is observed among the Muslim women and the situation between the other two categories is almost the same (68.4 percent for Hindus and 69.2 percent for Christians).

Status at Home and Involvement in Decision-making

Status at home is categorised as head of the household (HHH) and others. In this society a person need not necessarily be prime earning member of the household to be classified as head of the household. It can even be a position given to them as a mark of respect. In many such cases it could only be nominal. Thus, these heads of household need not necessarily be the decision makers/ involved in decision making. Many of those with assets or liquid cash also may not be the prime earners and may or may not be involved in decision making. Hence an analysis was made to explore the effect of financial status of the elderly and their status at home on decision making.

Fig. 8 gives the involvement of elderly in decision making by their status at home. It shows that as in all other characteristics, the proportion involved is less for women than men. It also shows that for both men and women, a higher proportion of those who are currently head of the household participate in decision making than others.

Fig. 8
Percent of elderly involved in decision making among head of households and others

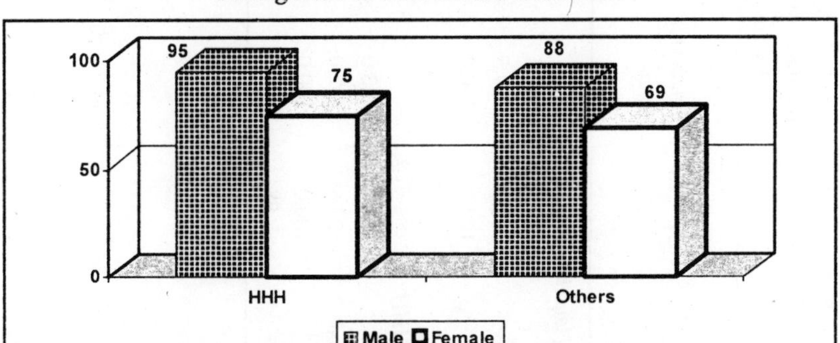

Table 8 shows the relationship between status at home and involvement in decision making for different categories of financial

Table 8
Percentage distribution of elderly in different financial status group by involvement in decision making and status at home

Status and involvement in decision making	Financial Status								
	Financially weak			*Liquid asset*			*Immovable asset*		
	Male	*Female*	*Total*	*Male*	*Female*	*Total*	*Male*	*Female*	*Total*
Head of the Household (HHH)									
Involved	87.5	70.5	77.6	98.1	87.5	96.7	91.3	71.7	84.8
Not involved	12.5	29.5	22.4	1.9	12.5	3.6	8.7	28.5	15.2
Total	100.0	100.0	100.0	100.0	100.0	100.0	100.0	100.0	100.0
	32	44	76	160	24	184	92	46	138
Other than HHH									
Involved	72.4	63.0	64.8	95.2	84.1	89.9	87.3	68.6	75.5
Not involved	27.6	37.0	35.2	4.8	15.9	10.1	12.7	31.7	24.5
Total	100.0	100.0	100.0	100.0	100.0	100.0	100.0	100.0	100.0
	58	257	315	124	113	237	71	121	192

status of elderly. The pattern of relationship is the same as other characteristics with higher level of involvement among those with liquid asset and a comparatively lesser proportion involved in the case of those without any financial means, with those with immovable assets falling in between. Elderly males enjoy a better position than females in their families even if they are financially weak.

Relation with caregiver and involvement in decision making

The closest relative with whom the elderly stays can affect the involvement in decision making, as the importance given to elderly himself/herself may differ in each case. Majority (72 %) of the elderly are staying with sons, and the rest with daughters (11%) and others like niece, nephew, brother or sister (17%).

Here again, male-female difference is noticeable (Fig. 9). Irrespective of the relation to care givers at least 90 percent of the men are involved in decision making. For women who are staying with persons other than their own children the proportion participating is comparatively low (63%), whereas for those who are staying with children, it is 71-72 percent. There is hardly any difference in the case of elderly men.

Fig. 9
Percent of elderly involved in decision making in each category of care giver

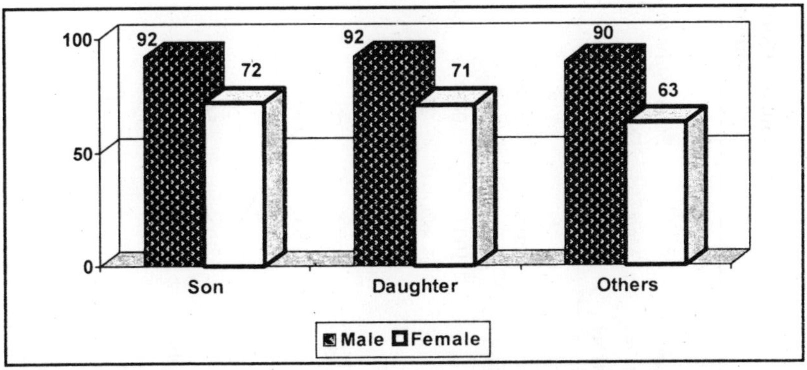

Table 9 gives the involvement of elderly in decision making controlling financial status and relation with care giver.

Table 9

Percentage distribution of elderly in different financial status group by involvement in decision making and relation with care giver

Relation with care involvement in decision making	Financial Status								
	Financially weak			Liquid asset			Immovable asset		
	Male	*Female*	*Total*	*Male*	*Female*	*Total*	*Male*	*Female*	*Total*
Son									
Involved	80.6	65.8	69.0	96.6	87.8	94.1	89.5	71.0	80.3
Not involved	19.4	34.2	31.0	3.4	12.2	5.9	10.5	29.0	19.7
Total	100.0	100.0	100.0	100.0	100.0	100.0	100.0	100.0	100.0
	62	219	281	207	82	289	133	131	264
Daughter									
Involved	72.7	69.0	69.8	100.0	76.9	88.5	91.7	68.8	78.6
Not involved	27.3	31.0	30.2	—	23.1	11.5	8.3	31.3	21.4
Total	100.0	100.0	100.0	100.0	100.0	100.0	100.0	100.0	100.0
	11	42	53	26	26	52	12	16	28
Others									
Involved	70.6	50.0	56.1	96.1	82.8	91.3	88.9	60.0	73.7
Not involved	29.4	50.0	43.9	3.9	17.2	8.8	11.1	40.0	26.3
Total	100.0	100.0	100.0	100.0	100.0	100.0	100.0	100.0	100.0
	17	40	57	51	29	80	18	20	38

At least 70 percent of the male elderly with no financial means are involved in decision making irrespective of with whom they are staying. The highest percentage reporting involvement among men with no financial means is those who stay with sons (80.6%). But this proportion drops drastically in the case of female elderly, with the lowest level being 50.0 percent among those who live with persons other than their children. However, having some financial assets improves their involvement in decision making, with those with liquid asset and staying with sons scoring a higher percentage (87.8%). There is some difference in the proportion involved in decision making among those women having only immovable assets. It is 60.0 percent among those staying with others and 68.8 percent in the case of those staying with daughters.

Standard of living and involvement in decision making

The relationship between standard of living and involvement is examined and the overall situation is given in Fig. 10.There exists a significant positive relationship with standard of living where elderly of higher standard of living had more involvement in decision making than other two categories.

Fig. 10
Percent of elderly involved in decision making in each category of standard of living

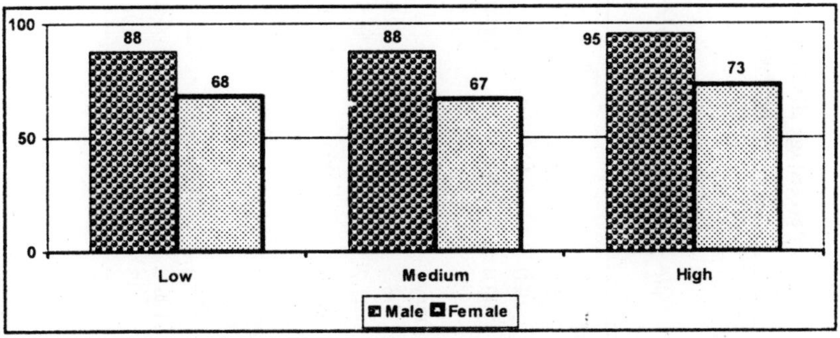

For both males and females the involvement is slightly high for those who are having high standard of living than those with low or medium level. Table 10 shows that financially weak male elderly having medium standard of living are least consulted (58.3%). Women in this financial status category show a direct

Table 10
Percentage distribution of elderly in different financial status group by involvement in decision making and standard of living

Standard of living and involvement in decision making	Financial Status								
	Financially weak			*Liquid asset*			*Immovable asset*		
	Male	*Female*	*Total*	*Male*	*Female*	*Total*	*Male*	*Female*	*Total*
Low standard of living									
Involved	81.0	59.3	63.4	91.8	76.1	85.0	86.3	77.6	82.8
Not involved	19.0	40.7	36.6	8.2	23.9	15.0	13.7	22.4	17.2
Total	100.0	100.0	100.0	100.0	100.0	100.0	100.0	100.0	100.0
	21	91	112	61	46	107	73	49	122
Medium standard of living									
Involved	58.3	65.6	63.5	98.4	72.2	92.5	89.5	66.7	77.1
Not involved	41.7	34.3	36.5	1.6	27.8	7.5	10.5	33.3	22.9
Total	100.0	100.0	100.0	100.0	100.0	100.0	100.0	100.0	100.0
	24	61	85	62	18	80	38	45	83
High standard of living									
Involved	86.7	66.4	71.1	98.1	93.2	96.6	94.2	65.8	77.6
Not involved	13.3	33.6	28.9	1.9	6.8	3.4	5.8	34.2	24.4
Total	100.0	100.0	100.0	100.0	100.0	100.0	100.0	100.0	100.0
	45	149	194	161	73	234	52	73	125

relation between involvement in decision making and standard of living. Among those men with liquid asset at least 90 percent are consulted irrespective of their standard of living. High standard of living and having liquid asset is having more or less the same effect on both men and women with 98.1 percent of males and 93.2 percent of females involved in decision making. For those with immovable asset involvement in decision making is showing a direct relation with standard of living for men and a negative relation for women.

Service contribution and involvement in decision making

Service contribution refers to any type of household work including house related outside work like grocery or provision shopping to meet the day-to-day requirements of the household. The elderly are classified into four categories: (i) those who do only household work (HHW), (ii) only child care (CC), (iii) household work and child care (HHW&CC) and (iv) no work at all. Most of the men who reported as engaged in household work are engaged in house related outside work like shopping.

Fig. 11 shows the relationship between service contribution and decision making. Though for men there is not a great difference in the proportion participating in decision making by service contribution (which ranges from 88 percent for those who are not

Fig. 11
Percent of elderly involved in decision making among those who participate in household work and others

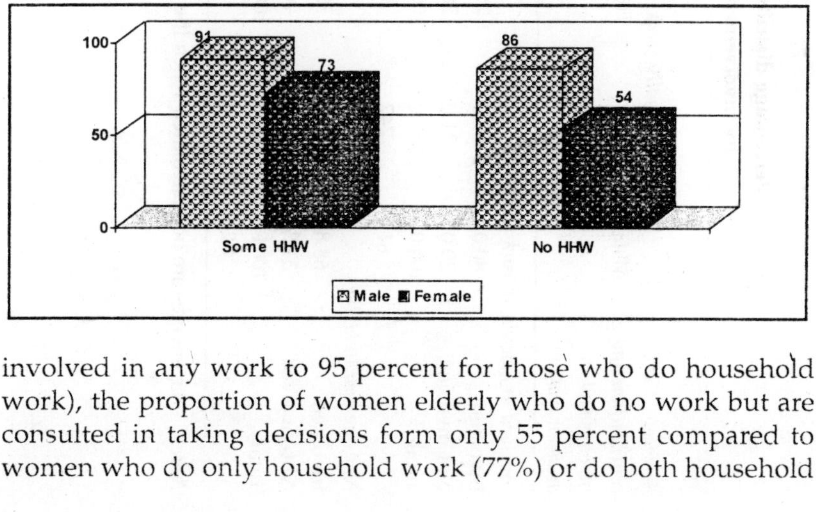

involved in any work to 95 percent for those who do household work), the proportion of women elderly who do no work but are consulted in taking decisions form only 55 percent compared to women who do only household work (77%) or do both household

Table 11

Percentage distribution of elderly in different financial status group by involvement in decision making and service contribution

Service contribution and involvement in decision making	Financial Status								
	Financially weak			Liquid asset			Immovable asset		
	Male	*Female*	*Total*	*Male*	*Female*	*Total*	*Male*	*Female*	*Total*
Involved in household work (HHW)									
Involved	80.0	69.0	71.2	94.7	84.1	90.9	88.0	71.6	79.1
Not involved	20.0	31.0	28.8	5.3	15.9	9.1	12.0	28.4	20.9
Total	100.0	100.0	100.0	100.0	100.0	100.0	100.0	100.0	100.0
	61	242	303	225	126	351	117	141	258
Not involved in HHW									
Involved	68.8	45.3	53.1	95.5	70.8	89.0	86.0	59.4	75.6
Not involved	31.3	54.7	46.9	4.5	29.2	11.0	14.0	40.6	24.4
Total	100.0	100.0	100.0	100.0	100.0	100.0	100.0	100.0	100.0
	32	64	96	68	24	92	50	32	82

Note: Percentages are not calculated when the number of cases is less than 15

work and child care (75%). In short, involvement in decision making is the lowest when the elderly are not rendering any type of help to the household, the percentage being 88 for males and 55 for females.

Table 11 gives the differences in involvement in decision making controlling for the financial status of the elderly. Only two categories of involvement are used here, viz. those involved in household work and those not involved in household work.

Among financially weak men, involvement is the lowest when the elderly are not rendering any type of help to the household – 68.8 percent. Again having immediate liquid cash in hand seems to be a great asset with almost no difference in their involvement in decision making for men, with 94.7 percent for those who do some work at home and 95.5 percent for those who do no work at all. Data for women shows a clear difference in being consulted on matters relating to household between those who render some work at home and those who render no work at all, the latter group being the losers. But even for women, having some asset particularly liquid asset, increases the chances of their being part of household decision making.

Current health status and involvement in decision making

If a person is not healthy, the chances of his/her involvement in decision making could be low. However, in this regard it should be mentioned that the seriousness of the illness or the type of illness is not taken into consideration here. The general assumption is that other things remaining constant, compared to a person who is ill, the chances of consulting one who is not ill will be high. This expectation is born out by this data only in the case of women as can be seen from Fig. 12.

Involvement in decision making by health status and financial status is given in Table 12. The combination of financially poor and unhealthy reduced drastically the chances of women being consulted (58.0%) compared to their healthy counterparts (75.0%). However, for women, the presence of liquid asset helps to increase their involvement in decision making even if they are unhealthy (87%). Same is the pattern for those with immovable assets (71.3%). For male elderly these differences are not very conspicuous.

Among elderly males and females, the possession of liquid asset improves their role in decision making and it is followed by

Table 12
Percentage distribution of elderly in different financial status group by their health status and service contribution

Health and involvement in decision making	Financial Status								
	Financially weak			Liquid asset			Immovable asset		
	Male	Female	Total	Male	Female	Total	Male	Female	Total
Healthy									
Involved	80.0	75.0	76.5	97.2	80.0	91.9	84.9	67.1	73.8
Not involved	20.0	25.0	23.5	2.8	20.0	6.6	15.1	32.9	24.6
Total	100.0	100.0	100.0	100.0	100.0	100.0	100.0	100.0	100.0
	40	108	149	144	45	197	53	73	126
Unhealthy									
Involved	76.0	58.0	61.0	96.4	87.0	89.0	91.8	71.3	81.0
Not involved	24.0	42.0	37.3	3.6	13.0	6.9	8.2	28.7	17.1
Total	100.0	100.0	100.0	100.0	100.0	100.0	100.0	100.0	100.0
	50	193	249	140	92	246	110	94	204

possession of immovable asset. But in the case of financially weak category, involvement in decision making is decided more by their health status. Comparatively elderly males have some supremacy in all categories with respect to decision making.

Fig. 12
Percent of healthy and unhealthy elderly involved in decision making

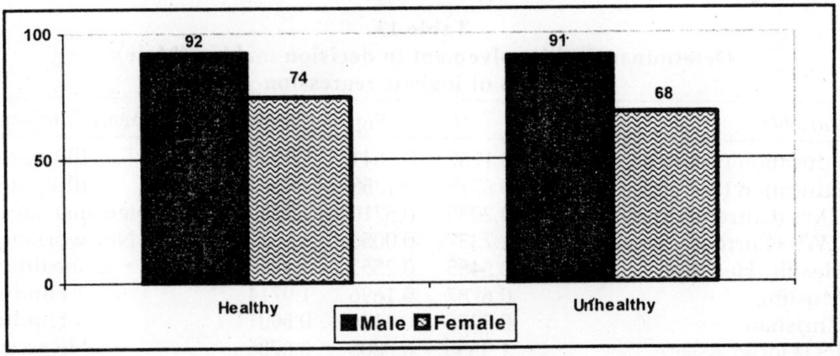

DETERMINANTS OF INVOLVEMENT IN DECISION MAKING

Using logistic regression an attempt is made to find the factors affecting the involvement of elderly in household decision making. The analysis is done separately for both men and women. The variables included in the model for elderly men are education, current marital status, current work status, health, religion, financial status, relationship with care giver and status at home. For elderly women all these variables except current work status have been considered in the analysis.

Table 13 shows the results of the analysis for men and Table 14 for women. The importance of liquid cash in this society has come out very clearly with the chances of being consulted increasing by a factor of 3.9 when one changes from a status of no asset to having liquid asset. Similarly, possession of immovable asset increases the chances of being consulted in household matters by a factor of two compared to those with no asset.

Current work status of the elderly males is also important with the likelihood of being consulted increasing by a factor of 5.66 compared to those who are not working. In short, the importance of the economic status of the elderly men in their involvement in household decision making comes out clearly from the analysis.

Two other significant variables in deciding the involvement of elderly in household decision making process are status at home and relation with care giver. Head of the households are twice as likely to be consulted compared to others which indicate the importance of status of a person at home. Similarly, if the care giver is son, the chances of being consulted increases by 82 percent compared to the other group.

Table 13
Determinants of involvement in decision making (Male): Results of logistic regression

Variable	*B*	*Sig.*	*Exp(B)*	*Reference category*
Education (1-4 yrs)	0.1787	0.6641	1.1957	Illiterate
Education (5+ yrs)	0.6715	0.1358	1.9571	Illiterate
CMS (Currently married)	0.2035	0.5710	1.2257	Disrupted marriage
CWS (Currently working)	1.7337	0.0058	5.6617	Not working
Health (Healthy)	0.3485	0.2552	1.4169	Unhealthy
Muslim	0.6787	0.1696	1.9714	Hindu
Christian	-0.5275	0.1190	0.5901	Hindu
FS (Liquid Asset)	1.3555	0.0005	3.8786	No asset
FS (Immovable .Asset)	0.7136	0.0525	2.0414	No asset
Care giver (Son)	0.5993	0.0915	1.8208	Other than son
SAH (Head of household)	0.6945	0.0362	2.0027	Other than HHH
Constant	-0.2133	0.6949	0.8079	

Note: The variable measurements are given in the chapter on methodology FS = Financial Status; CWS = Current Work Status; CMS = Current Marital Status; SAH = Status at Home.

Table 14
Determinants of involvement in decision making (Female): Results of logistic regression

Variable	*B*	*Sig.*	*Exp(B)*	*Reference category*
Education (1-4 yrs)	0.3607	0.0909	1.4343	Illiterate
Education (5+ yrs)	0.3290	0.2136	1.3895	Illiterate
CMS (Currently married)	-0.0206	0.9325	0.9796	Disrupted marriage
Health (Healthy)	0.6943	0.0002	2.0023	Unhealthy
Muslim	0.3508	0.2262	1.4202	Hindu
Christian	0.4032	0.0869	1.4966	Hindu
FS (Liquid Asset)	0.9690	0.0002	2.6353	No asset
FS (Immovable Asset)	0.1720	0.4244	1.1877	No asset
Care giver (Son)	0.3237	0.1144	1.3822	Other than son
SAH (Head of household)	0.5606	0.0248	1.7517	Other than HHH
Constant	-0.4682	0.0621	0.6261	

Note: The variable measurements are given in the chapter on methodology FS = Financial Status; CMS = Current Marital Status; SAH = Status at Home

Among women also possession of liquid asset makes a difference in decision making. That is, possession of liquid asset increases the chance of being consulted by a factor of 2.6 compared to those with no asset. Though health was not important for men to be involved in the decision making, it is not so in the case of women where healthy women have a better chance of being consulted than unhealthy women.

Other significant variables are education, religion and status at home. When compared to the illiterate, those with 1-4 years of schooling have a better chance of being consulted. However, having a higher level of education did not improve the situation. Elderly females of the Christian community have more likelihood of being consulted than women in Hindu community. Elderly women Head of households have 75 percent more chance for involvement in household decision making than others.

Note that religion is not an important variable for men while the relationship with care giver is not important for women in determining the involvement in decision making. Years of schooling also are not important in the case of men while some education increases the chances of the women being involved in household decision making.

The analysis indicates the existence of sex differential in the determinants of decision making. But possession of liquid asset and headship of household significantly contributes towards involvement of both men and women in decision making at household level.

6 FINANCIAL STATUS OF THE ELDERLY AND THEIR INPUT TO HOUSEHOLD RELATED ACTIVITIES

(Service Contribution)

INTRODUCTION

In any given household, there are many activities of varying importance, length of time required, effort involved and the degree of patience needed. This chapter looks at the type of work done by the elderly at home, which is referred to as service contribution. It refers to the help or assistance of any nature given to the household including child care. Elderly may make service contribution either to make use of their time or due to an eagerness to share the responsibility of the household or to reciprocate the help and care the elderly receive from the caregiver or forced by the need of the household.[1] This help could be a great boon to the family as there will be someone to share the household responsibilities. Among the elderly, it is found that 77 percent are involved in some type of household activities. The male-female difference in this matter, given in Fig. 1, shows that more women (81%) are involved in household activities than men (73%).

The household activities of the elderly are further classified into three types viz. only child care (CC), only household work (HHW) and both CC&HHW.

Child care helps the adult women in the household to take care of the other household activities without much interference from children as also without worrying about them as the children are being taken care of by the elderly persons. Besides, taking children to school and bringing them back is also included in child care.

Hence child care is a great help and its importance cannot be undermined. In this context it should be mentioned that in Kerala

Fig. 1
Percentage distribution of elderly by involvement in household work

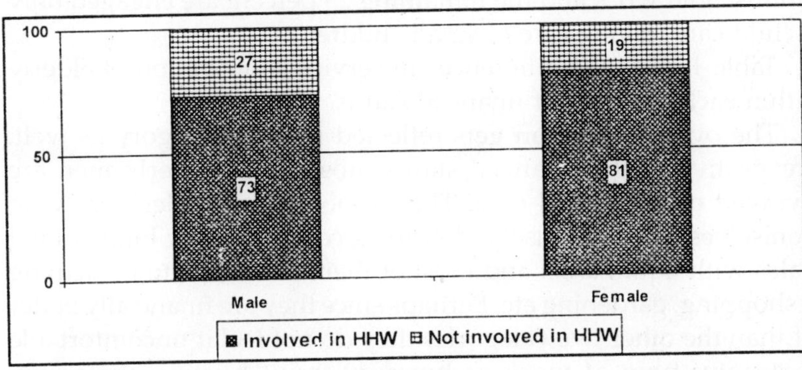

as in many other societies, taking care of very small children are considered as the work of women alone. Household work in this study include, besides regular work like cleaning, washing, cooking, sweeping, swabbing etc., activities like getting things from the market for household use, kitchen gardening, and the like.

Fig. 2 clearly shows the male-female differences in the participation in household activities. More than half of the elderly men (55%) who are involved in some kind of service to household are actually involved only in child care which is mainly to take the

Fig. 2
Percentage distribution of participating elderly by type of work at home

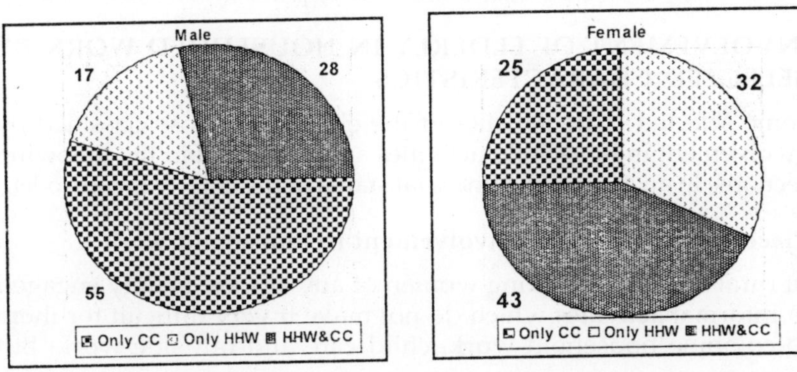

children to school and back. Seventeen percent of the men are engaged only in household work and the remaining 28 percent are engaged in both household work and child care.

Majority of the women (43%) are engaged in both child care and household work. Thirty two percent of them are engaged only in household work and the remaining 25 percent are engaged only in child care (taking care of small children).

Table 1 gives the differences in service contribution of elderly within each category of financial status.

The overall situation gets reflected in each category as well. Irrespective of the financial status most of the elderly men are involved only in child care. The proportion of males involving themselves only in household work is comparatively high among males with liquid asset and most of them are found to be helping in shopping, gardening etc. Perhaps since they are financially better off than the other two categories they do not feel it uncomfortable to do any type of work at home without hurting their ego. Moreover, they on their own, may also get some necessities for the household from their own financial resources. One-third of the men who are financially weak are not involved in any kind of work at home while 30 percent of those with only immovable assets fall in this category. A higher proportion of men with liquid asset are involved in one type of work or the other compared to the other two types of financial status.

More women are involved in household work as well as child care. Invariably, in the categories involving household work the proportion of women is higher than that of men. Further, the proportion of women who are not involved in any type of work at home is much less than their male counterparts in the same category.

INVOLVEMENT OF ELDERLY IN HOUSEHOLD WORK BY SELECTED CHARACTERISTICS

Some selected characteristics of the elderly are cross classified by involvement in household activities and presented in the following sections. In all aspects the financial status of the elderly is controlled.

Place of residence and involvement in household work

In rural areas the working women of any age are mainly engaged in informal activities which do not make it very difficult for them to combine household work, child care and out side work. But

Table 1
Percentage distribution of elderly in different financial status group by service contribution

Service Contributions	*Financial Status*								
	Financially weak			*Liquid asset*			*Immovable asset*		
	Male	*Female*	*Total*	*Male*	*Female*	*Total*	*Male*	*Female*	*Total*
Only CC	43.0	22.2	27.1	36.2	19.3	30.5	45.5	17.3	31.2
Only HHW	9.7	24.2	20.8	16.0	30.7	21.0	6.6	24.9	15.9
HHW & CC	12.9	32.7	28.1	24.6	34.0	27.8	18.0	39.3	28.8
No work	34.4	20.9	24.1	23.2	16.0	20.5	29.9	18.5	24.1
Total	100.0	100.0	100.0	100.0	100.0	100.0	100.0	100.0	100.0
	93	306	399	293	150	443	167	173	340

urban women are often found in formal activities and the need for healthy elderly women will be more, so that the working women can leave the household work in the hands of someone whom they can trust. Since taking the child to school and back also is part of child care, more men could be of use than women. Fig. 3 takes into account the place of residence of the elderly and shows the differences in the participation of the elderly in house work. In general, participation of both men and women in rural and urban areas are high. Between rural and urban areas male participation is high in rural and female participation is high in urban areas.

Fig. 3
Percent of elderly involved in household work in rural and urban areas.

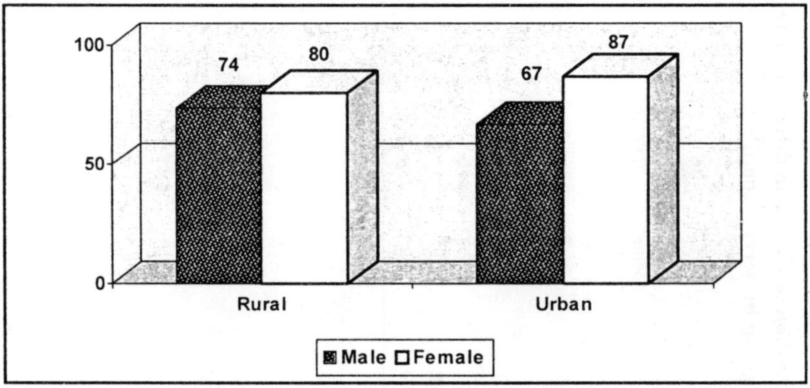

Table 2 shows the involvement of elderly in household work in each financial status category by place of residence to see whether the financial status of the elderly really make any difference in their involvement in household work.

The overall pattern is found to be the same as stated earlier in the case of both rural and urban areas for both men and women. Between rural and urban areas, urban men with no money are either involved only in child care (63.6%) or are not involved in any work at all (31.8%) whereas their rural counterparts are involved in household work as well.

Age and involvement in household work

Age could be a hindrance to participating in the household activities. As age advances active participation in household work

Table 2

Percentage distribution of elderly in different financial status group by involvement in household work and place of residence

Place of residence and service Contributions	*Financial Status*								
	Financially weak			*Liquid asset*			*Immovable asset*		
	Male	*Female*	*Total*	*Male*	*Female*	*Total*	*Male*	*Female*	*Total*
Rural									
Only CC	36.6	20.6	24.1	36.3	18.3	29.9	46.3	13.8	30.7
Only HHW	12.7	24.9	22.2	16.3	31.3	21.6	6.7	26.8	16.4
HHW & CC	15.5	32.8	29.0	26.3	32.8	28.6	18.1	39.9	28.6
None	35.2	21.7	24.7	21.3	17.6	19.9	28.9	19.6	24.4
Total	100.0	100.0	100.0	100.0	100.0	100.0	100.0	100.0	100.0
	71	253	324	240	131	371	149	138	287
Urban									
Only CC	63.6	30.2	40.0	35.8	26.3	33.3	38.9	31.4	34.0
Only HHW	—	20.8	14.7	15.1	26.3	18.1	5.6	17.1	13.2
HHW & CC	4.5	32.1	24.0	17.0	42.1	23.6	16.7	37.1	30.2
None	31.8	17.0	21.3	30.2	5.3	23.6	38.9	14.3	22.6
Total	100.0	100.0	100.0	100.0	100.0	100.0	100.0	100.0	100.0
	22	53	75	53	19	72	18	35	53

Note: In some cases percentage may not add to 100 because of the omission of no data cases

could be physically and in some cases mentally difficult. Since works are of different nature, it is worth seeing the type of work many of them are engaged in. On the whole it is found that 81 percent of the young old persons are involved in some HHW whereas the corresponding figure for those who are at least 75 years old is 71 percent. Fig. 4 shows the involvement situation for males and females separately. In 65-74 age group, the proportion of men participating, though high in itself, is lower than that of women in the same age category. A conspicuous difference in the involvement in house related work between the two age groups is noted for women with a drastic decline in the proportion of old-old women is observed (from 86% to 71%). However, there is no difference in the proportion engaged in household activities between men and women in the age group 75 years and above (71 % each).

Fig. 4
Percent of elderly involved in household work in each broad age group

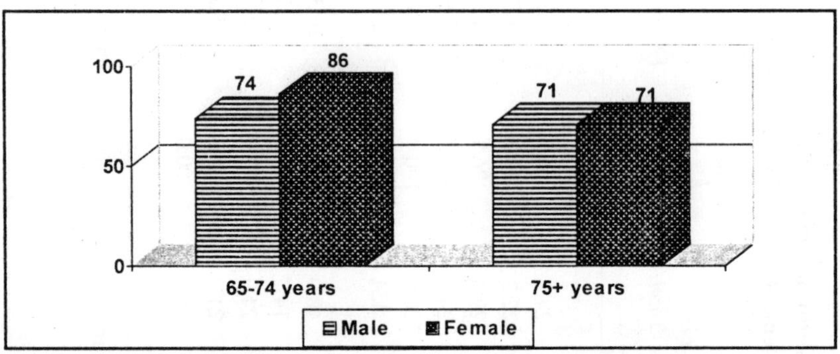

When the financial status of elderly is controlled with type of work details Table 3, it is found that irrespective of the financial status and age, a higher proportion of men are engaged only in child care. The noticeable difference is among those with liquid assets, where the proportion of men taking care of children is below 40 percent. Half the men over 75 years of age with only immovable assets are taking care of children. As stated elsewhere in this chapter child care includes taking children to school and back, playing with them, keeping them out of mischief, etc. and thus, it is not surprising to see more men involved in child care. For women who are engaged in household work and child care, the combined proportion (HHW and HHW&CC) varies by financial status; the

Table 3

Percentage distribution of elderly in different Financial status group by involvement in household work and age of elderly

Age and service Contributions	Financial Status: Financially weak Male	Female	Total	Liquid asset Male	Female	Total	Immovable asset Male	Female	Total
65-74 years									
Only CC	44.7	20.7	24.8	35.4	17.5	29.5	43.0	14.5	28.6
Only HHW	15.8	25.5	23.9	16.7	34.0	22.4	7.0	27.4	17.3
HHW & CC	7.9	39.4	34.1	24.7	36.1	28.5	20.2	44.4	32.5
None	31.6	14.4	17.3	22.7	12.4	19.3	29.8	13.7	21.6
Total	100.0	100.0	100.0	100.0	100.0	100.0	100.0	100.0	100.0
	38	188	226	198	97	295	114	117	231
75 years and above									
Only CC	41.8	24.6	30.1	37.9	22.6	32.4	50.9	23.2	36.7
Only HHW	5.5	22.0	16.8	14.7	24.5	18.2	5.7	19.6	12.8
HHW & CC	16.4	22.0	20.2	24.2	30.2	26.4	13.2	28.6	21.1
None	36.4	31.4	32.9	23.2	22.6	23.0	30.2	28.6	29.4
Total	100.0	100.0	100.0	100.0	100.0	100.0	100.0	100.0	100.0
	55	118	173	95	53	148	53	56	109

Note: Percentage may not add to 100 because of the omission of no data cases

variation among the young old is from 64.9 percent for those who are financially weak to 71.8 percent for those who have only immovable asset. Correspondingly, among the old-old women the variation is from 44.0 percent for the financially weak to 54.7 percent for those with liquid asset. Interestingly, where one would expect the old women with liquid asset to do less work, as they are not entire dependants, the opposite is observed among the old-old women in this survey. Also to be noted is the fact that more than two-thirds of the elderly (be it men or women) are involved in house related work in this society, be it willingly or forced by circumstances.

Literacy/Education and involvement in household work

The relationship between participation in household activities and literacy/education is given on the assumption that literate/educated persons will realise the importance of sharing responsibilities on the one hand and would like to remain active on the other. Fig. 5, where involvement and literacy are given for men and women separately, shows that the expected relationship is found only among the women where the proportion declined from 83 percent for literate to 78 percent for illiterate (the difference being to the tune of only 5 percentage points).

Fig. 5
Percent of literate and illiterate elderly involved in household work

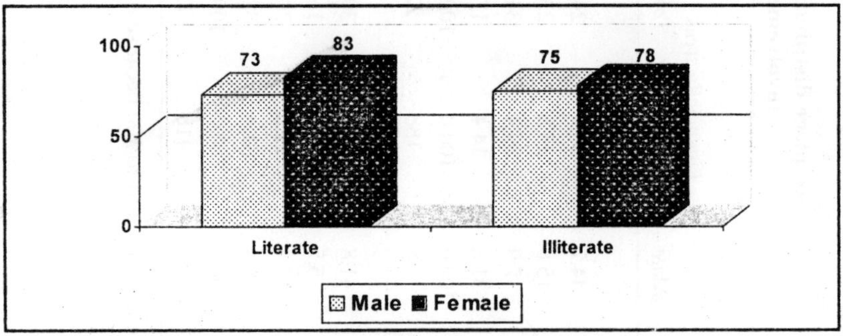

When the financial status is controlled for the literate and illiterate elderly Table 4, a higher proportion of illiterate men with no financial means had to do one type of work or the other compared to their literate counterpart (the proportion doing no work being 17.6 for illiterate and 37.3 for literate men).

Table 4

Percentage distribution of elderly in different financial status group by involvement in household work and literacy status of elderly

Literacy and service Contributions	Financially weak			Liquid asset			Immovable asset		
	Male	*Female*	*Total*	*Male*	*Female*	*Total*	*Male*	*Female*	*Total*
Literate									
Only CC	40.0	15.8	23.6	34.8	16.7	30.0	45.8	16.9	34.0
Only HHW	10.7	28.5	22.7	16.3	33.3	208	6.7	27.5	12.6
HHW & CC	12.0	36.7	28.8	24.2	35.4	27.2	20.0	45.3	31.2
None	37.3	19.0	24.9	24.2	14.6	21.7	27.5	16.9	22.3
Total	100.0	100.0	100.0	100.0	100.0	100.0	100.0	100.0	100.0
	75	158	233	264	96	360	120	95	215
Illiterate									
Only CC	58.8	29.1	32.1	48.3	24.1	32.5	44.7	15.4	26.4
Only HHW	5.9	19.6	18.2	13.8	25.9	21.7	6.4	30.8	21.6
HHW & CC	17.6	28.4	27.3	27.6	31.5	30.1	12.8	32.1	24.8
None	17.6	23.0	22.4	10.3	18.5	15.7	24.7	21.8	27.2
Total	100.0	100.0	100.0	100.0	100.0	100.0	100.0	100.0	100.0
	17	148	165	29	54	83	47	78	125

(Column group heading: *Financial Status*)

The same pattern is observed for the other two financial status categories for men, though the difference was quite negligible in the case of men with immovable asset (45.8% vs. 44.7%). Majority of men in all the categories are involved in child care. But the highest proportion was found among illiterate men with no asset (58.8%).

Women, on the other hand, behaved in the expected fashion with a higher proportion doing no work among the illiterate group than is the case with literate women. Even among those who did some work, a higher proportion of literate women were involved in household work, with or without child care. Fig. 6 relates to education of literate persons and their involvement in work. A negative relationship is observed with lesser educated persons participating more. Table 5 shows the participation by type within each category of financial status of the elderly.

Fig. 6
Percent of elderly involved in household work in the two categories of years of schooling

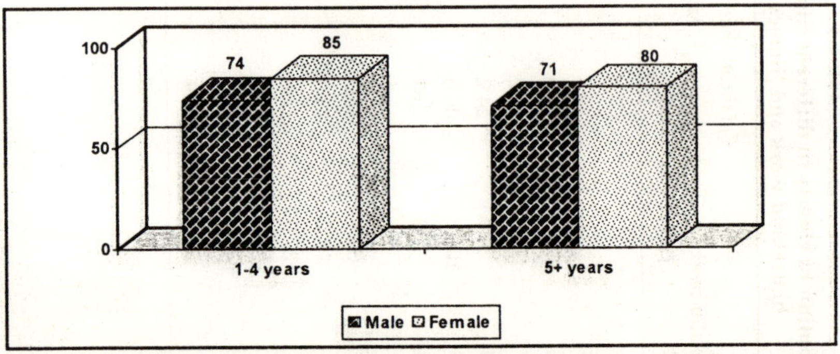

Among men with 1-4 years of schooling, half of the financially weak and almost half with immovable asset are engaged only in taking care of the children. The corresponding proportion for those with liquid asset is 40 percent. But the proportion doing no work is the lowest in this group. Among women, the distribution was almost equal in the different types of work with no asset and with only liquid asset. Women with 1-4 years of schooling and having immovable asset, almost 41 percent were engaged in child care and household work. The pattern is more or less the same for all the categories. Exception is women with five years of schooling

Table 5

Percentage distribution of literate elderly in different financial status group by involvement in household work and years of schooling

Years of schooling & service Contributions	*Financial Status*								
	Financially weak			*Liquid asset*			*Immovable asset*		
	Male	*Female*	*Total*	*Male*	*Female*	*Total*	*Male*	*Female*	*Total*
1-4 years									
Only CC	50.8	23.0	28.3	39.6	20.0	32.0	47.8	14.8	29.9
Only HHW	6.3	23.8	20.5	14.6	28.6	20.1	5.3	27.4	19.4
HHW & CC	11.1	32.3	28.3	26.8	35.2	30.1	15.0	40.7	29.1
None	31.7	20.8	22.9	18.9	16.2	17.8	31.9	17.0	21.6
Total	100.0	100.0	100.0	100.0	100.0	100.0	100.0	100.0	100.0
	63	269	332	164	105	269	113	135	849
5 + years									
Only CC	27.6	16.2	21.2	31.8	17.8	28.2	40.7	26.3	28.6
Only HHW	17.2	27.0	22.7	17.8	35.6	22.4	9.3	15.8	19.6
HHW & CC	17.2	35.1	27.3	21.7	31.1	24.1	24.1	34.2	25.9
None	37.9	21.6	28.8	27.9	15.6	24.7	25.9	23.7	25.6
Total	100.0	100.0	100.0	100.0	100.0	100.0	100.0	100.0	100.0
	29	37	66	129	45	174	54	38	332

and with liquid asset where the proportion engaged only in household work is higher than that of the other work categories.

Marital status and involvement in household work

As has already been shown, majority of men are currently married and majority of women have disrupted marriages[2]. Fig. 7 shows that there is hardly any currently married woman who is not involved in some work or the other. Among men, marital status did not make any difference as 73 percent of them were reportedly involved in some household work in both categories of marital status.

Fig. 7
Percent of elderly involved in household work in the two marital status categories

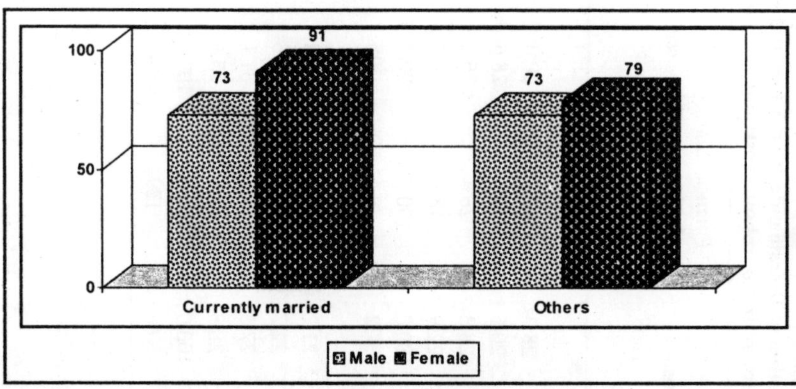

Table 6 shows the relationship between service contribution and financial status of the elderly in different marital status groups.

Differences in participation by marital status in the type of work done by financially weak elderly men are negligible. However, child care is the major work done by men in all categories of financial status, though a combination of having immovable assets and not being currently married increases their involvement. Similarly very few women with any asset are engaged only in child care while half or more are engaged in the category of HHW&CC (58.3% of women with immovable asset are engaged in HHW&CC). Irrespective of financial status, the proportion involved in household work in any category is high for women compared to

Table 6

Percentage distribution of elderly in different financial status group by involvement in household work and marital status

Years of schooling & service Contributions	*Financial Status*								
	Financially weak			*Liquid asset*			*Immovable asset*		
	Male	*Female*	*Total*	*Male*	*Female*	*Total*	*Male*	*Female*	*Total*
Currently Married									
Only CC	42.9	21.1	31.3	35.7	5.0	33.5	45.2	8.3	40.0
Only HHW	9.5	19.7	14.9	16.5	35.0	17.8	7.5	25.0	10.0
HHW & CC	11.1	49.3	31.3	24.3	50.0	26.2	17.8	58.3	23.5
None	36.5	9.9	22.4	23.1	10.0	22.2	29.5	8.3	26.5
Total	100.0	100.0	100.0	100.0	100.0	100.0	100.0	100.0	100.0
	63	71	134	255	20	275	146	24	170
Others									
Only CC	43.3	22.6	24.9	39.5	21.5	25.6	47.6	18.8	22.4
Only HHW	10.0	25.5	23.8	13.2	30.0	26.2	—	24.8	21.8
HHW & CC	16.7	27.7	26.4	26.3	31.5	30.4	19.0	36.2	34.1
None	30.0	24.4	24.9	21.1	16.9	17.9	33.3	20.1	21.8
Total	100.0	100.0	100.0	100.0	100.0	100.0	100.0	100.0	100.0
	30	235	265	38	130	168	21	149	170

men in the corresponding categories. Conversely the proportion of men taking care of only children is significantly high compared to their women counterparts.

Religious composition and involvement in household work

It is not clear whether there is any specific religious tenet which prescribes whether an elderly should be involved in household work or not. However, it is worth exploring. Fig. 8 shows the involvement of elderly in household activities in each religious group.

Fig. 8
Percent of elderly involved in household work in each religious group

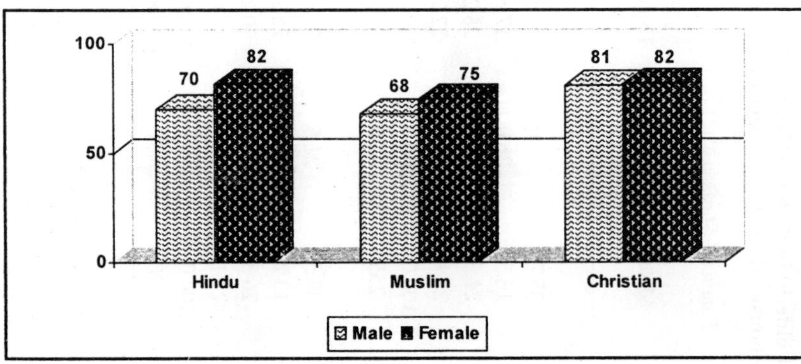

The maximum involvement of men is observed among the Christians (81%) with the Hindus (70%) and Muslims (68%) having more or less the same proportion. Among the women, both Hindus and Christians are having the highest proportion reporting involvement (82%) with Muslims the lowest (75%). It is also to be noted here that among the Christians, the proportion participating is not much different for both men (80%) and women (82%). The major difference by sex in the participation in household work is seen among the Hindus (70% for men and 82% for women).

Table 7 shows the participation of elderly in household work within each category of financial status by religion. Religion in combination with financial status shows some differences from the pattern so far observed in the case of Muslims. Fifty three percent of the men with some financial means are not involved in any household work. Similarly a fairly high percentage of women with

Table 7
Percentage distribution of elderly in different financial status group by involvement in household work and religion

Status at home and service Contributions	Financially weak			Liquid asset			Immovable asset		
	Male	Female	Total	Male	Female	Total	Male	Female	Total
Hindu									
Only CC	41.2	22.1	26.5	37.4	22.0	31.1	46.6	19.2	31.8
Only HHW	13.7	26.7	23.8	13.7	31.9	21.2	8.7	25.8	17.9
HHW & CC	7.8	30.8	25.6	22.1	34.1	27.0	14.6	34.2	25.1
None	37.3	20.3	24.2	26.7	12.1	20.7	30.1	20.8	25.1
Total	100.0	100.0	100.0	100.0	100.0	100.0	100.0	100.0	100.0
	51	172	223	131	91	222	103	120	223
Muslim									
Only CC	41.2	34.2	36.4	52.1	33.3	47.6	43.8	12.5	30.4
Only HHW	—	13.2	9.1	10.4	20.0	12.7	—	8.3	3.6
HHW & CC	5.9	34.2	25.5	14.6	6.7	12.7	21.9	54.2	35.7
None	52.9	18.4	29.1	22.9	40.0	27.0	34.4	25.0	30.4
Total	100.0	100.0	100.0	100.0	100.0	100.0	100.0	100.0	100.0
	17	38	55	48	15	63	32	24	56
Christian									
Only CC	48.0	17.7	24.0	28.1	9.1	22.8	43.8	13.8	29.5
Only HHW	8.0	24.0	20.7	21.1	31.8	24.1	6.3	34.5	19.7
HHW & CC	28.0	35.4	33.9	31.6	43.2	34.8	25.0	48.3	36.1
None	16.0	22.9	21.5	18.4	15.9	17.7	25.0	3.4	14.8
Total	100.0	100.0	100.0	100.0	100.0	100.0	100.0	100.0	100.0
	25	96	121	114	44	158	32	29	61

liquid asset (40%) also are not engaged in any work at home. Otherwise the pattern observed is the same for Hindus and Christians with a fairly high proportion of men taking care of children and women doing both household work and child care irrespective of the financial status.

Status of Elderly at Home and Involvement in Household Work

Taking part in household activities, to a certain extent, depends on the status of the elderly at home. It is assumed that a combination of low status at home and no asset, leads to performing loads of household chores in order to compensate for their perceived negative points.

Fig. 9 shows that other things remaining constant, as far as women are concerned, the status at home made no difference at all in their participation in household work. But the case of elderly men appears to be different. Whereas only 68 percent of those who are household heads are involved in household work, the corresponding percentage is 78 for those who are not heads of household – a clear 10 percentage points increase.

Fig. 9
Percent of elderly involved in household work among heads of household and others

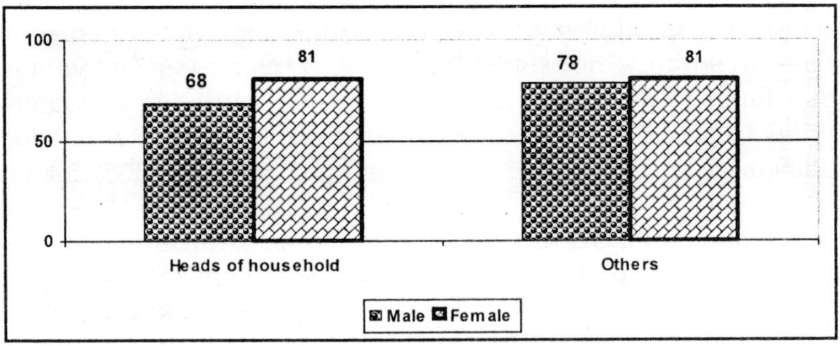

Table 8 gives the percentage distribution of elderly in different financial status group by involvement in household work and the status of the elderly at home.

It is found that the highest proportion of men who are not involved in any work are those who are head of households with

Table 8

Percentage distribution of elderly in different financial status group by involvement in household work and status at home

Status at home and service Contributions	Financially weak Male	Financially weak Female	Financially weak Total	Liquid asset Male	Liquid asset Female	Liquid asset Total	Immovable asset Male	Immovable asset Female	Immovable asset Total
Head of the household									
Only CC	39.4	18.8	27.2	33.3	21.9	31.5	41.9	18.0	33.6
Only HHW	6.1	29.2	19.8	19.4	46.9	23.9	6.5	22.0	11.9
HHW & CC	9.1	29.2	21.0	17.6	21.9	18.3	20.4	38.0	26.6
None	45.5	22.9	32.1	29.1	9.4	25.9	31.2	22.0	28.0
Total	100.0	100.0	100.0	100.0	100.0	100.0	100.0	100.0	100.0
	33	48	81	165	32	197	93	50	143
Other than head of the household									
Only CC	45.0	22.9	27.0	39.8	18.6	29.7	50.0	17.1	29.4
Only HHW	11.7	23.3	21.1	11.7	26.3	18.7	6.8	26.0	18.8
HHW & CC	15.0	33.3	29.9	33.6	37.3	35.4	14.9	39.8	30.5
None	28.3	20.5	22.0	14.8	17.8	16.3	28.4	17.1	21.3
Total	100.0	100.0	100.0	100.0	100.0	100.0	100.0	100.0	100.0
	60	258	318	128	118	246	74	123	197

Note: HHW = Household work; CC = Child care

no financial means. But such conspicuous differences are not found among women.

Almost half (45.5%) of the financially weak male head of the households are not participating in any household activities and almost 40 percent of them are engaged only in child care. In other words, household work is not their fort. But more men with liquid asset do household work and the proportion doing only household work is high among the heads of households (19.4%).

Though no specific pattern is observed among women even when controlled for financial status, almost three-fourths are involved in household work, irrespective of their financial status. About 50-60 percent of women are engaged in one or the other type of household work leaving one-fifth of women to take care of the children. Almost half of the women with liquid assets (46.9%) are involved in only household work and the proportion involved in no activity is below 10 percent – the lowest observed in any group.

Relationship Of The Elderly With The Care Giver And Involvement In Household Work

The person with whom the elderly is staying is categorized into three: living with son, living with daughter and living with persons other than one's own children. Seventy two percent of the elderly are staying with sons. This includes 75 percent of men and 70 percent of women. Traditionally sons are expected to take care of elderly parents and thus staying with daughters is not that common. This situation is slowly changing with a reduction in the family size and also increased migration particularly among males. Some of the elderly who may not have sons or have sons who are staying away from home do stay with daughters. Eleven percent of elderly who are staying with daughters consists of 9 percent male and 13 percent female elderly. The remaining 17 percent are staying with persons other than children (16% men and 17% women). The proportion of the elderly who contributes towards household work is more when they stay with son or daughter. Fig. 10 shows that the highest proportion of men involved in household work is found among those living with sons (76%), which is an only two percentage point more than those living with daughters (74%). However, the proportion is comparatively low for those men living with persons other than their own children (60%). For women, however, the person with whom they stay did not make any difference with four out of five women being involved in household work.

Fig. 10
Percent of elderly involved in household work in each category of care giver

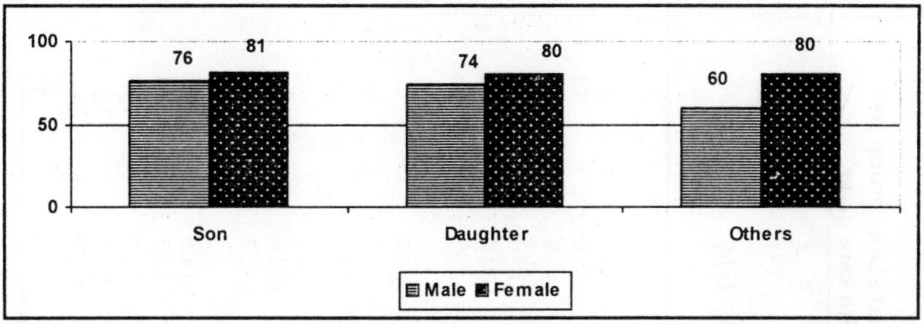

Table 9 shows that though majority of men staying with sons are involved only in child care, the proportion is low for men with liquid assets (41.7%) than for men with no assets (46.2%) or with only immovable asset (50.7%). The proportion doing only household work or household work and child care is high for those with liquid assets. Those who are not involved in any work are also low for this group of persons.

A higher proportion of men staying with daughters or others are found to be doing only household work compared to those who are staying with sons, irrespective of their financial status, with a comparatively higher proportion for those with liquid assets. Since household work involves getting things from outside also, men who are staying with daughters/others may be feeling it their responsibility to take up this matter. Women, on the other hand, also may be feeling like helping their daughters more than their daughters-in-law.

Health And Involvement In Household Work

To do household work/child care one should be fairly healthy and this comes out clearly from Fig. 11. The proportion involved declined from 78 percent for healthy to 63 percent for unhealthy men. The corresponding proportion for women is 90 percent to 67 percent respectively. That is, almost all healthy women are involved in one type of work or the other, compared to three out of four

Table 9
Percentage distribution of elderly in different financial status group by involvement in household work and relation with care giver

Relation with care giver and service Contributions	Financial Status								
	Financially weak			Liquid asset			Immovable asset		
	Male	Female	Total	Male	Female	Total	Male	Female	Total
Son									
Only CC	46.2	21.7	27.3	41.7	22.6	36.3	50.7	16.5	33.8
Only HHW	6.2	19.5	16.4	10.4	15.5	11.9	5.1	23.3	14.1
HHW & CC	15.4	37.6	32.5	28.4	47.6	33.9	16.9	42.9	29.7
None	32.3	21.3	23.8	19.4	14.3	18.0	27.2	17.3	22.3
Total	100.0	100.0	100.0	100.0	100.0	100.0	100.0	100.0	100.0
	65	221	286	211	84	295	136	133	269
Daughter									
Only CC	45.5	28.6	32.1	30.8	23.1	26.9	—	18.8	28.6
Only HHW	18.2	31.0	28.3	26.9	38.5	32.7	—	18.8	10.7
HHW & CC	9.1	21.4	18.9	15.4	23.1	19.2	—	31.3	32.1
None	27.3	19.0	20.8	26.9	15.4	21.2	—	31.3	28.6
Total	100.0	100.0	100.0	100.0	100.0	100.0	100.0	100.0	100.0
	11	42	53	26	26	52	12	16	28
Others									
Only CC	29.4	18.6	21.7	17.9	10.0	14.6	10.5	20.8	16.3
Only HHW	17.6	41.9	35.0	32.1	57.5	42.7	21.1	37.5	30.2
HHW & CC	5.9	18.6	15.0	14.3	12.5	13.5	15.8	25.0	20.9
None	47.1	20.9	28.3	33.9	20.0	28.1	52.6	16.7	32.6
Total	100.0	100.0	100.0	100.0	100.0	100.0	100.0	100.0	100.0
	17	43	60	56	40	96	19	24	43

healthy men. A detailed examination of the data showed that 10 percent healthy women who are not involved in household work of any nature are staying in joint families with children and grand children and almost all are in rural areas. The decline in the proportion from healthy to unhealthy is sharper (23 percentage points) for women than for men in the corresponding category (15 percentage points).

Fig. 11
Percent of elderly involved in household work among the healthy and the unhealthy

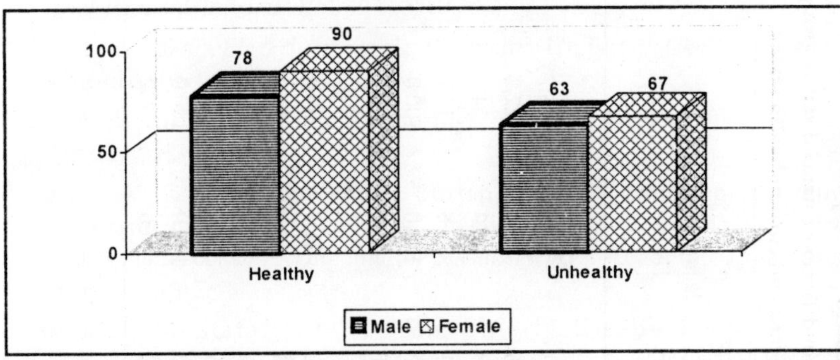

Table 10 shows that more unhealthy persons are involved in child care than healthy ones. In general, the proportion doing household work is less for unhealthy than healthy persons in the different financial status category as it is more strenuous. Further in each category of financial status the proportion of men taking care of children is more than that of women.

Standard Of Living And Involvement In Household Work

Fig. 12 gives the percentage distribution of elderly in different levels of standard of living and the involvement in household work. It is assumed that a higher proportion of those who are in the low standard of living may be involved in household work compared to the other two groups, with those in the high standard of living having the lowest proportion. The logic being, in households having a better living standard there may be paid assistants to take care of the household work which may not be the case with those in the low standard of living, an idea that can not be tested with the data set used.

Table 10

Percentage distribution of elderly in different financial status group by involvement in household work and current health status

Status at home and service Contributions	Financial Status								
	Financially weak			Liquid asset			Immovable asset		
	Male	*Female*	*Total*	*Male*	*Female*	*Total*	*Male*	*Female*	*Total*
Healthy									
Only CC	43.1	13.4	20.0	30.3	17.8	26.7	34.1	13.9	22.6
Only HHW	13.7	31.8	27.8	18.6	31.1	22.2	12.2	27.8	21.1
HHW & CC	23.5	45.8	40.9	30.8	43.3	34.4	28.0	46.3	38.4
None	19.6	8.9	11.3	20.4	7.8	16.7	25.6	12.0	17.9
Total	100.0	100.0	100.0	100.0	100.0	100.0	100.0	100.0	100.0
	51	179	230	221	90	311	82	108	190
Unhealthy									
Only CC	42.9	36.4	36.7	54.2	21.7	39.4	56.5	23.1	42.0
Only HHW	4.8	13.4	11.2	8.3	30.0	18.2	1.2	20.0	9.3
HHW & CC	—	14.2	10.7	5.6	20.2	12.1	8.2	27.7	16.7
None	52.4	37.8	41.4	30.6	28.3	29.5	34.1	29.2	32.0
Total	100.0	100.0	100.0	100.0	100.0	100.0	100.0	100.0	100.0
	42	127	169	72	60	132	85	65	150

Fig. 12
Percent of elderly involved in household work in each category of standard of living

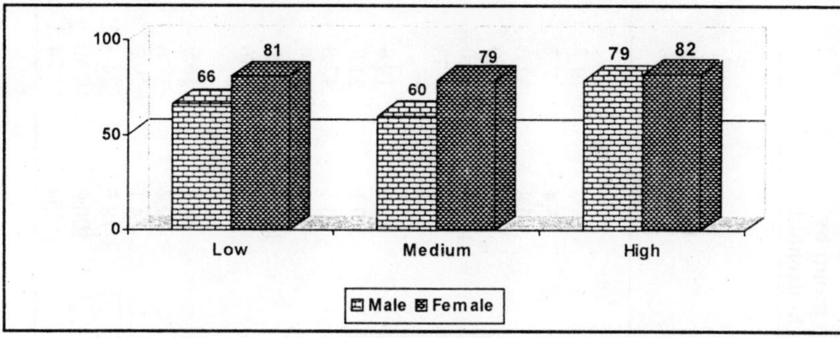

The Figure actually shows that there is no difference in the household work participation of women in all the three categories of standard of living. For men the reverse pattern is observed. Since majority of men are found engaged in either child care or getting things for the household from out side, it is possible that such work is less in poor households because of poverty and the easiness with which the women can combine the informal activities (they may be involved in) and child care.

Table 11 shows the situation of involvement when differentiated for different financial status category and standard of living. At least three-fourths of the women are engaged in some sort of work in all the categories. But for men, the findings above and the logic given seems to be clearer when one looks at the financially weak elderly and their involvement in household work in different standard of living categories. There is a systematic decline in the proportion of elderly men who are not doing any work as the standard of living of the household increases.

DETERMINANTS OF SERVICE CONTRIBUTION

To find the factors that affect the involvement of elderly in household work, two separate logistic regression analyses were carried out for elderly men and elderly women.

The variables entered in the model for men are current work status, health of the elderly, status at home, education, financial status, current marital status and the relationship with the care giver. For women also all except the current work status are included in the model.

Table 11
Percentage distribution of elderly in different financial status group by involvement in household work and standard of living of the household

Standard living and service Contributions	Financial Status								
	Financially weak			*Liquid asset*			*Immovable asset*		
	Male	*Female*	*Total*	*Male*	*Female*	*Total*	*Male*	*Female*	*Total*
Low									
Only CC	33.3	23.2	25.0	30.2	20.0	25.4	45.9	19.7	32.3
Only HHW	4.8	21.1	18.1	22.2	34.5	28.0	5.4	37.7	18.9
HHW & CC	9.5	32.6	28.4	25.4	30.9	28.0	10.8	32.0	19.7
None	52.4	23.2	28.4	22.2	14.5	18.6	37.8	17.0	29.1
Total	100.0	100.0	100.0	100.0	100.0	100.0	100.0	100.0	100.0
	21	95	116	63	55	118	74	53	127
Medium									
Only CC	42.3	22.6	28.4	38.7	25.0	35.4	41.0	19.6	29.4
Only HHW	3.9	21.0	15.9	12.9	30.0	17.1	5.1	21.7	14.1
HHW & CC	11.5	29.0	23.9	22.6	20.0	22.0	23.1	47.8	36.5
None	42.3	27.4	31.8	25.8	25.0	25.6	30.8	10.9	20.0
Total	100.0	100.0	100.0	100.0	100.0	100.0	100.0	100.0	100.0
	26	62	88	62	20	82	39	46	85
High									
Only CC	47.8	21.5	27.7	37.5	17.3	31.3	48.1	18.9	31.3
Only HHW	15.2	27.5	24.6	14.9	28.0	18.9	9.3	17.6	14.1
HHW & CC	15.2	34.2	29.7	25.0	40.0	29.6	24.1	39.2	32.8
None	21.7	16.8	17.9	22.0	14.7	19.8	18.5	24.3	21.9
Total	100.0	100.0	100.0	100.0	100.0	100.0	100.0	100.0	100.0
	46	149	195	168	75	243	54	74	128

Health, as one would expect, is the major factor that decide the participation of the elderly in the household work (Table 12). Compared to unhealthy men, healthy men are more likely to be involved in household work. The other significant variable is status at home showing a negative relationship. The likelihood of doing household work reduces by 41 percent as one moves from a status of non-head to head of household. Similarly financial status has a significant relationship with participation in household work. Though not expected the elderly males with liquid asset participate about 76 percent more than those without any asset. Perhaps, the elderly with liquid asset feel part of the household and therefore, is involved in household activities. It is also found that those who are staying with sons are more likely to get involved than those who are staying with daughters or others.

Table 12
Determinants of involvement in household work (Male): Results of logistic regression

Variable	*B*	*Sig.*	*Exp(B)*	*Reference category*
CWS (Currently working)	0.1006	0.6993	1.1059	Not working
Health (Healthy)	0.7106	0.0009	2.0353	Unhealthy
SAH (Head of the household)	-0.5183	0.0169	0.5955	Not HHH
Education (1-4 years)	-0.3561	0.2340	0.7004	Illiterate
Education (5+ years)	-0.4329	0.1516	0.6486	Illiterate
FS (Liquid Asset)	0.5692	0.0427	1.7669	No asset
FS (Immovable Asset)	0.3004	0.3101	1.3503	No asset
CMS (Currently Married)	-0.0879	0.7534	0.9158	Disrupted
Care giver (Son)	0.4429	0.0503	1.5572	Other than sons
Constant	0.5284	0.2063	1.6962	

Note: The variable measurements are given in the chapter on methodology FS = Financial Status; CMS = Current Marital Status; CWS = Current Work Status; SAH = Status at Home

There are only two statistically significant variables in the model for women and they are health status of the women and her marital status (Table 13).

Compared to the women who perceive their health to be bad, the healthy women are 4.6 times more likely to be involved in household work. Current marital status of the women is another statistically significant variable with the chances of participation of currently married women being 2.5 times more than the women who are not currently in wed lock. None of the other variables are statistically significant. But the direction of relation indicates that unlike in the case of men, women who are considered as head of

Table 13
Determinants of involvement in household work (Female): Results of logistic regression

Variable	*B*	*Sig.*	*Exp(B)*	*Reference category*
Health (Healthy)	1.5361	0.0000	4.6464	Unhealthy
SAH (Head of the household)	0.2936	0.2891	1.3413	Not HHH
Education (1-4 years)	0.0621	0.8010	1.0640	Illiterate
Education (5+ years)	-0.2763	0.3522	0.7586	Illiterate
FS (Liquid Asset)	0.4653	0.1017	1.5925	No asset
FS (Immovable Asset)	0.1679	0.5208	1.1828	No asset
CMS (Currently Married)	0.9121	0.0101	2.4895	Disrupted marriage
Care giver (Son)	0.1829	0.4462	1.2007	Other than sons
Constant	0.2687	0.3305	1.3083	

Note: The variable measurements are given in the chapter on methodology FS = Financial Status; CMS = Current Marital Status; SAH = Status at Home

the households are more likely to do household work than those who are not head of the households. Unlike in the case of men, financial status made no difference in the participation of women in household work.

NOTES

1. This information is not available in the data used in this study. Perhaps this is an area that need more detailed study.
2. Unmarried persons, who form only a very negligible proportion, are included in the "other" group.

7 SUMMARY AND DISCUSSION OF MAJOR FINDINGS

SUMMARY

General

Ageing of population raises financial challenges to the family and the society. In this context an understanding of the financial status of the elderly and its relation with basic aspects of life assumes importance. This study is an attempt in that direction. The basic aspects studied are limited to three, viz. the health status of elderly as perceived by them, involvement in decision making and involvement in the household work.

Though one chapter (chapter II) was devoted entirely to analyze the available census data for the major states in India to show the fact that the population of Kerala is ageing faster than all other major states in this country, the data for the main analysis were taken from a study on aged conducted in 1996-97 in Ernakulam and Kozhikode districts of Kerala. The information relating to the economic status of the elderly was classified into three categories based on the availability of liquid cash (asset) to meet day-to-day needs and availability of property or house in the name of the elderly. The categories are (i) "financially weak" indicating no asset, (ii) "immovable asset" indicating those with only property and (iii) "liquid asset" which included all others, with or without immovable asset, but having liquid cash. The status level was measured in ascending order, with the financially weak at the bottom and liquid asset at the top with immovable asset falling in-between these two extremes.

The census analysis revealed that the Indian population had been ageing fast during the recent past and is expected to age faster in the coming decades. The percent of aged population in India increased from 5.6 in 1961 to 7.4 in 2001. This lead to a change in the shape of the population pyramid from a very broad based one in 1961 to a pyramid with shrunken base in 2001. The base is expected to shrink further in the years to come.

The rate of growth of the elderly varied from state to state. The proportion of the aged in 2001 varied from 5.9 percent in Assam to 10.5 percent in Kerala. The proportion of the aged population in Andhra Pradesh, Karnataka, Kerala, Punjab, Haryana, Orissa, Maharashtra and Tamil Nadu was equal or higher than that of the national average. Among these states, the tempo of ageing of population is highest in Kerala. The share of elderly women increased more than that of elderly men. The median age in all the major states was at least 20 years in 2001 except Bihar and Uttar Pradesh and a consistent increase is observed over the years 1971-2001 for all the states except in Uttar Pradesh. The highest median age of 27.5 was noted in Kerala. The highest index of ageing is also prevailing in Kerala, which increased from 13.7 in 1961 to 40.2 in 2001. Kerala's expectation of life at birth in 1999-2003 was the highest, with the female expectation of life at birth (76.0) higher than that of males (70.9). On the basis of expectation of life at age 60, Kerala stands second only to Punjab with a residual length of life of 21 years. Even at the age of 70 there is a residual life of 13 years remaining for an elderly in Kerala (Registrar General of India, 2006). Age pyramid of Kerala for 2001 showed a narrow base with expanded middle portion and expanding apex. This constriction is expected to continue and by 2021 Kerala's age structure will turn to a more or less cylindrical shape – a shape depicting an ageing population.

Subsequent chapters of this study had used survey data. An examination of the general characteristics of the elderly revealed that there were 1182 elderly persons aged 65 years and over comprising of 553 men and 629 women coming from 1060 households. Majority of both men and women were in the 65-74 age group, belonged to Hindu religion and were literates. Among the literates, a higher proportion had 1-4 years of schooling. Only about 13 percent were engaged in any economic activity at the time of survey. A larger proportion of workers was engaged in agriculture and related activities. There was a preponderance of currently married men while the majority of women were widowed. A large number of elderly had 3 or more living children. Seventeen percent of men and 49 percent of women were financially weak. Whereas 30 percent of men and 27 percent of women had only immovable asset, the remaining 53 percent of men and 24 percent of women fell into the liquid asset category.

The household population details showed that of the total of 6239 persons enumerated from the 1060 selected households included 2925 men and 3314 women giving a sex ratio 883. Mean household size was 5.9 persons with 2.8 males and 3.1 females. Eighty-eight percent of those aged 10 years and above were literate. Sixty two percent of those aged 15 years and above were currently married. Among the working population 29 percent were involved in non-agricultural labour. Nearly half of the 1060 households were living in semi-pucca houses and almost all the houses were owned by one of the residents. Electricity facility was available in nearly three-fourths of the houses. Similar is the case with drinking water (piped into the house or well water within the compound) and flush toilet facility. Majority of the houses were having 3-4 rooms. Medium standard of living was noted for forty five percent of households. A large proportion of elderly with liquid asset were having high standard of living with facilities and amenities like electricity, safe water piped into the house or well water within the compound, flush toilet, and more than 3 rooms in the house.

Health and financial status

In order to understand the inter-linkages between health and financial status of elderly, the health status as assessed by elderly is made use of. Sixty-two percent of the elderly were in good health. Their proportion is higher in the liquid asset category compared to the financially weak category, as one would expect.

More elderly in urban area were found to be healthy than their rural counterparts. The proportion of healthy men was lesser in the immovable asset and financially weak categories in rural area compared to women. The gap in the proportion of healthy men and women was highest in the liquid asset category. However, there was not much difference in the health status of women across the different financial status categories in rural area.

Elderly in the "young old" age group (65-74 years) were found healthier than the oldest age group of 75 years and above. Proportion of healthy men in the liquid asset category was highest for both the age groups. More of the financially weak men were healthy compared to those with immovable assets. Financial status made no difference on the health status of women aged 65-74 years.

Literate elderly were healthier than illiterate elderly. The proportion in the other two categories remained more or less equal. The proportion of healthy among literate women in the financially weak category and possessing immovable asset were found to be higher compared to men in the corresponding categories. A combination of being literate and having liquid asset appeared to be in favour of good health with a higher proportion of men reporting to be so. Among literates, a higher proportion of those with at least 5 years of schooling was found to be healthy. Proportion of healthy was lesser among men educated 5 years or more in financially weak category and among women in immovable asset category. In sum, level of education is found to be very important in maintaining better health status of the aged.

A higher proportion of currently married elderly reported themselves to be healthy compared to others. An exception observed is for men in the financially weak category where the proportion healthy was lower for currently married men compared to others. A higher proportion of Christians were healthy and the lowest proportion was reported by Muslims. Financial status made a difference for Christian men where the highest proportion of healthy was found among those with liquid asset. Financial status did not make any difference in health among Hindu women. Muslim women with liquid asset had the highest proportion healthy, followed by those with immovable asset and no asset in that order.

The proportion of healthy was the lowest among those who did not involve themselves in household work. The highest proportion of healthy was found among those men and women who were doing both child care and household work. That is, service contribution and health status have a significant direct relationship.

The determinants of health as assessed with the help of logistic regression for elderly men had shown that the current work status, involvement in household work, having at least five years of schooling, staying with son, having liquid asset, having at least a few hours with care giver and visiting places of worship like temple or church or mosque increased the chances of being healthy. A similar analysis for women also showed the importance of doing household work, visiting temple/church/mosque and having at least some education to favour health with statistically significant relation. To be noted here is the fact that while for men having liquid asset, living with son, and having some time with the care giver were found important determinants of health, that is not so for women. Thus the study indicates sex differential in the determinants of health among the aged.

Involvement in decision making and financial status

Involvement in decision making, which suggest the importance given to a person in the household, showed that nine out of ten elderly men and seven out of ten elderly women were involved in decision making. Differentials by financial status on their involvement in decision making indicated that nearly all elderly men and 85 percent of the elderly women with liquid asset were consulted in making household decisions. Percentage consulted in decision making decreased with decline in financial capability. The study observed a significant relationship between financial status and involvement of the aged in decision making.

In the case of elderly men literacy status did not play any role whereas more literate women were consulted than illiterate women. It was found that involvement in decision making by women elderly varied with difference in the financial status: the highest proportion being for those with liquid asset and the lowest for those who are financially weak.

The level of education has significant influence on the involvement in decision making though the degree of involvement varied with financial status and sex of the elderly. Elderly women with at least five years of education had a higher proportion of those who were consulted than those with less than five years of schooling. Almost all elderly men with liquid asset were consulted irrespective of their educational level. A higher proportion of currently married elderly men were involved in decision making. The level of involvement in decision making was higher for currently married women having immovable asset. More Muslim men were consulted in decision-making than Hindu men or

Christian men. But among women the highest proportion of Christian women were consulted followed by Muslims and Hindus in that order. Proportion of elderly in decision making varied much among religion especially in the case of those in the financially weak category. But as a whole there is a significant relationship between religion and involvement of the aged in decision making.

The study observed a significant dependence between the status of the aged at home and involvement in decision making, where being the head of the household increased the chance of participation in decision making. Among elderly head of the households, the highest proportion involved in decision making was found among those with liquid asset, which was followed by those with immovable asset, and those with no asset in that order.

The relationship of the elderly with the care giver is found to have a significant relationship with the involvement of the aged in decision making. More elderly who stay with sons were consulted in taking decisions than those who stay with daughters/others.

More elderly in high standard of living category were involved in decision making than others. Elderly men with no asset and having medium standard of living had the lowest proportion consulted. For men there was not much difference in the proportion participating in decision making by service contribution. When service contribution and involvement in decision making was examined for elderly within the category of immovable asset there was a negative relation with the different categories of service contribution. A combination of financially poor and unhealthy reduces drastically the chance of being consulted for women compared to their healthy and financially betters off counterparts.

The determinants of involvement in decision making as emerged from the logistic regression analysis brings out clearly the importance of economic aspects in day-to-day life in the case of men. The most important variables were current work participation and possession of liquid asset which increased the chances of being consulted. Besides these, being head of households and staying with son also increased the chances of being consulted. For women having liquid asset and being healthy increased the chances of participation in the household decision making. Other variables of importance were having at least 1-4 years of schooling, being a member of Christian community and being the head of households.

Financial status and involvement in household work

Of the 1182 elderly, 77 percent participated in household activities of one nature or the other. The corresponding percentage was higher for women where majority of them were engaged in both child care and household work. Most of the men were involved only in child care. Proportion of men involved in household work was high among those with liquid asset. One-third of the financially weak men and almost a third of those with immovable asset was involved in some kind of work at home.

In both rural and urban areas a noticeable proportion of older persons participated in household work, though participation was high among rural men and urban women. Urban men with weak finance involved only in child care more than their counterparts with liquid asset or immovable asset.

Proportion of women involved in household activities is lesser among those aged 75 years and above while male participation was not much different between the two age groups. A higher proportion of illiterate men did one type of work or the other compared to their literate counterparts in all the three financial status categories. A higher proportion of women did not involve in any work among the illiterate group compared to the literate. Lesser educated men with liquid asset participated more in the household work. Almost all currently married women were involved in household activities. But the corresponding percentage *per se* among women who were not currently married also was not too small (79%).

More Christian men were involved in household activities. But among women a higher percentage of Hindus and Christians were involved. Half of the men with some financial asset and a higher percentage of women with liquid asset participated in the household activities. It was found that among men, those who were not involved were comparatively high among the head of households with no financial means than others, whereas that kind of difference was not found among the women. Almost half the men with no asset who were head of the households did not participate in any household activities while almost two-fifths of the elderly were engaged only in child care. But more men with liquid asset did household work. There is no specific pattern observed among women.

A major proportion of elderly were living with sons. Involvement in household work was found highest among them compared to those living with daughters and others. But in the case of women, this proportion did not vary much between financial status categories. Men were involved mainly in child care. Between men involved in household work in the various financial status categories, a higher proportion of men with liquid asset were involved in household work.

Almost all healthy women and three-fourths of healthy men contributed to household activities. The proportion contributing to household work was higher among healthy elderly in all the three different financial status categories. No difference was found in the proportion that did household work among women across different levels of standard of living. But among men, service contribution increased with increase in standard of living.

The results of the logistic regression showed that the service contribution of men were determined by their health, status at home, financial status and the relationship with care giver. For women only two variables were statistically significant and they were health of the women and her marital status. Thus there was just one common variable, viz. health, that determined the participation of both men and women in household activities.

DISCUSSION OF MAJOR FINDINGS

This study had brought out clearly the importance of financial status, particularly having liquid asset, in treating the elderly as part of a household by involving them in household decision making and household work. It is also found to be of immense importance in their perception of own health. This is true particularly for men. However, there are foggy areas where more studies are required to understand the exact relationship of these factors.

One such area is the relationship between perceived health of the elderly and some of its determinants. Work participation, be it in terms of household activity or economic activity, indicated a relation such that men with no activity were found to be less likely to be healthy than those who are active. However, whether activity leads to better health or vice versa could not be established with the available data set. This calls for further exploration. Similar is the case with respect to those who visit religious places like temple/ church/mosque. One way of looking at the relationship is that they could go over to these places, as they are healthy enough to do that. Another view could be that going to religious places give them peace of mind and the courage and ability to cope with the difficulties of life in addition to having opportunities for interaction with friends or similar category of persons. Thus such persons may report themselves as healthy. But one is not sure about the real situation, which needs to be further investigated to have a clear picture of the direction of relationship.

Another interesting finding that calls for explanation is the fact that more men with liquid asset were involved in household activities than those who do not have any asset, and hence are financially weak. The expectation was that those who are financially weak would try to compensate for this deficiency by doing household work of one nature or the other, while those who have asset, particularly liquid asset, would involve less in household work as they are not a complete burden to those with whom they co-reside. But the findings belied this expectation with a significant relationship indicating men with liquid asset being almost twice as likely to be involved in household work than those with no asset. Perhaps the low participation of the elderly with no asset in household work could also be explained. First explanation could be that the members of the household want to avoid hurting the feelings of the financially weak elderly and thus disallow them from involving in household work. A third way of looking at it could be that the members of the household deliberately want to ignore the elderly with no asset by not allowing him/her to make any service contribution. Though one would like to believe the first explanation, the actual situation in real life is not clear.

A higher proportion of the elderly with liquid asset involving themselves in household work could suggest the absence of ego problem, as they are free to involve or not involve in household work. Moreover, since shopping for household requirements also form part of the household work, men with means could do that with out waiting for some one to suggest and provide the means.

Another important finding that was not expected related to the head of households participating in household work more than others. Perhaps when one already holds an important position in the household, one's self esteem is not going to be affected by involving in any work, be it household or otherwise. Also whether these heads are really heads actually taking care of the household members or holding only a nominal position is also not clear.

It is also of importance to note that women, irrespective of their financial status, have to involve themselves in household work as long as their health permits. That is, in this society household work is part of the socially assigned work for the women and that is less likely to change due to the possession of some asset.

While considering the involvement of elderly in household decision making again the possession of liquid asset came out as a significant factor for both men and women. One wonders whether this finding suggests that the caregivers are not just interested in getting opinion from the elderly but would expect them to contribute financially, if necessary, as they are also party to the decisions taken in the household.

The main finding of this study is that having some asset, mainly liquid asset, really enhances the chances of the elderly being made a part of the household generating a feeling of belonging which is of immense importance in old age. Hence the policy prescription would be that the Government should spread the net of social welfare schemes to increase the number of elderly receiving monetary benefits. Perhaps it is a kind of buying services from the caregivers, mostly children, which from the point of view of the elderly, will be better than being left in an old age home or being ignored at home. This, it is hoped will lead to a healthy and dignified ageing in all its differing angles.

REFERENCES

Ara, Shabeen., (1995), "Old Age Homes: The Last Resort", *Research and Development Journal,* Vol. 2(1):3-10.

Asharaf, A., (2000), *Elederly in Kerala: Productive Units with Challenges Ahead,* Unpublished Ph.D. Thesis.

Beck, Barbara, (1996), "The Economics of Ageing", *The Economist,* 27 January.

Bengtson, V., C. Rosenthal and L. Burtan, (1990), "Families and Ageing: Diversities and Heterogeineity", in Binstock, R. H. and L. K. George (eds.) *Handbook of Ageing and the Social sciences,* Academic Press, New York.

Benyaklef, Mustafa, (1991), "The Elderly Disabled and Ageing Populations: How to Conduct Sample Surveys", *BOLD,* Vol.1 (4):2-4.

Cangping, Wu (1994), "The Ageing Process and Income Security of the Elderly Under Reform in China", *The Ageing of Asian Population,* (Proceedings of the United Nations Round Table on the Ageing of Asian Populations, Bangkok, May 1992).

Census of India, (2001), *Age Tables,* Office of the Registrar General of India, New Delhi.

Chaddock, Robert E., (1936), "Age and Sex in Population Analysis", The Annals of the American Academy Political and Social Sciences, 188:185-193, (Nov. 1936), Clark, R. L. and J. J. Slengler (eds.), *Economics of Individual and Population Ageing,* London Cambridge University, 1980.

Chan, A., (1997), "An Overview of Arrangements and Social Support Exchanges of Older Singaporeans", *Asia- Pacific Population Journal,* Vol. 12(4):35-50.

Clark, Robert L. and Joseph J. Spengler, (1980), *Economics of Individual and Population Ageing,* London Cambridge University.

Coale, A. J., (1956), "The Effect of Change in Mortality and Fertility on Age Composition", *Milbank Memorial Fund Quarterly,* 34(1): 79-114.

Cruz, G. T. and J. N Natividad, (1997), "Patterns in Living Arrangement and Familial Support for the Elderly in Philippines", *Asia- Pacific Population Journal*, Vol. 12 (4):17-39.

Dandekar, Kumudini, (1996), *Elderly in India*, Sage Publications India Pvt. Ltd., New Delhi.

Decker, David. L. (1980), *Social Gerontology: An introduction to the dynamics of ageing*, Little Brown, Boston.

Desai, K. G. and R. D. Naik, (1982), *Problems of Retired People in Greater Bombay*, TATA Institute of Social Sciences. Bombay.

Dharmalingam, A., (1994), "Old Age Support : Expectations and Experiences in a South Indian Village", *Population Studies*, 48 (1): 5-19.

D' Souza, Victor S., (1985), *Economic Development, Social Structure and Population Growth*, Sage Publications, New Delhi.

Easwarmoorthy, M. and N. K. Chadha, (1999), "Quality of Life of Indian Elderly: A Factor Analytical Approach", *Social Change*, vol.29 (1&2): 32-46.

El Badry, M. A., (1986), *Ageing in Developing Countries: One More Population Problem?* Working Paper no. 13, Cairo Demographic Centre.

Fultz, E. and M. Ruck, (2001), "Pension Reform in Central and Eastern Europe: Emerging issues and Patterns", *International Labour Review*, Geneva, Vol. 140(1):19-44.

Government of India, (1998), *The Aged in India: A Socio-Economic Profile*, NSS 52nd Round, July 1995-June 1996, National Sample Survey Organization, Dept. of Statistics, Ministry of Planning and Programme Implementation, Govt. of India.

Government of India, (1998), *National Policy on Older Persons*, New Delhi Ministry of Social Justice and Empowerment.

Government of Kerala , (2004), *Economic review 2004* , State Planning Board, Trivandrum. Government of Kerala, 2006 *State Old Age Policy*.

Government of Kerala, (2007), *Economic review*, State Planning Board, Trivandrum.

Goyal, R. S., (1997), "Implication for the Elderly of the Demographic Transition: An Illustration from India", *Bold*, Vol. 7(2):2-10.

Gulati Leela, (1993), "Population Ageing and Women in Kerala State, India", *Asia Pacific Population Journal*, Vol. 8 (1): 53-63.

Gulati, Leela and S. Irudaya Rajan, (1988), *Population Aspects of Ageing in Kerala*, Centre for Development Studies, Trivandrum.

Guruswamy, M., (1986), *Social and Economic Activities Influencing Fertility Regulation: A Micro Demographic Study of Two Villages in Tamilnadu*, unpublished Ph.D. Thesis, Australian National University.

Guruswamy, Mohan and Ronald Joseph Abraham, (2006), 'Myth of the Poverty Line', in *Redefining Poverty: A New Poverty Line for a New India*, Center for Policy Alternatives, New Delhi, India, April 1.

Halli, S. S. and K. V. Rao, (1992), Advanced Techniques of Population Analysis, Plenum Press, New York.

Hobson, W. and J. Pemberton, (1976), *The Health of the Elderly at Home*, CBGS Report No.13, Brussels.

Hussain, M. G., (1997), *Changing Indian Society and Status of the Aged*, Manak Publications, New Delhi.

International Labour Organization, (1998), LABORSTA, Economically Active Population Estimates and Projections, Version 5:1980-2020, Geneva.

Jamuna, D., (2001), *Intergenerational Issues in Elder Care, Ageing and Development: Global Perspectives*, Ishwar Modi (Ed.), Rawat Publications, New Delhi.

Jones, Gavin K. (1990), "Consequences of Rapid Fertility Decline for Old Age Security in Asia", Working Paper in Demography, Australian National University, Olshansky, Jay and others (eds.), *Reading for Ageing Intergenerational Transfers*.

Joseph, J., (1991), *Aged in India, Problems and Personality*. Churg Publications, Allahabad.

Kamin, Ghulam Farouq, (1994), *A Demographic Study of Afghan Refugees in India*, Unpublished Ph.D. Thesis.

Kanbargi, R., (1985), Old Age Security and Fertility Behaviour: Some Research Issues, *Journal of Indian Anthropological Society*, 20 (3): 226-237.

Karkal, Malini (1999), *Elderly in India, Healthy? Happy? Helpless? Respected? Rewarded? Rejected*, Centre for Health Studies, Tata Institute of Social Sciences, Mumbai-88.

Keynes, J. M., (1948), "Population Policy in Great Britain," *Political and Economic Planning*, London:16 Queen Annes Gate, 1948, Quoted in Clark L. Robert, and Joseph J. Spengler, *Economics of Individual and Population Ageing*, Cambridge University Press, Cambridge, 1980.

Knodel, J. and N. Chayovan, (1997), "Family Support and Living Arrangements of Thai Elderly", *Asia- Pacific Population Journal*, Vol. 12 (4):51-68.

Kono, Shigemi, (1993), *Social, Economic and Demographic Consequences of Ageing of Population*, International Population Conference: Montreal, 1993, Vol.3, pp.3-7. International Union for the Scientific Study of Population [IUSSP]: Liege, Belgium.

Krishnan, T. N., (1976), "Demographic Transition in Kerala, Facts and Factors", *Economic and Political Weekly*, Vol 11 (31, 32, 33):1203-1224.

Krishnaraj, Maithreyi, (1999), "Ageing Women in a Welfare State: Cracks in the Utopia?", *Economic and Political Weekly*, Vol XXXIV (44):WS75-WS88.

Laslett, Peter, (1978), "The History of Ageing and the Aged" in Carver, Vida and Penny Liddiard (eds.)", *An Ageing Population*, Open University Press, Great Britain.

Laura Rudkin, (1993), "Gender Differences in Economic Well-Being Among the Elderly of Java", Demography, Vol.30 (2):209-226.

Long, Clarence D., (1958), *Labour Force Under Changing Income and Employment*, Princeton University Press, Princeton.

Lorimer, F., (1951), "Dynamics of Age Structure in Population with Initially High Fertility and Mortality", Population Bulletin, United Nations, New York, 1:31-41.

Martin, Linda G, (1990) "The Status of South Asia's Growing Elderly Population", *Journal of Cross-cultural Gerontology*, vol.-5(2):93-117.

Naik, V. Sarveshwara, (2001), "Economic Empowerment of the Socially Disadvantaged: State's Agenda", *Social Welfare*, Vol. 48 (9):26-30.

Ogawa, N. and R. D. Retherford, (1997), "Shifting Costs of Caring for the Elderly Back to the Families in Japan, Will it Work?", *Population and Development Review*, Vol. 23(1):59-94.

Okazki, Yoichi, (1967), *Analysis of Decline of Birth Rate in Japan*, English Pamphlet Series No. 65, Institute of Population Problems, Ministry of Health and Welfare, Tokyo, Japan.

Pant, Devendra Kumar, (1997), *Human Development, Demographic Transition and Economic Growth Linkages: An Economic Analysis with Indian Data*, National Council of Applied Economic Research, Working paper No. 67, New Delhi.

Phillips, Bernard S., (1957), "A Role Theory Approach to Adjustment in Old Age", *American Sociological Review*, vol. 22 (2):212-217.

Pratt, James B., (1959), *Review of Religion Research*, New York, Macmillan, quoted in P. K. Dhillon, "Religiosity and Death Among the Aged", *Research and Development Journal*, 1996, Vol. 2(2):33-40.

Radha Devi, D., (1998), "The Aged in India: Some Quantitative Aspects" *Asia Pacific Development Journal*, vol. 5(2):67-97.

Radha Devi, D.; S. Santhosh; A. Asharaf, and T. K. Roy, (2000), *Aged in a Changing Society : A Case Study of Kerala*, Research Report No. 24-2000, International Institute for Population Sciences, Mumbai.

Rajan, S. Irudaya; U. S. Mishra, and P. S. Sarma, (1999), Indian Elderly: Burden or Challenge, New Delhi, Sage Publications.

Registrar General of India, (1984), *SRS Based Abridged Life Tables 1970-75*, Vital Statistics Division, Office of the Registrar General of India, Ministry of Home Affairs, New Delhi.

Registrar General of India, (1989), *SRS Based Abridged Life Tables 1981-85*, Vital Statistics Division, Office of the Registrar General of India, Ministry of Home Affairs, New Delhi.

Registrar General, (1996), *Report of the Technical Group on Population Projections*, Office of the Registrar General, India, New Delhi.

Registrar General of India, (1998), *SRS-Based Abridged Life Tables 1990-94 and 1991-95*, SRS analytical Studies Report, No.-1 of 1998.

Registrar General of India, (1998), *Sample Registration System Bulletin*, Vol. 32-35, Vital Statistics Division, New Delhi.

Registrar General of India, (1999), *Ageing Population of India – An Analysis of the 1991 Census Data*, A Study Report in the Analytical Study Report Series Based on the 1991 Census Data, Registrar General of India, New Delhi.

Registrar General of India, (2000), SRS Based Abridged Life Tables 1992-96 and 1993-97, Registrar General of India, New Delhi.

Registrar General of India, (2006), *SRS Based Abridged Life Tables 1999-2003*, Vital Statistics Division, Office of the Registrar General of India, Ministry of Home Affairs, New Delhi.

Registrar General of India, (2006), *Sample Registration System Bulletin*, Vol. 40, Vital Statistics Division, New Delhi.

Registrar General & Census Commissioner, (2006), *Population projections for India and states 2001-2026*,(Revised December 2006), Report of the Technical Group on Population Projections Constituted by the National Commission on Population, May 2006, Office of the Registrar General & Census Commissioner, India.

Retherford, R. D. and M. K. Choe, (1983), *Statistical Model for Causal Analysis*, Wiley Inter-science Publication, John Weily and Sons, New York, pp. 119-150.

Rosow, Irving, (1976), "Status and Role Change Through the Lifespan", Binstock R. H. and E. Jhanas(eds.) *Handbook of Ageing and the Social Sciences*, Van Nostrand, New York, pp. 457-482.

Santhosh , S, (1994), *Population Ageing in Kerala: Present and Prospect,* Unpublished Ph.D thesis submitted to University of Kerala, Trivandrum.

Sauvy, Alfred, (1948), "Social and Economic Consequences of the Ageing of Western European Population", *Population Studies* 2:115-24 (1948) quoted in Clark R. L. and J. J. Splenger (eds.), *The Economics of Individual and Population Ageing,* Cambridge University Press, Cambridge, 1993.

Seligman, E. R. A. and A. Johnson, (1959), "Status", *Encyclopedia of Social Sciences,* Volume 13, New York, The Macmillan Co.

Shah, Bela, (1993), *Health Status of the Ageing Population,* Indo-UK Workshop on the Public Health Implications of Ageing in India-Convened by the ICMR.

Shantakumar G., (1990), *Census of Population,* Monograph No. 1, National University of Singapore, Singapore.

Shryock, H. S, and J. S. Siegel. (1980), The Methods and Materials of Demography. U. S. Government Printing Office, Washington, D. C.

Sidney, Goldstein, (1968), "The aged segment of the market 1950-1960", *Journal of Marketing,* Vol. 32 (2): 62-68.

Srinivasan, K., (1995), "Lessons From Goa, Kerala and Tamil Nadu - Three Successful Fertility States in India", *Demography India,* Vol. 24(2):163-194.

Sureender, S.; M. Vaithilingam and A. G. Khan (1996), "Distress of the widows in rural Tamil Nadu", *Research and Development Journal,* Vol.2 (2):41-46.

Thompson W. S. and P. K. Whelpton, (1933), "Population Trend in the United States", New York: Mc Graw-Hill Book co., quoted in Clerk, Robert L. and Joseph J. Splenger (eds.), *The Economics of Individual and Population Ageing,* University of Cambridge, Cambridge.

Townsend, Peter, (1963), *The Family Life of Old People,* Penguin Publications, Harmondsworth.

United Nations, (1983), *Vienna International Plan of Action on Ageing,* World Assembly on Ageing, United Nations.

United Nations, (1991), *Ageing and Urbanization: Proceedings of the United Nations international conference on ageing populations in the context of urbanization,* Sendal, (Japan), 12-16 September 1988, New York.

United Nations, (1992), *Economic Aspects of Population Ageing in Kerala, India,* Economic and Social Affairs, United Nations, New York.

United Nations, (1996), *Population Ageing in Asia and the Pacific,* United Nations, ESCAP, New York.

United Nations, (2002a), *World Population Ageing: 1950-2050*, New York.

United Nations, (2002b), *Population Ageing: 2002*, UN, ST/SER.A/208 (Wall Chart).

United Nations, (2005), *World Population Prospects*: 2004 Revision, New York.

United Nations, (2007), *World Population Prospects: The 2006 revision*, New York.

Vijayakumar S. and M. Suryanarayana, (1989), "Problems of the Aged in Rural Sector", Pati, R. N. and B. Jena (eds.), *Aged in India - Socio-demographic Dimensions*, Ashish Publications, New Delhi.

Visaria, Pravin, (2001), "Demographics of Ageing in India", *Economic and Political Weekly*, Vol. 36 (22): 1967-1975.

Vukovich, Gabriella, (1994), "Economic and Social Implications of Aging in Hungary, Social Aspects and Country Review of population Ageing", *Economic Studies*, No.6, United Nations.

Wise, David A., (1989), *Economics of Ageing*, University of Chicago, Chicago.

World Bank, (1994), *Averting the Old Age Crisis*, A World Bank Policy Research Report, Oxford University Press, New York.

Zachariah, K. C.; E. T. Mathew and S. Irudaya Rajan, (2001), "Impact of Migration on Kerala's Economy and Society", *International Migration*, Vol.39 (1):63-88.

INDEX

[F]

[G]

[H]

[I]

[J]

[K]

[L]

[M]

[N]

[O]

[P]

[R]

[S]

[T]

[U]

[V]

[W]

[Y]